YORUBA
RITUAL

AFRICAN SYSTEMS OF THOUGHT

GENERAL   EDITORS
Charles S. Bird
Ivan Karp

CONTRIBUTING   EDITORS
James Fernandez
Luc de Heusch
John Middleton
Roy Willis

YORUBA
RITUAL

PERFORMERS, PLAY, AGENCY

MARGARET
THOMPSON
DREWAL

INDIANA UNIVERSITY PRESS
Bloomington and Indianapolis

This book is a publication of

Indiana University Press
601 North Morton Street
Bloomington, IN 47404-3797 USA

http://www.indiana.edu/~iupress

Telephone orders 800-842-6796
Fax orders 812-855-7931
Orders by e-mail iuporder@indiana.edu

The Northwestern University Research Grants Committee has provided
partial support for the publication of this book. Indiana University
Press gratefully acknowledges this assistance.

The paper used in this publication meets the minimum requirements of American
National Standard for Information Sciences—Permanence of Paper for Printed
Library Materials, ANSI Z39.48-1984.

Manufactured in the United States of America

Library of Congress Cataloging-in-Publication Data

Drewal, Margaret Thompson.
    Yoruba ritual : performers, play, agency / Margaret Thompson
Drewal.
        p.   cm.—(African systems of thought)
    Includes bibliographical references (p.   ) and index.
    ISBN 0-253-31817-3 (cloth).—ISBN 0-253-20684-7 (paper)
    1. Yoruba (African people)—Rites and ceremonies. 2. Yoruba
(African people)—Folklore. 3. Rites and ceremonies—Nigeria.
4. Folklore—Nigeria—Performance. I. Title. II. Series.
DT515.45.Y67D75   1992
398.2'08996333—dc20   91-8414

    4   5   6   7   8   9   05   04   03   02   01   00

CONTENTS

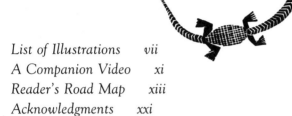

Illustrations

Yoruba Ritual: A Companion Video

Written accounts cannot fully convey the sounds, colors, energy, contingency, physicality, and playfulness embodied in the Yoruba ritual performances described in this book. In part to capture more permanently their vitality, in part for future review and study, and finally with the possibility of classroom use in mind, I videotaped various Yoruba ritual performances. A thirty-minute video cassette featuring segments of the performances analyzed in *Yoruba Ritual* has been prepared and is available to accompany this text. The video includes sequences from Agẹmọ, Egungun, and Jigbo masking and dancing; divination rituals; an Osugbo elders' dance evoking "life's journey"; a Muslim Yoruba celebration of 'Id al-Kabir; and a new festival, the Imewuro Annual Rally, combining traditional and contemporary elements. Subtitles key the performances to chapters of this book.

For information about ordering this cassette, contact Indiana University Press, 601 North Morton Street, Bloomington, Indiana 47404-3797.

Reader's Road Map

Until now, Western interpreters as well as African analysts have been using categories and conceptual systems which depend on a Western epistemological order. [. . .] Does this mean that African *Weltanschauungen* and African traditional systems of thought are unthinkable and cannot be made explicit within the framework of their own rationality?

V. Y. Mudimbe (1988:x)

How, and in what perspective, objects appear to me depends upon me. Only because, at this moment, I am here, where I am, do they appear to me in the way in which they do. Should I change my perspective, the aspect of things would also change.

Michael Theunissen (1986:28)

Yoruba peoples of southwestern Nigeria conceive of rituals as journeys—sometimes actual, sometimes virtual. In elaborate funeral rituals, the elders transfer the deceased's spirit to its otherworldly domain, while in rituals performed after the birth of a child, a diviner strives to settle the newly arrived infant on earth. Ritual incantations tell of the journeys of ancient diviners, deities, and spiritually powerful women as they came from heaven to earth. Diviners journey to the sacred grove of the deity Odu to perform initiations. In masking rituals, trained specialists bring spectacles of cloth, dance, and music into the world from their otherworldly domain and send them away again to close the performance (H. Drewal and M. Drewal 1983:2–4). The deities, too, journey into the world, by mounting the heads of their priests, who go into states of possession trance and dance (M. Drewal 1986, 1988). Elaborated transitional stages mark the deity's arrival and withdrawal. Wherever Yoruba religion thrives—Brazil, Cuba, the United States—this practice has persisted. Cast in performance in a myriad of ways—as a parade or a procession, a pilgrimage, a masking display, or possession trance—the journey evokes the reflexive, progressive, transformative experience of ritual participation.

Transformational, or generative, processes are embedded in African performance practices through acts of re-presentation, or repetition with critical difference. Thus, ritual performance necessarily involves relations between the past and individual agents' interpretations, inscriptions, and revisions of that past in present theory and practice. Scholars have long recognized the transformational capacity of ritual (see Meyerhoff 1990). Ritual has been said both to transform human consciousness and to alter the social statuses of participants, such as in rites of passage. This is true for the Yoruba cases examined here. In addition to these two kinds of transformation, I argue that ritual practitioners as knowledgeable human agents transform ritual itself through play and improvisation. Studies that place emphasis on the transformation of consciousness and changes in social status tend to attribute agency to the ritual structure, as in Victor Turner's tripartite model of ritual process (1977a). From this point of view, the ritual is successful only if the participants fulfill or complete all the stages of the ritual structure (see Fernandez 1986:43). In this study, I have examined instead the power of human agents to transform ritual through performance. This extends the perspective of W. Arens and Ivan Karp (1989). Rather than privileging ritual structure as if it were some *a priori* "thing," I stress the power of participants to transform ritual itself.

In the temporal flow of situated human interactions, knowledgeable actors make choices and take action based on their assessments of the moment and in order to influence their circumstances. Virtually everything in one's environment and experience is potentially usable to this end. This does not mean, however, that *everybody always* exercises his or her options. But, as I hope to show, performers exercise their options frequently enough to undermine the dominant notion in scholarly discourse that ritual repetition is rigid, stereotypic, conventional, conservative, invariant, uniform, redundant, predictable, and structurally static (see, for example, Bloch 1974; Gell 1975:217–218; Moore 1975:41, 219; Peacock 1975:219; Goody 1977:30; Rappaport 1979:172, 175–176, 183, 208; Ortner 1984:154; Tambiah 1985:131–166; and, more recently, Lincoln 1989).

Using a performance paradigm, I attempt to make an African system of thought explicit from the vantage point of its practitioners' theories and embodied practices. Terms such as *ritual* have traditionally defined the gaze of the anthropologist and the historian of religion more so than they have defined what their subjects of study actually do and think (de Certeau 1986:129). What I have written has a dialectical relationship with the literature on ritual by anthropologists and historians of religion. Had I not flagged my intent as dialectical, my writing might otherwise have constituted a [hidden] polemic in Mikhail Bakhtin's sense (see Todorov 1984:70–71). Thus, I have written ever mindful of the discourse on ritual, even stimulated by it, at times establishing an adverse relation to it. My study of Yoruba ritual practice resonates most strongly with poststructuralist theories of performance, social process, and literature.

Throughout the following pages, I have given prominence to the intentionality of actors as knowledgeable agents (Giddens 1986). As an agent myself, a manipulator of textual fragments, I want to state my own intentions. Whether or not I have accomplished what I intended is for the reader to judge.

The central problem of ethnography is translation. Each language comes impregnated with its own peculiar past, loaded with its own ontology and epistemology. The English I am writing is inadequate to translate the conceptual patterns of other languages. The words that correspond most closely with Yoruba ones, for example, are not equivalent (equi-valent); they do not really fit.

It was Rowland Abiọdun who first confronted me with this problem, expressing his dissatisfaction with my translation of the Yoruba word *ọrun* as "otherworld" or "heaven." "What is the best translation?" I asked. His suggestion was that once I had defined the concept I should continue to use the Yoruba term instead of any English translation of it. He pointed out that in English it is commonplace to adopt foreign terms when no translation of them gives the appropriate connotations, terms such as *milieu, gemeinschaft, gesellschaft,* and so forth.

There was a complication however: I soon realized, apart from the problem of readability as more and more Yoruba words crop up in an English text, that English-speaking Yoruba, whom I quote extensively, say "heaven." Should I translate their English back into Yoruba? I am not unaware that their translation has its own history in Christian missionary education and colonialism.

The problem arose again when my use of terms such as *ritual* and *play* kept colliding with my readers' preconceptions. How can ritual at the same time be play? That sounded like a strange configuration. Perhaps it is inappropriate to use the term *ritual* at all? If that would be the case, then Yoruba peoples have no kind of performance that corresponds to "ritual." How else then might I translate the term *etutu*, based on the verb *tu*, "to cool." Perhaps an *etutu* is more accurately "a coolant" or "a cool out"? But these are equally loaded terms and in my opinion trivialize and marginalize what Yoruba do. After all, Yoruba themselves translate *etutu* as "ritual."

Abiọdun felt strongly that, rather than translate any Yoruba concepts, I should have required an English readership to deal with them on their own terms. For political reasons, I sympathize with his position. But I have another overriding agenda.

The irony is: the literature has always referred to Yoruba religious performances as "ritual," much of it without ever indicating the Yoruba term. What this has meant in effect is that what Yoruba do has been understood in terms of our own preconceived notion of what ritual in so-called "preindustrial societies" is, or ought to be. For example, Sally Moore (1975:219) has written that rituals represent "fixed social reality" and "stability and continuity acted out and re-enacted." She continues, "by dint of repetition they deny the passage of time, the nature of change, and the implicit extent of potential indeterminacy in social relations" (Moore 1975:221). What Moore failed to take into account is the indeterminacy of improvisation as praxis in ritual, that is, the transformational capacity of repetition itself.

But as James Fernandez among others has acknowledged, "the overall strategy of most anthropology is to take the student's too individuated awareness and demonstrate system to him—in some sense to return him or her to the whole" (Fernandez 1986:210; see also Goody 1977:33; Bruner 1986:8). Within its rules, patterns, and processes, ritual at once encapsulates the world of social relationships and the cosmos. For anthropologists and historians of religion, ritual has been a model *par excellence* of the return to the whole, a romantic longing for a mythical time and place where communality, coherence, connectedness, collective conscience, and efficacy characterized the social order. What I know of Yoruba performance that has heretofore been labeled "ritual" convinces me that the term as we have been led to think it reflects more our own intellectual history, conceptual patterns, and ways of looking than it does any kind of African performance.

In attempting to move closer to an African epistemological locus, I have adopted an actor-centered approach that privileges not only what people do, but what ritual specialists say about what they do, their intentionality. In taking this approach, I hope to provoke us to rethink the concept of ritual as it has been applied cross-culturally and, by extension, to question how that concept has shaped the way we see. My orientation does not presuppose that the power of ritual to transform experience lies somehow outside human agency in either its structure, its process, its context, or its symbols. Nor does it assume that human agency is itself normative. Rather, it assumes the instrumentality of performers in invoking or even breaking rules, producing structures, and mobilizing resources and support. Particularly in ritual, actors are engaged in framed, rule-oriented action as well as in the exercise of power to accomplish something (cf. Karp 1986:136–137, footnote 1).

The approach I have adopted reveals the relationship between actors and the forms they operate on. It is a perspective that in my opinion comes closest to conveying how Yoruba understand and experience ritual and how they express those understandings and experiences, all of which are then mediated by my own experiences. The level and quality of Yoruba exegesis is particularly sophisticated, demonstrating a remarkable reflexivity rarely revealed in the literature on ritual. I am talking about the degree to which practitioners conceptualize and explain their own practices. Perhaps the most stable aspect of ritual is the knowledge that each performer brings to a given performance. Specialists tended to talk about what they "do"; their accounts were normative and presented in the present tense, unless they were asked specifically about a particular performance and what they and others "did." The most direct access to the performer's interpretive process, apart from actual performance, is through her or his own explanation of that process.

My understanding of ritual has been shaped by my experience in southwestern Nigeria with Yoruba practitioners and their performances. Following my initial visit in 1970, I have been back five times for extended periods. I also spent the summer of 1974 in Salvador, Brazil, studying Yoruba-derived Candomblé performance (M. Drewal 1989). And more recently I have attended ritual parties (*bembe*) in New York with John and Valerie Mason, both priests of the Yoruba deity Ọbatala. I was especially interested in learning how these practices related to their Yoruba prototypes (see M. Drewal, in press).

Quite apart from my own personal experience with ritual specialists and their performances, there is a vast literature. The Baldwins' 1976 bibliography contains nearly 3,500 references. By now, I estimate the literature has more than tripled. Much has been written by Yoruba themselves—some of it in the Yoruba language. Nor is the discourse limited to academics. It includes the writings of practitioners of Yoruba ritual as well—both Yoruba and American (see, for example, Epega 1987; Edwards and Mason 1981, 1985; Mason 1985; Ọṣitọla 1988).

After more than twenty years as a student of Yoruba ritual, continually moving between the literature and personal interactions with people in Yoruba country and elsewhere, I am sufficiently steeped in what is called "Yoruba culture" that I cannot always isolate *how* I know what I know. At the same time, certain concepts, institutions, and practices are so widely known by practitioners and scholars alike that it would be unruly to list all sources. Knowledge is cumulative, a progressive blending of personal observations and experiences with readings of the writings and listenings to the tellings of ritual specialists and other participants. In addition, the theories of Michel de Certeau and Anthony Giddens on social process, Richard Schechner on the restoration of behavior, Linda Hutcheon on parody, and Henry L. Gates, Jr., on signifyin(g) proved particularly relevant to the Yoruba cases examined here.

The development of the chapters is unconventional: cumulative rather than linear. I have selected different performances to illustrate the range of operations specialists perform on ritual. As I shift from one ritual to another, I also shift modes of analysis. The rituals invite this approach because of differences in style, the relationships between participants, and the kinds of materials available for study in each case. In making these strategic shifts, I also call attention to my own writing practices as rhetorical play. I throw forward multiple threads simultaneously in layers; some I elaborate and expand, some I suspend or withdraw, others I introduce, or reintroduce, later and unevenly. As will become apparent, the rituals themselves work this way, a kind of ritual intertextuality—or should I say interrituality?

In chapters 1 and 2, I lay out my theoretical concerns on the issues of repetition and improvisation and follow with a more detailed treatment of my methodology. In the second chapter I am equally concerned with translating and qualifying some key Yoruba terms, at the same time working against what they normally signify in English. This has to be if the English language is going to convey anything about Yoruba performance.

In chapter 3, I explicate the Yoruba notion of ritual as a journey with a synecdochic relationship to the ontology of the human spirit journeying through birth, death, and reincarnation. The journey is an organizing theme throughout. I get at this with a patchwork of sources—a Yoruba parable a diviner "gave" me about a journey, which he related to a personal experience of mine; a divination verse and a gloss on it by the same diviner; examples of ritual journeying; and a specialist's step-by-step account of funeral performance concerned with the journey of the human spirit to the otherworld of ancestors.

In the midst of this, I introduce Kọlawọle Ọsitọla, a seventh-generation diviner, drummer, and member of the society of elders known as Oṣugbo who served as the precolonial judiciary in Yorubaland. Ọsitọla is a scholar of oral tradition, a ritual practitioner and healer, a master performer, and an intellectual. By virtue of his training and knowledge, he is the equivalent of a Western-trained scholar. His thoughts on life and his explications of rituals emerged from our interactions. He was as interested in the questions I would ask as I was in his answers, and he frequently evaluated the quality of my questioning. I have tried to give an idea of our relationship and way of working because it is important for the reader to understand that in everyday life, as in ritual, people operate *on* their situations, whatever they may be, and are always taking stock of those others who happen into them. Yoruba consciousness of what it means to be a stranger in a strange land is implicit in stories about the experience of journeying.

In chapters 4 through 9 I move from ritual to ritual, first considering relatively simple rituals that focus on the definition of the individual, performed by specialists for children and their parents, before treating more complex performances Yoruba also call "spectacle." Chapters 4 and 5 focus on divination rituals that Ọṣitọla performed—what he did and what he said about what he did. In these two chapters I try to convey something of Yoruba ideas about the individual, the process of individuation, the ongoingness of interpretation as a lifelong exercise, and situational innovations in ritual that reflect, in Ọṣitọla's terms, a concern for "the changing world."

In turning to a masking performance that is explicitly entertaining and playful in chapter 6, I explore the relationship of myth to ritual, modes of representation, and the manipulation of ritual form by performers; I conclude with a case study of one individual's successful commandeering of a ritual performance. In chapter 7, my presentation of another masking ritual in which conflict among the participants is endemic must take into account more than sixteen strong personalities. The theme of the journey persists in the form of a pilgrimage. Indeed, in both rituals discussed in chapters 6 and 7, participants shifted their orientations in the performance, altering their perspectives as well as their operating assumptions.

In contrast to the rituals in the previous chapters, the rituals I treat in chapters 8 and 9 are twentieth-century introductions. The first is the Yoruba version of 'Id al-Kabir, a Muslim festival commemorating Abraham's sacrifice to God. The other, called a "rally," is a composite form derived from disparate other rituals. In these cases I provide some historical depth to indicate *how* individual interests get transformed into performance practices. Because these ritual spectacles have recoverable pasts, the changes they have undergone are set in clear relief. Older rituals probably also went through such changes, but, in the absence of historical evidence, the new is often indistinguishable from the old. What the twentieth-century examples suggest is that the choices people make in ritual are not always temporary, quirky, indexical adaptations to the environment or adjustments to changes in society. Rather, optionality in ritual practice is itself transformational, altering not only the ritual form but also the very canons on which particular rituals presumably rest.

In all of the rituals, issues of sex and gender are implicit concerns for Yoruba performers. This is apparent in each of the chapters, and yet I did not want to cast Yoruba ritual practices solely in terms of gender. Therefore, in the last chapter I turn specifically to the issue of gender, culling relevant data from earlier chapters, and with this I am able to compare different modes of performance—divination, masking, and possession trance—and to return ultimately to Yoruba ontology in relation to the issue of gender. I suggest that Yoruba themselves are conscious that gender is a construction. Reflecting this, ritual participants engage in gender play as another dimension of performance discourse.

Finally, Yoruba sensitivity to the indeterminacy of life as lived and of ritual as practiced is thoroughly embedded throughout. Michael Taussig pointed this out to me. I was not thinking in those terms; I did not seek it out. Indeterminacy revealed itself as an unintended outcome of my processual approach of tracking what individuals do in specific situations. Indeterminacy is implicit in Yoruba transformational processes of play and improvisation as modes of operation; it is anthropomorphized as the trickster deity Eṣu, whom scholars have fondly called the principle of unpredictability. It is also evident in the practice of Ifa divination, although scholars prefer to call Ifa the principle of predictability. But Ifa does not predict the future; rather, as a system of knowledge it provides models for action and suggests modes of behavior that allow for a breadth of interpretation and application by individuals to their personal situations.

Yoruba performers regard themselves as "people of action." The idea inheres in a Yoruba theory of action termed *aṣẹ*, which I discuss in greater detail in chapter 2. And although I cannot claim to understand it fully—it is one of those concepts like "will" that philosophers write entire books about—it is at a very fundamental level understood by Yoruba performers as "the power to bring things into existence," or "the power to make things happen." Performers succeed in influencing their situations, although they cannot always determine the consequences. In part this is because, in a highly competitive society of operationally strong individuals, everybody is engaged in the same exercise to alter their current conditions, seizing opportunities, jockeying for position, extending their power and influence, "playing" situations to turn them to their own advantage, in short, "making things happen." As the oft-seen adage painted on trucks and lorries in Nigeria asserts, "NO CONDITION IS PERMANENT."

To evoke the intricacies of the goings on, I load all circuits—overloading them—to "complex" the text, to *dalu* = "split the rhythms" (into polyrhythms and meters), with the challenge to the reader that simultaneity and multifocality in ritual are, in the words of one Yoruba ritual specialist, "just a test on how your brain can be prepared to do many things at a time" (Oṣitọla, #86.79).

Acknowledgments

I take this opportunity to thank the National Endowment for the Humanities for their continued confidence and institutional support in the form of research grants for fieldwork in both 1982 (#RO-20072-81-2184) and 1986 (#RO-21030-85), for which I was a co-recipient with Henry Drewal and John Pemberton III.

In Nigeria, I am indebted to several institutions for providing me appointments as Visiting Research Associate. They are the Institute of African Studies, University of Ibadan (1977–78); the Department of Fine Arts, University of Ife—now Ọbafẹmi Awolowo University (1982 and 1986); and the Nigerian National Museum (1970–71, 1975, 1977–78, 1982, 1986).

I could not have written this text without the hospitality and generosity of my performer colleagues and collaborators in Nigeria, many of whom I have quoted. Kọlawọle Ọsitọla shared openly his experience of Yoruba religious practice and gave me great insight into his system of thought. For my understanding of individual performance traditions, I owe much to various individuals: my fellow Oṣugbo members in the towns of Imodi, Imọsan, and Ijẹbu-Ode; Raimi Akaki Taiwo, an expert on Egungun masking; Iya Ṣango, child of Ṣango and a consummate performer; the priests and chiefs of Agemọ and their families; Ọtun Balogun M. O. Ṣọtẹ and his family; the late Chief Philip B. Rennaiye and the members of the Imewuro Development Council; and the Olọriṣas of Igbogila.

All along the way I have also benefited from advice and discussion with my elders in academia, especially Wande Abimbọla, Rowland Abiọdun, Lamidi Fakeye, Ọyin Ogunba, and Ọlabiyi Yai. I am especially indebted to Rowland Abiọdun and Ọlabiyi Yai for reading and evaluating individual chapters. Any shortcomings are my own.

Other individuals have provided hospitality and many other courtesies during my various stays in Nigeria. I single out Lamidi Ṣofenwa; Rhoda Johnston; Larry Amy; Buffy Amy; Reverend Ron Howarth; Ekpo Eyo; Bode Ladejobi; Chief Bayo Kuku and Brother; Alhaji S. A. Ọnafuye; the Ajalọrun of Ijẹbu-Ife; the Idoko of Ijẹbu-Mushin; Mr. Olufowobi; the Ọmọ Awo of Kọlawọle Ọsitọla's group; Iya Are; and the members of the Egungun societies of Ilaro and Ijado, among others. Especially, I want to express my deep appreciation to the Longe and Abiọdun families for their close friendship and sustained support and encouragement over the years.

On the western side of the Atlantic, John and Valerie Mason have contributed indirectly to this study, sharing with me their own perspectives on Yoruba religious practice. I also extend my gratitude to Ms. Theresa Adepoju for assisting me with Yoruba orthography, which is continually being refined. I take responsibility for any mistakes.

For their advice and comments on an earlier version of this study, I wish to thank Richard Schechner, Barbara Kirshenblatt-Gimblett, Marcia Siegel, Michael Taussig, and Sandra Barnes, each of whom contributed to this text in ways that are not always obvious. Also, for their support and encouragement during the final preparations of this manuscript, I am grateful to my colleagues at Northwestern University, especially Dwight Conquergood and Carol Simpson Stern. And to Morris Meyer, Forrest Inslee, and Sarah von Fremd, I express my thanks for their useful comments; they are really more like colleagues than graduate students. Finally, there are no words sufficient to express what Henry Drewal's companionship and love have meant over the years. The scope of this study I think is in large part attributable to successful teamwork.

YORUBA
RITUAL

1. Theory and Method in the Study of Ritual Performance

A program announced for the 1977 anniversary celebration of the Ọjẹ Improvement Society, Lagos, which sponsors masked performances called Egungun honoring the ancestors: "BUSH GROOVE [sic] PROCESSION & PARADE of ALL EGUNGUN from Berkley St. Lagos to Oju Olobun in Isale-Eko area. [. . .] ALL EGUNGUN (ancient as well as modern) will take part in the Procession and Parade with their respective BANNERS." Not only is there a concept of "modern" Egungun, but the establishment of an "Improvement Society" (one of whose improvements was considered to be the printed program) is testimony to the idea that Yoruba performers of ritual do not intend to create an exact reproduction of some original. A fundamental problem with the study of ritual has been our understanding of the nature of repetition, which has heretofore been seen as structurally restrictive or—at the very least—confining. Below I theorize repetition as a way to understand the transformational capacity of performance praxis.

Repetition is by definition a re-presentation (Derrida 1978:247–248), indeed, a representation. It represents an earlier period of time, which itself may have been a repetition. As a representation of an earlier segment of time, repetition embodies creativity, for representation itself is a form of creativity (Wagner 1972:4). As a representation of time, repetition may create the illusion of recurrence, but, in the words of Antonin Artaud (1958:75), "an expression does not have the same value twice, does not live two lives; [. . .] all words, once spoken, are dead and function only at the moment when they are uttered, [. . .] a form, once it has served, cannot be used again and asks only to be replaced by another, and [. . . .] a gesture, once made, can never be made the same way twice." Not only would the performance be different, but the audience—even if it were essentially the same—would experience the performance differently. In other words, phenomenologically a thing repeated is never the same as its, or any other, "original." In this sense, each repetition is in some measure original, just as it is at the same time never totally novel. Or, as Clifford Geertz (1986:380) has put it, "it is the copying that originates." This is because time does not repeat itself; rather, repetition operates within time to represent it,

to mark it off, to measure it, to imbue it with a feeling of regularity and permanency, or even to substantiate its existence.

MODES OF REPETITION

It is useful to distinguish two modes of repetition that operate differently,
although they are conceptually related. The broader mode of ritual repetition is
the periodic restoration of an entire performance, as in annual rituals scheduled
to correspond in some way to seasonal change (Schechner 1985:35–116). In
this mode, the unit to be repeated is a complete whole, and long gaps of time
exist between the repetitions. The other mode is the repetition that occurs
within a single ritual performance, and is experienced in a steady, unbroken
flow, as in regular, persistent drumming or vocalizing of the sort ethologists,
psychologists, and others cite to explain ritual trance (Lex 1979). The practice
of *dhikr*, repetitive vocalization that induces trance in Arabic dervish brother-
hoods from India to Morocco, is but one example (Rouget 1985:263, 300–301,
317). Indeed, one of the confusions in the literature on ritual is that scholars
often apply the concept of repetition to ritual without ever making this distinction explicit (cf. Tambiah 1985:137–146).

Repetition within ritual serves to represent (re-present) time concretely, providing a continuous temporal reference. It has a unifying potential, or rather it
provides a common denominator for actions and events. Its binding potential is
what makes it particularly crucial to any collective action. Repetition *within*
ritual may induce a sense of stability and predictability (Moore and Myerhoff
1977:17). But to what extent does ritual employ this mode of repetition? Repetition may be seen as an attempt to impose a predictable order on what Edmund
Husserl (1964:48) refers to as the "running-off phenomena" of time. But, "just
as every temporal point (and every temporal interval) is, so to speak, different
from every other 'individual' point and cannot occur twice, so also no mode of
running-off can occur twice." Repetition within ritual would seem to have the
illusory effect of impeding the running-off potency of time, for it allows its
subscribers to re-capture a moment as many times as they wish. Yet, simultaneously, repetition is the common denominator for differentiation.

The best published discussions to date of the dialectic between repetition
and variation, between the collective and the individual within the ritual
process, comes from those who involve themselves in the "doing" of ritual, its
actualization. In this methodology, the researcher masters a technique which
enables him/her to participate in the collective action, thereby gaining access to
its internal dynamics, in contrast to merely "observing" ritual or "interviewing
about" ritual.

John Miller Chernoff (1979:125), for example, studied drumming technique
in Ghana for ten years. With that experience, he was able to understand that
which escapes a mere observer; that is, "we fail to understand the music because
we have difficulty participating with adequate sophistication within the *rhythmic
framework* of a specific event. The aesthetic requirement of participation in such

a context is the ability to stand back from the rhythms of the scene and find an additional *rhythm* which complements and mediates those other rhythms." Although Chernoff does not mention repetition explicitly, it is understood that the participants' dynamic relatedness is based on a constant pulse either sounded percussively or sensed. Variety can be understood only against constancy, and vice versa. In a flow of shifting relationships, participants initiate and respond to the rhythmic development spontaneously, whether in song, in dance, or in drumming.

In comparison, the periodic repetition of an entire ritual is what Richard Schechner calls "restored behavior" (1982a:40; 1985:35–116). According to him, restored behavior is characteristic of all performance; it is never for the first time, but for the second to the nth time. Jacques Derrida (1978:247–248) alludes to this feature when he asserts that dramatic representation itself (re-presentation), or mimesis, is repetition. Thus, "nowhere else is one so close to the stage as the origin of repetition, so close to the primitive repetition which would have to be erased, and only by detaching itself from itself as if from its double." Performers recover through memory (of myth, of rehearsal, of the last performance) organized sequences that they then re-behave. Thus a performance is based in actuality on an earlier performance. In this sense, performance is by its very nature intertextual by virtue of the embodied practices of the performers.

At best, any given performance can bear only a likeness to previous performances, even when the performers have acquired sophisticated techniques to achieve duplication. Consider Schechner's comment that

> my very existence as a "theatre person" who "makes plays"—experiences that can't be kept, that disappear with each performance, not with each production but with each repetition of the actions I so carefully plan with my colleagues; each repetition that is never an exact duplication no matter how closely scored, how frozen by disciplined rehearsals—this very existence in/as theatre is postmodern. For the theatre is a paradigm of "restored behavior"—behavior twice behaved, behavior never-for-the-first-time—ritualized gestures. (1982b:110–111)

A frustration for many directors is that duplication is an impossibility. But is duplication any more possible in ritual practice? Indeed, is duplication even a primary concern?

REPETITION WITH CRITICAL DIFFERENCE

In two recent theories of repetition, transformation is a fundamental principle. One is Linda Hutcheon's theory of parody (1985, 1988). Hutcheon defines parody not in terms of satire, but rather as repetition with critical distance (1985:6, 20). In her words (1988:26, 35), parody "allows ironic signalling of difference at the very heart of similarity," paradoxically indicating both cultural continuity and change, authority and transgression, involving both creator and partaker in a participatory hermeneutics.

In certain Yoruba masked performances in honor of ancestors, for example, human beings are represented as stereotypes and parodied (see chapter 6). It is as if the spirit world comes to tell the phenomenal world about itself. In the Awori town of Ilogbo on March 7, 1982, a masker representing a British colonial officer chucked his wife under the chin; she put her head on his shoulder; then he pulled her toward him and kissed her on the lips (fig. 1.1). The scene was a parody of the European propensity to display affections publicly. There are infinite possibilities for rendering whites to show how they are variously read and perceived by the performers/interpreters. In the 1820s in New Oyọ, explorer Hugh Clapperton (1829:55) witnessed a parody of a European male "miserably thin, and starved with cold." The masker walked around in an awkward, tender-footed gait, dipped snuff, and rubbed his hands together. The European maskers that Ulli Beier observed (1964:197–198) had enormous hooked noses and black hair made of the pelt of the Colobus monkey. They shook hands, saying "how do you do," and mocked ballroom dancing. In another variation, a mask depicting a white man shook Kacke Gotrick's hand (1984:94–95) and kept looking conspicuously at his wristwatch. A spectator told her he sometimes also carried a teacup or a transistor radio. Virtually anything in one's experience of the white man is potentially usable for commentary.

Similarly, repetition with revision, or repetition that signals difference, is in an Afro-American tradition known as signifyin(g), according to Henry Louis Gates, Jr. (1988:xxiv, 63–65). Signifyin(g) can include any number of modes of rhetorical play.[1] Whenever meaning is constant or repeated, Gates argues, the play of the signifier is foregrounded. He takes his example from jazz, citing Jelly Roll Morton's 1938 recording "Maple Leaf Rag (A Transformation)," which signifies on Scott Joplin's 1916 signature piece "Maple Leaf Rag." Whereas Joplin's musical form was AABBACCDD, Morton swung the introduction, which he borrowed from the end of A, and then played ABACCD, the latter in a style reminiscent of the tango, and then repeated D, this time in a New Orleans "stomp" variation (Martin Williams, cited in Gates 1988:63). Imitating Joplin, pianist Morton played the trumpet/clarinet part with his right hand and the trombone rhythm with the left. As Gates points out (1988:63–64), "Morton's composition does not 'surpass' or 'destroy' Joplin's; it complexly *extends and tropes* figures present in the original."

What is especially interesting to me is that Afro-Americans take the concepts of signifiers and signifieds (objects—persons, places, and things) and turn them into a verb "signify," simultaneously turning the static equation between two related "things" into a double-voiced process. "To signify" is to revise that which is received, altering the way the past is read, thereby redefining one's relation to it.

Revision can take place within one or more wide-ranging features—form, style, content, medium, sequence, qualitative aspects such as dynamics and timing, and so on. The range of possibilities is different depending on what is being revised, whether music, dance, oral narrative, maskers, or whatever. In order for any one of the above to comment on the past, it would have to maintain some recognizable relationship to it. Thus some arbitrary feature, or cluster of features, would have to be retained and reproduced, while all others could diverge—to be displaced and replaced by other features, cross-referenced, extended, embellished, or omitted altogether. From the description of Morton's transformation of Joplin's musical composition, for example, it appears that the form was recast, the style was altered radically in the A and D sections, and the instrumentation was changed completely. What is unspoken, but understood, is that the melody retained its thematic identity.

For me, one of Gates's most important points is that the revision of the signifier disrupts the signified/signifier equation and opens up meaning. Another Yoruba example will serve to illustrate the point. Associated with the dry season and body sores that seem to occur frequently at that time, Jigbo masks represent bush spirits. Ordinarily, they wear skirts and tunics made of cloth from local markets and strands of fresh palm fronds draped around their necks, evoking the environs they supposedly emanate from.[2] At the 1986 Imewuro Annual Rally, on the second day, when the Jigbo masks performed, one with the typical palm frond strands and cloth face covering came out wearing a Western style men's hat and a tuxedo complete with satin lapels and stripes down the outer sides of the legs (fig. 1.2). People laughed and called the mask Jigbo Oyinbo, that is, "White Man's Bush Spirit." Later that evening, driving back to Ijebu-Ode with the performer, I asked why he wore the tuxedo. He told me it used to be his uniform when he worked in a Lagos gambling casino, and he had decided to wear it on that day just for fun. There was no more explanation than that. Disrupting the signifier, in this case the Jigbo form, the performer opened the meaning to new interpretations.

The Jigbo mask and the tuxedo are both special dress; neither is for ordinary, everyday use. In only one other sense are they similar. Both refer to exotic Others, either as spirits or as foreigners. What would happen if the performer switched contexts, going to the casino with elements of the Jigbo mask incorporated into his work uniform? And to what extent was the performer conscious of the implications of his manipulations? I cannot say. Artists in our own society cannot always verbalize exactly why they choose to do what they do. It is often their critics who make those determinations. But the mere fact that the performer exercised this option to bring the materials from two diverse domains together, and others in attendance enjoyed it, tells us something about the openness of Yoruba ritual, the power of performers to improvise, and the willingness of participants to entertain alternate possibilities. Below, I will explore Yoruba ritual praxis as *repetition with revision* (Gates 1988:63–64), what Yoruba call *ere* and translate into English as "play," and what I understand in terms of performance as improvisation. Broadly defined, improvisation is rhetorical play.

1.1 White Man chucks Wife's chin in a parody on European couples. Awori area, town of Ilogbo, 7 March 1982.

1.2 Three Jigbo maskers perform during the Imewuro Annual Rally. The one in the foreground is decorated with plastic toys, while the middle wears a Western hat and tuxedo that the owner acquired when he worked in a gambling casino in Lagos. Ijẹbu area, village of Imewuro, 25 August 1986.

IMPROVISATION

By improvisation I mean more specifically moment-to-moment maneuvering based on acquired in-body techniques to achieve a particular effect and/or style of performance. In improvisation, each move is contingent on a previous move and in some measure influences the one that follows. Improvisation requires a mastery of the logic of action and in-body codes (or strips of behavior to be re-behaved, in Schechner's words) together with the skill to intervene in them and transform them (de Certeau 1984). Each performance, each time, is generated anew. Periodically repeated, unscripted performance—including most ritual, music, and dance in Africa—is improvisational. Most performers—maskers, dancers, diviners, singers, and drummers alike—have been trained from child-hood in particular techniques enabling them to play spontaneously with learned, in-body formulas. This kind of mastery distinguishes a brilliant performer from a merely competent one. Improvisation can be parodic, that is, it can signal ironic difference from the conventional or the past, a past experience, the past performance.

Improvisation is transformational, often participatory and competitive, in which case it constitutes a multidimensional process of argumentation. Dancers and drummers, for example, negotiate rhythmically with each other, maintaining a competitive interrelatedness. This is particularly critical because of the close conceptual and formal link between music and dance in Africa.[3] Drummers can increase the rhythmic complexity of the music, pressing dancers to the limits of their skill, or they can simplify the music to suggest that the dancer cannot measure up. Dancers can also move beyond the limits of the drummers' skill, to underscore their superior knowledge. Meanwhile drummers negotiate rhythmi-cally with one another, each finding his own path in relation to his co-players.[4] Just as each improvisation has a recognizable identity formally and stylistically, it also has an element of newness. The interrelatedness of drummers and dancers establishes a situation whereby individual performers can either support, rein-force, impede, or even subvert other performers and thus commandeer the entire ritual. The work of interpretation is often immediate and spontaneous because of the multilogics of performance and the interrelationships between performers and between the various performative genres—drumming, singing, dancing.

Improvising, participants intervene spontaneously in the ritual framework at their whims. I will deal with this specifically in chapter 6, although it emerges in one way or another in all the chapters. Improvisors risk transgressing the bound-aries of appropriateness. These boundaries are not hard and fixed, however, so that negotiating appropriateness is itself another dimension of improvisation.

Whenever improvisation is a performative strategy in ritual, it places ritual squarely within the domain of play. It is indeed the playing, the improvising, that engages people, drawing them into the action, constructing their relation-ships, thereby generating multiple and simultaneous discourses always surging between harmony/disharmony, order/disorder, integration/opposition, and so on. Contrary to Don Handelman's suggestion (1977:187), then, the domains of ritual and play are not necessarily mutually exclusive. Acknowledging correctly that play can be dangerously explosive, even subversive, Victor Turner (1986:168) likewise distinguishes it from ritual. Elsewhere he argues (1982:85) that there is room for play in ritual and that the liminal phase of ritual is particularly conducive to it. But play in ritual, as Yoruba conceive it, is not at all synonymous with, or confined to, Turner's "antistructural" phase of the ritual process (1977a). I concur with Gates's suggestion (1988) that both signifyin(g) and improvisation among Afro-Americans are formal manifestations of African traditions, and more specifically of a self-reflexive tradition of rhetorical play in cultural and performance practices.

ON CHANGE IN RITUAL

Practitioners of Yoruba religion are aware that when ritual becomes static, when it ceases to adjust and adapt, it becomes obsolete, empty of meaning, and eventually dies out. They often express the need to modify rituals to address current social conditions. Sometimes change is the result of long deliberations; oftentimes it is more spontaneous. Many revisions are not particularly obvious, unless the observer is thoroughly familiar with the ritual process by having followed a number of its performances, much in the same way a critic follows the productions of a dance or theater piece. Other kinds of modifications are more glaring.

An example: a Yoruba priestess in Ilaro, 1978, had to decide whether to ride in a car to a ritual. After an involved discussion with her peers, she decided that she could ride only so far, after which she would bear her ritual loads on top of her head as her predecessors had done. On the one hand, she reasoned that the deities themselves keep up-to-date, now demanding Gordon's gin and Beefeaters as libations, instead of the local brew. At the same time, it was her obligation to bear the ritual loads to demonstrate her devotion. The priestess compromised. She rode as far as the crossroads—the junction at the edge of the town—then she began to walk.[5] The logic of these adjustments is not always apparent unless the observer has access to a particular participant's extremely personal experience. Unless the observer tracks the practices of individuals, such alterations will not be evident, because they do not necessarily occur on a grand scale.

Western goods and technology are evident everywhere in Africa. Anthropologists have often associated such change with modernization, beginning with the colonial period, or before, through to the present.[6] One of the problems is that they tend to see modernization as the antithesis of ritual. James Peacock (1975:219), for example, notes that

> modernizing movements, whether Protestant, Muslim, or Buddhist reformations, Melanesian cargo cults, or Communist revolutions all endeavor to purge traditional ritual. The obvious reason is that ritual which has supported the

established order must be destroyed. A more basic reason is that ritual action by its very repetitive rigidity celebrates the eternal, the socio-cosmic structure that was, is, and ever shall be. The modernizing activity that relentlessly thrusts toward harnessing new means to valued ends unavoidably opposes a symbol of the unchanging.

But ritual is a symbol of the unchanging for whom? For the so-called "modernizing movement," or for the cultural relativist?

Peacock pits modernizing movements against ritual—movements which themselves incorporate ritual—and modernity against ritual action, that is, the changing versus the unchanging. It seems equally plausible, however, that these movements attempt to purge ritual precisely because its generative force runs counter to the one that the movement is attempting to set into action. In that case, the conflict is not between movement and stasis but, perhaps more accurately, between two opposing generative forces—the established ritual and the establishing movement.

Sometimes individuals apply established rituals to new situations or create new rituals that partake of old ideologies. These were the issues for one Ijẹbu Yoruba king and deacon in the Cherabim and Seraphim Church who once related to me the story of his trip abroad. The king turned to Christianity because, as he pointed out, "Jesus is quicker." The king explained that he knows "the secret names of Jesus" and can therefore call him at any time and "Jesus will answer." He does not have to go through a priest, wait for divination, or offer a sacrifice. Quicker, yes, and less expensive.

But even though he is a Christian, when the king wanted to go to England to visit his daughter and son-in-law, he claimed to have consulted a priestess in charge of the deity of his forebears, who prepared medicine to protect him on his journey. When he arrived at his destination, he told his son-in-law that the first thing he had to do was to go to the center of London (which he perceived to be St. Paul's Cathedral) to pay homage to its founding father. The king explained to me that it would be dangerous for him to enter another king's domain without paying proper respect. Reportedly, his son-in-law warned him to be careful because the London police would not understand what he was trying to do. So the king decided to perform this ritual in the alley beside St. Paul's in the middle of the night. At midnight his son-in-law waited in a taxi while he went up the alleyway to perform an act of homage to the ancestors. There he invoked "the founder of London" and "stepped" his left foot on the ground three times, as he does annually at home in a festival honoring the founder of his own kingdom.[7]

In the king's story, Jesus, by implication, assumed the status of a Yoruba deity. The rituals he reportedly performed shifted emphasis. Instead of going through a priest or diviner, the king invoked Jesus directly. Yet, when the king traveled on foreign soil he reinstated his ancestors' deity for protection and appropriated a ritual ordinarily performed in his own kingdom, transposing it to the center of London. It seemed logical to the king that the police might give him trouble. After all, what could the London police be expected to think on catching such a powerful man as the king surreptitiously performing ritual in the heart of their city?

The king shaped ritual to suit his immediate need. Grounded in a tradition, he freely evaluated, adapted, transposed, and transformed ritual, applying old meanings to new contexts and creating new meanings from old ones, totally reconstituting the conventional. And he knew precisely what he was doing. He was mastering and manipulating power and symbols through ritual action, inserting himself into the royal domain of the Other, even if London and the Queen were unaware of it. And, in telling me the tale, he impressed on me his ability to perform these kinds of critical transformations.

METHODOLOGY

To understand the dynamics of ritual demands an interdisciplinary perspective that takes into account the temporal nature of performance (M. Drewal 1990:77–78). This means making a paradigmatic shift from structure to process (from an essentially spatialized view to a temporal one); from the normative to the particular and historically situated (from the timeless to the time-centered); and from the collective to the agency of named individuals. Only then can ritual as praxis be historicized.

Shifting from the normative to the particular means focusing on *how* ritual practitioners operate, observing *what* they actually do in specific performances and then listening to what they *say* about what they do, their intentionality. It means studying the transmission of modes, techniques, and styles for setting into process the generation of meaning and the construction of authority. It means distinguishing particular performances of a ritual from *the* ritual as an event encapsulating culture or an ideology. Dance and theater critics in the West have always been attentive to particular performances of a theater piece, at the same time evoking some essence of that particular performance (Siegel 1979:xi).

Adopting a temporal perspective means following repeated performances of the same ritual by the same people and between different groups of people. It means focusing on individuals in specific performances as they *use* structure and process and then locating that performance within a larger body of performances and in history, society, and politics. This is a fundamental reorientation in the study of ritual. But rather than losing sight of structure, as skeptics might imagine (Kapferer 1986:192), the performances illuminate structuring properties all the more brilliantly, indicating at the same time how performers handle them.

Acquired, in-body techniques for use in performance do not necessarily constitute structures or systems of reproduction. Rather, techniques of the body should be understood as resources for negotiation that are deployed in performance by knowledgeable agents. It is thus not sufficient to observe that performance is emergent. Rather, it is crucial to understand *how* particular performances situated in time and place emerge through discursive practices and the rhetoric of human action and agency. For tradition is, as Raymond Williams

(1982:187) has observed, a process of the selection of—not necessary, but desired—continuities, and thus it involves choice-making.

With these shifts to the particular and the individual, I was able to study ritual as transformational process, as improvisation, in contrast to the more standard approach as a process of regularization or reproduction in which ritual is viewed more or less as reproducing the past or the cosmos in stable fashion with relatively little, or only gradual, change (see, for example, Moore 1975:41; Peacock 1975:219; Ortner 1984:154; Tambiah 1985; and, more recently, Lincoln 1989). In such a shift, what becomes readily apparent is that in ritual there are no predictable or verifiable constants endlessly or mindlessly repeated by performers. Performance is a multilayered discourse employing multiple voices and perspectives. And as we recognize this, it should also be apparent that fieldwork itself is performance.

Treating fieldwork as performance means placing the emphasis on the participant side of the participant/observer paradigm; breaking down the boundaries between self and other, subject and object, subjectivity and objectivity; and engaging in a more truly dialogical relationship with our subjects of study so that both researcher and researched are coeval participants in performance discourse (Fabian 1983). Like performance, fieldwork is a mode of the production of knowledge. It is based on learned techniques for doing research, or rather it should be. And fieldwork is largely improvisational. It is repetition with revision. That, I hope, will also be transparent in the following pages.

2. Yoruba Play and the Transformation of Ritual

Yoruba-speaking peoples number approximately twenty-five million, constituting Nigeria's second largest language group (Abiọdun 1990:64) (Map 1). Composed of some twenty-five distinct subgroups, which extend approximately three hundred kilometers in from the Atlantic coast, the Yoruba have a certain linguistic coherence, but in many ways they are culturally and socially diverse. This in part led J. S. Eades (1980:ix) to suggest that writing a general account of the Yoruba is foolhardy. The term "Yoruba" as a cultural designation dates only to mid-nineteenth-century colonialism (Law 1977:5). People identify with hometowns or areas first and foremost and with being Yoruba only in relation to outsiders. The significance of this will be more apparent chapter by chapter as I consider specific Yoruba performances, but first let me qualify my English translations of some Yoruba categories of performance.

YORUBA PERFORMANCE: RITUAL, SPECTACLE, FESTIVAL, PLAY

Throughout these pages I use the words "ritual" for *etutu*, "festival" for *ọdun*, "spectacle" for *iran*, and "play" or "improvisation" for *ere*. In the way Yoruba use these terms, they are not discrete, bounded categories as folklorists and anthropologists tend to think of them (Ben-Amos 1976; Handelman 1977; MacAloon 1984). Instead, they are overlapping and interpenetrating (fig. 2.1). Whether Yoruba-speakers invoke one or another of the above terms in any given context is a matter of emphasis and/or orientation.

Yoruba often use ritual, festival, spectacle, and play interchangeably—which is how I use them throughout—so that any generic distinctions have to acknowledge that as categories of performance they are open and inclusive rather than closed and exclusive. My cross-application of terms in this text will no doubt disturb scholars preoccupied with genre theory and taxonomic classifications. But as Dan Ben-Amos (1976) has acknowledged, there is often a discrepancy between the analytical categories applied by scholars and those operative on the ground as applied by the "folk." Throughout I have cross-applied terms as Yoruba cross-apply them. I do this to resist readers' inadvertent attempts to

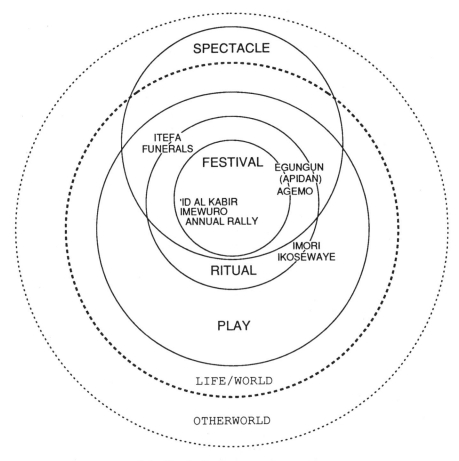

2.1 Yoruba Performance Categories

impose rigid classifications, and to preserve instead the openness, inclusivity, and interchangeability of the Yoruba concepts.

The Yoruba categories of play and spectacle are broadest.[1] Yoruba conceive spectacle as a permanent, otherworldly dimension of reality which, until *revealed* by knowledgeable actors, is inaccessible to human experience. Indeed R. C. Abraham (1958:317) translates *iran* as "theatrical performance." Yoruba, however, apply the term to most religious rituals. Intrinsic to the meaning of the Yoruba word *iran* (spectacle) is repetition and transformation (Ọlabiyi Yai, personal communication, 1990). Thus *iran* derives from the verb *ran*; so, for example, *ranti (ran eti)* = to remember; *ranfa (ran Ifa)* = to recite Ifa verses; and *ranṣẹ (ran iṣẹ)* = to send a message via a messenger. In the latter case, according to Yai, the message delivered is the messenger's interpretation of the original. In each case, the repetition is a revision of whatever was repeated. The Yoruba word for a visual representation (*aworan*) is likewise based on this same root, as is the

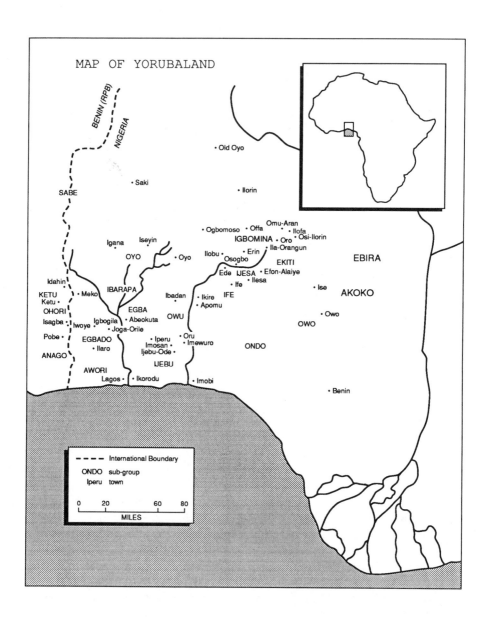

MAP OF YORUBALAND

same Yoruba term used for spectator (*aworan*), the viewer of a spectacle. It is the role of knowledgeable performers to bring spectacle into the world periodically from its otherworldly domain so that it can be experienced and contemplated. In this sense, then, Yoruba spectacle is by definition restored behavior based in the embodied practices of performers.

Such performances meet all but one of John MacAloon's four criteria for spectacle (1984:243–244): 1) the primacy of visual sensory and symbolic codes, 2) monumentality and an aggrandizing ethos, 3) institutionalized bicameral roles of actors and spectators (that is, presentational action set in opposition to passive spectating), and 4) dynamism in the performance that engenders excitement in the audience. The difference is that in the Yoruba notion of spectacle *there are no fixed bicameral roles*. Yoruba spectacle is participatory; it is not set off as a unitary object of the spectator's gaze. The relationships between spectators and spectacle are unstable, one always collapsing into the other. Participatory spectacle does not set up fixed unequal power relationships between the gazer and the object of the gaze; rather, the participatory nature of Yoruba spectacle itself means that subject and object positions are continually in flux during performance.

The absence of institutionalized bicameral roles means at the same time that Yoruba spectacle does not have a destructive effect on the status of either rituals or festivals (cf. MacAloon 1984:268). This is because rituals, festivals, and spectacles are all participatory; participants move in and out of the action, moving at the same time between autotelic[2] and reflexive experience. Taussig (1987:443) has experienced this too in shamanism, "standing within and standing without in quick oscillation." Precisely for this reason, Yoruba performance accommodates optionality and individual choice much more so than do forms of spectacle, like the Olympics or those on the proscenium stage, in which the very bicameral roles about which MacAloon writes only serve to make the unified, rationalist approach to representation more thoroughly rigid and confining (Wagner 1981:116; M. Drewal 1987).

Play is a broader, more generic concept than spectacle. All Yoruba spectacle is play, but all play is not spectacle. What Yoruba mean by play, *ere* [noun] or *şere* [verb], is much more difficult to communicate because of the cultural baggage the capitalistic notion of play carries, which often sets it in opposition to work. Performing ritual is at once "hard work" and "playing."[3] What play is *not* for Yoruba is unserious, frivolous, and impotent. Yoruba have a different term for what we might call frivolous play—*yeye*—usually translated into English by Yoruba-speakers simply as "nonsense." *Yeye* is useless or gratuitous play, a trifle.[4] When Yoruba-speakers use the English word "play," however, it is a direct translation of *ere* or *şere*. The Yoruba presupposition is that play is dialogical in which a certain *"égalité de départ"* operates among the players (Ọlabiyi Yai, personal communication, 1990). Play—like Yoruba spectacle—is, more specifically, an engaging participatory, transformational process that is often, but not always, competitive. Below I try to evoke the transformational capacity of Yoruba play by citing particular instances and giving examples.

Yoruba Play

A Yoruba acquaintance of mine arrived at a friend's house announcing, "I made the police work today oh!" A policeman had stopped him at a checkpoint on the road to examine all his "particulars"—his driver's license, car registration, insurance, and so forth. Playing the situation, my acquaintance warned the policeman that if he turned off the car's engine, he was going to have to work (that is, to get it started again). Nevertheless, the policeman insisted that he pull over and get out. Once back in the car, my acquaintance feigned that the engine would not turn over and the car would not start. The policeman felt compelled to help him, as my acquaintance well knew when he spontaneously improvised the ruse. Since the policeman had no car at the checkpoint, it meant he had to exert himself physically. For about thirty minutes the policeman pushed the car before my acquaintance finally allowed the engine to kick in. Thanking the policeman for his help, my acquaintance was on his way again. When my friend Kọlawọle Ọsitọla narrated this incident to me, as reported to him by our mutual acquaintance, he prefaced the story by reminding me, "you know, he is a Yoruba man." The fact of "being Yoruba" he presented as the basis for me to understand the ruse and the man's ability to pull it off.

The above example is not atypical of Yoruba tricks and ruses. Such trickster scenarios are common in the verbal arts as well as in the practice of everyday life. In one version of a popular story about the Yoruba trickster deity, Èṣù/Ẹlẹgba, he turns lifelong friends into enemies, sets fire to the townspeople's houses reducing them to ruins, and, pretending that he is going to protect the fire victims' possessions, he instead gives them away to passers-by (Wescott 1962:330–331; see also pp. 29–30). Similar scenarios abound with regard to Èṣù's Brazilian counterpart, Exu. Victor Turner (1986:54) sees Exu's potential for unexpected intrusions into Umbanda ritual as a manifestation of the danger of frame slippage. Frame slippage is dangerous because it destabilizes a situation and throws it into a zone of ambiguity. At the same time, it sets up opportunities for alterations.

But the very notion of frame slippage presupposes a "frame" from which to "slip." A frame in Erving Goffman's sense (1974) is a spatial metaphor for time, as is his use of the term "strip." Following Henri Bergson, David Parkin (1982:xxxi) has argued that such metaphors are embedded in language, where space denotes time, that is, a linear passage between fixed points that are measurable and finite. Parkin (1982:xxxi) suggested further that spatial metaphors for temporal phenomena may explain "the sway of positivist assumptions of fixity, set and measurable distance, and of observable objectivity." Frame analysis, it seems to me, exemplifies this sway, that is, our drive to isolate and identify the boundaries of situations so as to contain and control them, thereby preventing slippages and keeping the really real distinguishable from play, the serious from the unserious (Bateson 1972).

Goffman's frame analysis attempts to show how people distinguish the really real from make-believe, the indicative from the subjunctive. Play is then relegated to the latter. This model may help explain how Goffman's subjects of study attempted to structure their experience, but it cannot explain a structure of experience in which events and people are never taken to be simply what they seem. Frame analysis cannot cope analytically with a view of reality as unknowable, ambiguous, unpredictable, uncertain, and indeterminate. Indeed, indeterminacy is the very condition of the possibility of free play and is what empowers the players. It is inconceivable in frame analysis that play as the mode of everyday praxis is by definition serious and efficacious, shaping what reality is and how it is experienced. The unpredictable trickster stationed at the crossroads, whether in Nigeria or in Brazil, is a symbol of the efficacy of play, and narratives that focus on him are models *of* and *for* its practice.

What is significant is that to play a situation is to intervene in it—to transform it. When the policeman originally pulled my acquaintance's car over, he had no idea of the work he was going to do as a result. He interfered with my acquaintance, but my acquaintance reciprocated, turning the situation back on the policeman and taking pleasure in doing so. The ruse was not mere possibility cast in a "play frame"—certainly not from the policeman's point of view; it was nevertheless what Yoruba call play, what Schechner (1988) calls "dark play."

Yoruba play need not always involve ruses. In the Yoruba context, playing involves spending time with people for its own sake (indulging in time), engaging them in a competition of wits verbally and/or physically, and playing it out tactically to disorient and be disoriented, to surprise and be surprised, to shock and be shocked, and to laugh together—to enjoy. In conversations with my diviner friend and colleague Ọṣitọla, he would often insist, "All work and no play makes one become dull," in order to appeal to my Western perception of an unplayful Jack as "a dull boy." The following incident was a spontaneously improvised riddling encounter in which Ọṣitọla and I collaboratively explored our working relationship (taped interview #82.71). Recapping what we, together with Henry Drewal and John Pemberton III, had just discussed,

I reiterated: So when a six-year-old child goes through [an Itẹfa ritual], it is his mother who goes with him.

Ọṣitọla: Yes, his mother.

Me: He would be touching his head to each of those *ebe* [earthen mounds prepared with medicines].

Ọṣitọla: Yes, but . . .

Me: And the mother would follow.

Ọṣitọla: Will follow . . .

Me: And touch her head to . . .

Ọṣitọla: She will help him. She will be the helping hand. And, yes, any more questions? [Laughter.] Yes. The mother will be doing the work of the wife. And the question is, when you marry how will you [that is, me—a wife] have authority with the Ifa? That is the next question. Uh huh?

Me: Uh huh. [Laughter.]

Ọṣitọla:	The question, I know that is the . . .
Me:	Well, answer! [Laughter.] Answer your own question now!
Ọṣitọla:	Um um. Is it my question or your question? [Laughter.]
Me:	Well, I'll take it. I'll take it.
Ọṣitọla:	No! Who owns that question? [Uproarious laughter.] Well, I keep the answer within me.
Me:	You own the question.
Ọṣitọla:	Then I keep the . . .
Me:	I second the question. I will second the question.
Ọṣitọla:	I thank you for seconding my question, then I will take the answer for myself. [Laughter.] Because when I own the question, then I have to hold the question because I need the answer. [More laughter.] Then I will have to keep the answer for myself. [We laugh again.]
Henry:	That means we can't let him [Ọṣitọla] ask any more questions. [Laughter.]
Me:	No, we can't let him ask any questions because we will never know the answer.
Ọṣitọla:	Uh huh! So, maybe, I want you to ask the question, then I [will] give the answer.
Me:	Ah ha!
Ọṣitọla:	Let's agree it's not my question now, then you ask the question.
Me—resuming with *my* question:	So it's the mother that goes through the ceremony with the six-year-old son. What happens again when he is married?
Ọṣitọla:	When he is married?
Me:	And takes a wife?
Ọṣitọla:	When—thank you!—when he has married the wife, we have to associate the wife with the Ifa like this [. . . etc.].

Such play is reflexive. In the case above, it was about our mutual roles as—to use Ọṣitọla's creative English—"questionaire" (someone who has questions like a millionaire has millions) and respondent. By mutual agreement the ownership of the question was transferred to fit the roles we had set up for ourselves in the process of the doing. In this kind of play, nobody formally wins or loses, although Yoruba play is an exercise of power and it is fundamentally exploratory. The trajectory of the process, as well as the outcome, is unpredictable.

The object is to turn one condition into another through a series of exchanges that bring revelations, altered perceptions, or even a reorientation of the participants. It is the process itself that is critical, whereby each spontaneous response turns on the previous one and to some degree directs the one that follows. This process is also at times autotelic. When it involves competition between people, the activity itself organizes their relationships.

Such play is integral to the practice of everyday life, a "mode of activity" occurring at any time or any place (Schwartzman 1982:328; Schechner 1988). Over years of research, Yoruba friends have time and again advised me to "play with people" as a strategy "to get what you want," i.e., to do successful research. What they meant is that in order to establish the kind of relationship with people in which there is an open exchange of ideas and points of view—a prerequisite for working successfully with them—it is crucial to engage in play.

People who do not know how to play will ultimately be tricked because the play will proceed in any case without their awareness. Westerners, for example, are not generally known for their ability to play. Consequently, there is a well-known saying in Yorubaland that "you can always get a white man to fool." Or, more literally, you can easily "circumcise a white man" without his realizing it (*d'ako fun oyinbo*). Individual acts such as this may not have subverted colonialism, but could on occasion undermine a colonialist.

Play as a mode of activity is by nature tactical. It also demonstrates how individuals handle themselves and manipulate situations. Engaging in competitive play is probing; it probes individuals' personalities and ways of operating, revealing at once their strengths and weaknesses. As keen observers of human behavior, Yoruba are also extremely conscious of the value of exposing opponents and of the dangers of being exposed oneself. The Yoruba concern with appearances is expressed in their acute awareness of *oju aye*, "the eyes of the world" (Adedeji 1967:62). The implications of probing individuals' ways of operating transcends any notion of a bounded "play frame." Play in the Yoruba sense is an interactive exploration of the inner heads (*ori inu*) of the players, a creative, engaging, ongoing strategy for testing the stuff opponents are made of. The insight one gains in this kind of play is applicable to any life situation.

THE PLAY OF RITUAL

Yoruba rituals (*etutu*) are propitiatory performances for the deities, ancestors, spirits, and human beings. They propitiate, or "cool" (*tu*), in that they entail both sacrifice (*ebo*) and play (*ere*), and in this they are socially and spiritually efficacious. What an *etutu* shares with the Indo-European root of ritual, *ri*—apart from its sacred dimension—is the notion of counting or enumerating (see Klein 1967:1351). Thus Yoruba specialists went on at great lengths enumerating the order of discrete segments (*aito* or *eto*) that make up their conceptual models of particular *etutu*. As a broad category of performance, the Yoruba concept of ritual subsumes annual festivals (*odun*), weekly rites (*ose*), funerals (*isinku*), divinations (*idafa*), and initiations and installations of all kinds—known by various Yoruba names according to the particular context.[5] Performances in each subcategory vary radically from place to place and from time to time. When Yoruba "perform ritual" (*se etutu*) they often say in English that they are going to "play." The concept has endured even in Yoruba-derived ritual practices in Brazil.[6]

In relation to ritual, what I understand Yoruba to mean by "play" is, more specifically, that they improvise. I do not use the term "improvisation" strictly in relation to music and dance, although in certain rituals Yoruba name and frame such activities as "play." In reference to ritual practice broadly, I use the term "improvisation"—as Yoruba use the English word "play"—to refer to a whole gamut of spontaneous individual moves: ruses, parodies, transpositions, recontextualizations, elaborations, condensations, interruptions, interventions, and more.

Improvisations are easiest to spot cross-culturally when they involve the incorporation of mass-produced items into new contexts for which they were never intended, as for example when maskers wear Western tuxedos, imported latex Halloween false faces, or World War II gas masks and sneakers (fig. 2.2), or when they carry pocketbooks in their hands and assemblages of plastic toys on top of their heads. In a similar vein, an Egungun masker in the Egbado Yoruba town of Imasai in 1978 used his raspy, guttural spirit voice to speak Pidgin English in imitation of a popular Nigerian radio and television comedian named Baba Sala.

More difficult to recognize, unless the observer knows carving styles over a wide area, are masks produced in neighboring cultures, such as masks made by Ibibio people of southeastern Nigeria for foreign tourists, but used in ritual by Yoruba performers. As representations of ancestral spirits, such masks refer to the past, but the newly incorporated items mark divergence from the conventional rather than similarity to it. In this sense, each mask is a "formal analogue to the dialogue of past and present" in which the past as referent is modified, signaling new meaning (Hutcheon 1988:24–25).

As in the ruse my acquaintance pulled on the police or in my agreeing to agree with Ositola that his question was really my question, the subjunctive gives way to the indicative by playing a situation, a code, a learned conventional pattern, or a form. The performance is a restoration of an earlier performance and, at the same time, a new actualization (Schechner 1985:35–116). I believe it is not purely coincidental that the Yoruba word for spectacle is the same word used to speak of a generation of people born into the world at the same time.[7] In ritual performance as in the notion of descent, there is at once a continuity and a transformation. A World War II gas mask becomes the spirit's face, or plastic dolls become spiritual accoutrements. They do so in synthesizing practices. Mere possibility or potential becomes a newly synthesized representation. When new syntheses are popular, they can spread widely, effecting change in the entire masking complex. In such cases, the new synthesis may eventually become conventional.

Unfixed and unstable, Yoruba ritual is more modern than modernism itself. During the 1970s, oil revenues brought prosperity, increasing the economic power of Nigerians to stage rituals in urban areas, for example. In Lagos, a cosmopolitan city, masks became posh and elaborate, made of imported damask, brocade, and velveteen. One I saw in the Egbado Yoruba town of Ilaro in 1977 was sewn with about sixty meters of velveteen—longer than the house where it was stored—reflecting the combined cash contributions of lineage members (according to two men in the household) (fig. 2.3). If verticality in

2.2 A small Egungun wears tennis shoes, gloves, and a World War II gas mask. Ẹgba/Ẹgbado area, Itoko Quarter, Abẹokuta, 23 April 1978.

2.3 A lineage's Egungun mask that dates to the early 1950s when the price of cocoa reached its peak. It is made of approximately sixty meters of imported velveteen and finished off with hand-woven strip cloth. Ẹgbado area, Agosaga Quarter, Ilaro, ca. 2 December 1977.

2.4 A lineage's Egungun mask whose train of imported brocade is carried by other family maskers. Isalẹ-Eko Quarter, Lagos, 15 October 1977.

New York City speaks visibly of corporate power (Kirshenblatt-Gimblett 1983:186), then the horizontality of these masks called *baba parikoko* visualizes another kind of corporate power for Yoruba—large cohesive descent groups.

Baba parikoko masks represent spirits of "the original" Egungun lineages in the town. Each has a personal name deriving from lineage praise epithets (*oriki*). When *baba parikoko* parade around the town in slow, stately fashion, other family masks accompany them to carry and position their trains, to translate their gestures, and to chant their personal praise epithets. The procession acquires power and eminence for the masks, and by extension for the lineage they represent, through sheer visibility in space. In procession, the entourage becomes a monumental spectacle, particularly as a *baba parikoko*'s enormous flexible form continually changes (fig. 2.4). The performance is an exercise of power that constructs for the participants a sense of self, both individually and collectively (Tuan 1977:173, 175). Many different groups representing various lineages parade the town simultaneously—but not as a unified group—thereby setting themselves competitively against each other.

Since ritual is at various levels a joint sacrifice, the amount of money participants put into their performances should ideally represent their economic conditions at that moment. As economists see it, people invest their incomes in ceremonies such as funerals and installations to reinforce relations of seniority and patronage as a strategy for competing for wealth and influence.[8] In her study of Yoruba economics, Sara Berry (1985:192–194) concludes that such strategies "promoted unproductive patterns of accumulation and resource use and management." Thus people dissipate their surplus pursuing the means of competition rather than building the means of production, in a process that has mitigated against unimodal economic development and one that, in her words, "is not likely to be arrested by the unilateral action of any single class, community, or institution." But investing income in performance is "unproductive" according to whose system of values? Economic prosperity in the 1970s during Nigeria's oil boom did not necessarily make costumes and performances better, but it enabled them to proliferate and flourish. Likewise, *baba parikoko* masks took on monumental proportions during the peak of Ilaro's cocoa industry in the early 1950s. The monumentality of the form was itself a revision: an improvisation that was contingent on economic conditions at the moment of its creation.

When Yoruba people say that they perform ritual "just like" their ancestors did it in the past, improvisation is implicit in their re-creation or restoration. Innovations in ritual, then, do not break with tradition but rather are continuations of it in the spirit of improvisation. In practice, improvisation as a mode of operation *destabilizes* ritual—making it open, fluid, and malleable. The progression of the action as well as the meanings it generates are unfixed, "trajectories obeying their own logic" in de Certeau's words. These trajectories have a dialectical relationship to each individual's conceptual model of a particular ritual, and, in a kind of ongoing process of evaluation, a lot of the discussion *about* ritual centers on discrepancies between those models and what in fact "happened."

Since what Yoruba performers "do" in ritual reflects their assessments of the moment, it would be naive and reductionistic to think of their performances as a preformulated enactment or reenactment of some authoritative past—or even as a reproduction of society's norms and conventions. As I attempt to show, Yoruba ritual is not a rigid structure that participants adhere to mindlessly out of some deep-seated desire for collective repetition in support of a dominant social order. If that were true then perhaps culture itself should be defined as hegemonic. And if the Yoruba perception of the white man's general incapacity to engage in play, or even to recognize it, can be taken as empirical evidence, it suggests that more attention should be given to improvisation as *praxis* and to its potential to test propriety, to challenge convention, and even to commandeer and transform ritual structures.[9]

RITUAL KNOWLEDGE, TRAINING, AND EXPERIENCE

People participate in ritual with varying degrees of performance knowledge, effort, and understanding. In this particular study, I have not given equal attention to all participants. I am specifically interested in the practice of ritual specialists—the conceptualizers, principal interpreters, and directors of performances, whom other participants then join. The generic term in Yoruba for ritual specialist is *alawo* or simply *awo,* that is, one who possesses specialized, esoteric knowledge and wisdom (*awo*).

The concept of *awo* has often been trivialized in the literature on Yoruba religion as "secret." Although Yoruba use the term generically in this sense, it implies deeper levels of meaning in relation to ritual. Thus the opposite of *awo* is *ogberi,* the naive or uninitiated, or *ologberi,* "one who possesses a naive perspective." The latter term is often used by *alawo* or *omo awo,* "students specializing in ritual knowledge," to speak of those who have not been trained and therefore lack skill and understanding. Most Yoruba ritual incorporates the naive in one way or another. In many, they outnumber the specialists.

The distinction Yoruba make between the experienced specialist and the naive often means that ritual is exclusive. Not only that, but the restricted parts of performances often contain further restrictions that certain ritual specialists themselves do not even have access to. Indeed, restricted access to ritual has probably led to a misunderstanding of *awo* as "secret." But it is not secrecy *per se* that is at issue so much as the idea that a little performance knowledge can be a dangerous thing. Why? Because action is linked to power. This is true from a Yoruba perspective as well as from the perspective of contemporary social theory (Giddens 1982:38–39; 1986:14–16).

Acquiring techniques for producing ritual action is mostly a rote exercise demanding sustained effort and concentration. Ọṣitọla described to me how his grandfather used to make him sit attentively for hours at a time studying the oral texts of divination and ritual processes in action. Some techniques require more effort than others to master. To acquire such techniques—in other words, to know how something is accomplished, particularly if it can be picked up easily—without simultaneously learning the values and ethics operating behind that knowledge can lead to misuse and even abuse. This is particularly critical in rituals performed to effect change, as in rites of passage, divination, and healing. Insofar as ritual action is related to power, it also privileges those capable of deploying such power.

Specialists learn their craft with sustained, formal exposure to a ritual process, perseverance, and the contemplation of ritual knowledge. If this were not the case, then anybody could become an instant specialist by reading a "how-to" book or by observing behind the scenes. But appearances can deceive the inexperienced. What distinguishes ritual specialists from each other, and from charlatans, are their particularized ritual roles, which they have often inherited and for which they have been specifically selected and trained. It is the transformative power of this kind of sustained experience that is essential, which is why Ọṣitọla often voiced to me his concern that "you can't learn everything in a day," in response to my persistent questioning.

The fact is, nobody can witness a Yoruba performance in its entirety, not even ritual specialists themselves. This is true not only because of the exclusivity of many ritual segments, but because of the simultaneity of ritual action generally. Many Yoruba performances are so exclusive at many different levels that the only reality participants have access to, including the performers themselves, is saturated through and through with secondhand representations of it. If I could observe every aspect of a ritual firsthand, or any other kind of performance for that matter, I would have observed undoubtedly more than any other participant.

This kind of fragmented experience—and everybody's is different—means at the same time that even constructing a narrative description of what happens in ritual is in some sense faulty since no one could ever experience a ritual in its "totality." At the same time, each participant has some conception of the whole and its performative sequence. And nobody seems to be at a loss to narrate it. Whether or not things actually happen in just that way is not the point of the narration. It is more about returning to the whole, in Fernandez's terms (1986), and returning to one's own personal whole at that, because no two conceptions of *the* ritual are usually the same.

Each participant in this way has her or his own portion of culture (Schwartz 1978). The portions are shaped by many things—individuals' motives and self-interest, their levels of knowledge, their relationships to each other, their formal ritual roles, and their access to the various parts. It is the combined force of people's personal interactions and representations of them, whether gained firsthand or based on hearsay, that shapes the entire experience for each participant, including myself. The very incompleteness of the experience engenders creativity as each person attempts to construct a sense of the whole. Thus, knowledge of any given ritual performance comes equally from experiencing the performance and from what Ladislav Holy and Milan Stuchlik (1983:99) call representations of social reality. Apart from the fact that representations constitute social reality, the distinction is nevertheless important in understanding ritual. In other words, the talk about ritual is as important as what people actually do.

During the 1986 Agẹmọ festival in lmọsan, Nigeria, rumors spread that a tree had fallen in a restricted sacred grove moments after the ritual priests left (see chapter 7). Apparently nobody actually saw the tree fall. Colleagues of the priest who is considered the owner of the grove explained that his enemy—another priest, who refused to participate in the performances that year—had used his power to fell the tree. It was the power of their colleague, they insisted, that prevented it from falling until after everyone had gone. By another account, it was the owner of the sacred land himself—not his enemy—who caused the tree to fall as a demonstration of his personal power in the midst of the conflict. Whether or not the tree actually fell was not as important as the interpretations given. Part of what people do in the midst of performing ritual is to talk about what is happening and gossip about what particular individuals are thought to have done. The representation takes on its own reality.

URBANISM AND AGENCY

Yoruba rituals take diverse forms and styles, to a certain extent a reflection of their urbanism.[10] People live in relatively large, dense, permanent settlements that are heterogeneous.[11] It is largely through ritual performances of diverse kinds that Yoruba celebrate urban life.

Yoruba political structure was historically based on an open, representative government in which conflict and competition operated both between descent groups and between the various Yoruba sacred kings and their chiefs (Lloyd 1965:99–102). Yoruba ritual functions politically, often excludes certain categories of people, and involves power plays among participants or between participants and other groups. The power of Yoruba deities varies in direct proportion to the power of their devotees, that is, in the number of a deity's supporters, their social statuses, and their abilities to mobilize support (Barber 1981b). Even prior to the introduction of Christianity and Islam more than a century ago, religion in Yorubaland was pluralistic (Eades 1980:118; Barber 1981b).[12]

In Yoruba thought, the otherworldly domain (*ọrun*) coexists with the phenomenal world of people, animals, plants, and things (*aye*).[13] *Ọrun* includes a pantheon of uncountable deities (*orisa*), the ancestors (*osi, egun*), and spirits both helpful and harmful.[14] The world and the otherworld are always in close proximity, and both human and other spirits travel back and forth between the two. The Yoruba adage "the world is a market, the otherworld is home" (*aye l'ọja, ọrun n'ile*) conveys the idea of the journey between the two and the permanency of existence in the latter in contrast to the former, where people and spirits merely visit. The crossroads (*orita, ori ita*), "a point of intersection," the juncture of three and sometimes four roads, is a physical representation of the intersection of the phenomenal world and the otherworld. Thus the crossroads is a prime spot to place sacrifices so that they will be taken to the otherworld, a practice that has been retained by both Cuban and American practitioners of Yoruba religion. For similar reasons, the crossroads also figures significantly in funerals, as the point of transfer of the deceased's soul to its otherworldly domain.

The life cycle of an individual constitutes only a segment in a larger ontological journey—a continuous, unending movement of the human spirit from the world to the otherworld and back again, to be reincarnated in the bodies of descendants (chapters 3 and 4). This otherworld of undisclosed realities is mediated by specialists through diverse representational acts—divination, masked performance, possession trance. Throughout the following chapters, it should become apparent that Yoruba ritual specialists are quite conscious that they are engaged in acts of interpretation and representation through diverse kinds of performative acts. Rituals in all their various permutations are strategies for invoking autonomous forces, bringing them into existence to be experienced, marshaling them, setting them into action one against the other, and then playing with them to suggest that things are not always what they appear to be.

The agency of performers is implicit in the Yoruba concept of power known as aṣẹ. Variously defined as "a coming to pass [. . .] effect; imprecation" (Crowther 1852:47), "power, authority, command" (Abraham 1958:71), aṣẹ has no moral connotations; it is neither good nor bad. Rather, it is a generative force or potential present in all things—rocks, hills, streams, mountains, plants, animals, ancestors, deities—and in utterances—prayers, songs, curses, and even everyday speech.[15] Aṣẹ is the power of transformation. Humans possess this generative force and through education, initiation, and experience learn to manipulate it to enhance their own lives and the lives of those around them.

The concept of aṣẹ presupposes the instrumentality of actors as agents in structuring, in processing, in contextualizing, in playing tropes off one other, at once performing operations on structure, process, and context and improvising on, in, with, and around them (see also Arens and Karp 1989). At its most effective, aṣẹ must also be accompanied by aba, the ability to reveal one's aṣẹ through masterful manipulation, negotiation, and persuasion (Ọlabiyi Yai, personal communication, 1990). Improvisations take diverse forms: transformations of esoteric verses into narratives, spontaneous interpretations, recontextualizations, drumming, dancing, chanting, parody, ruses, reconstitutions of conventions, competing interests, and individual interventions into the ritual event. All are rooted in Yoruba concerns with aṣẹ—the power to bring things into existence, to make things happen. This is the real "work" of a ritual performer; indeed, it is in essence what the act of representation is all about. There is no ritual specialist among the Yoruba who does not possess aṣẹ, the proto-concept of the axe of Brazilian Candomblé, the ache of Cuban Santeria and Lucumi, and the aṣẹ of New York City's "Yoruba reversionist" movement (Edwards and Mason 1985:v; M. Drewal in press).

Aṣẹ is the power of performers to generate ritual spectacles, or rather spectacular rituals, that operate as style wars, for style is meaning and competing styles generate uniqueness, virtuosity, and inventiveness (Kirshenblatt-Gimblett 1983:205, 220). The traditional Yoruba religious system itself engenders extreme diversity through its processes of divination and performance, emphasizing differentiation and the heterogeneity of citizens' origins and religious practices.[16] If performance through its symbolic representations constructs the cultural configurations and identity of a civilization, as Milton Singer (1972:165) would have it, then surely Yoruba ritual performances as a group construct multiple configurations and identities that are always in discourse with each other.

The malleability of Yoruba ritual practice has enabled it to tolerate both Christianity and Islam. It also had the capacity to survive in the oppressive slave societies in which it landed in the New World, operating clandestinely initially and now more openly. Indeed, Yoruba religion has taken hold and is growing today among well-educated, middle-class black and white Americans in a so-called liminoid society (Edwards and Mason 1985; Mason 1985).

If rituals can be said to be strategic in that they are organized by trained specialists—that is, subjects of will and power (de Certeau 1984:xix)—then who or what are the objects being worked upon? Playing is the power Yoruba actors exercise in transforming ritual itself, and indeed it may be more precise to say that ritual structures, or strategies, have no existence apart from the tactics, or play, of actors. It is in play that ritual's very efficacy resides. Indeed, play is the integrative mechanism driving Yoruba ritual action, thus introducing contingency into ritual process.

Continuously under revision, Yoruba ritual is molded and remolded by creative performer/interpreters who, acting both independently and in concert, reformulate it. That is essentially what the following pages are all about. Ritual, like the larger society in which it operates, is shaped by the competitive pulls and tugs of a multitude of manipulators. In this, Yoruba performances diverge radically from scholars' traditional assumptions about ritual's rigidity, stereotypy, conventionality, conformity, uniformity, predictability, invariance, structural stasis, and redundancy.[17]

As media of change and transformation, rituals are conceived as "journeys," a metaphor that runs like a leitmotif throughout these pages. In Yoruba usage, the journey highlights crucial dimensions of ritual that most of the literature on the subject does not reflect, that is, the subjective experience of participants, their capacities for reflexive self-monitoring, and their transformations of consciousness through play and improvisation.

3. The Ontological Journey

"In a muddy land, a person slips and falls easily. Those who follow behind beware." These were the words of wisdom spoken to Ọrunmila when he was traveling in a strange land called Ejibọnmẹfọn.

Before he set out, his diviners warned him to perform a sacrifice [erubo] so that he could be disgraced only to be later blessed. He sacrificed animals, birds, yams, palm oil, and all sorts of foodstuffs. The diviners put everything in a clay bowl, instructing Ọrunmila to carry it on his journey. He followed their instructions. Thank goodness he made the sacrifice. On the way, he first passed through the market on the outskirts of the town. There, Eṣu decided to humiliate him.

Causing it to rain heavily, Eṣu made the land slippery, but Ọrunmila persevered. As he reached the marketplace he slipped and fell down. The animals' blood, the palm oil, the food splattered all over his body. It was not pleasant to be so dirty. When the women and children in the market saw what happened, they began to laugh and ridicule him.

Ọrunmila did not know anybody. Ashamed and disgraced, he sat down feeling sorry for himself. That night when the marketwomen and their children went to sleep, Eṣu made them dream of blood spilling over their bodies. They were startled. Some woke up in fright, some became ill, some fell unconscious. Their husbands and fathers worried. Eṣu suddenly appeared inquiring:

What happened?

Husbands: The women woke up frightened and now they are ill.
Eṣu: Oh! You must consult a diviner.
Husbands: But there is no diviner around.
Eṣu: Yes, there is. You don't know? He is in the market.
Husbands: Take me to him.
Eṣu: Well then, bring a ram, a cow, some fish, a he-goat, a she-goat, and plenty of money.

Everybody went, one-by-one, each taking the prescribed animals and cash. Ọrunmila received everybody and helped them. In addition to the wealth he accumulated in that strange land, he also became famous.

Ọrunmila decided to thank the diviners who had advised him on his journey. During his thanksgiving service, he described how his beloved, learned diviners, in interpreting Ifa for him so wisely, had given him the words of wisdom that slippery land slips people up. Those who follow behind take note and be cautious.

But Ọrunmila's diviners said they were not to be thanked, that they themselves had to thank Ifa for giving them their wisdom. Then Ifa interjected that he is with God and God is with him.[1] Thus he too must not be thanked, but he must thank God Almighty.

In celebration, Ọrunmila's diviners summoned *apere* musicians from Ilara, *apesi* musicians and dancers from Ikija, and *iṣerimọle* dancers from Kijikiji, gathering them from different quarters.[2] As they played, Ọrunmila sang:

> I fell down and everybody saw me.
> They ridiculed me.
> Who knew what the result would be?
> I fell down and everybody saw me.
> They ridiculed me.

***

> Mo ṣubú, wọ́n rí mi ò.
> Ẹ̀ li sì mù'gbè yìn.
> Ẹ̀ li sì mù'gbèhìn eti mi o?
> Mo ṣubú o, wọ́n rí mi ò.
> Ẹ̀ li sì mù'gbè yìn.
>   (Ọsitọla #86.75)

Stories such as this often narrate the experiences of ancient diviners or animals on their distant journeys. "Words of wisdom" begin the verses, framing the story, teaching lessons about life. But these words require interpretation and contemplation. Thus the wisdom of the story above is not to beware of slipping and falling, but has to do with humility, humiliation, and reciprocity. Ọrunmila withstood humiliation only to be blessed with fame and wealth. He thanked his diviners, who thanked Ifa, who in turn thanked God. Who slipped—Ọrunmila or those who ridiculed him? And who gained most from the humiliation? Ọrunmila learned humility through the experience of humiliation, while the ones who humiliated him suffered most and in the end paid the greater price. This journey is only one among the many represented in Ifa literature that posit uncountable life situations. Such stories are always told in relation to an individual's personal problem.

Ọsitọla, my diviner friend who lives in the town of Imodi only a few kilometers outside Ijẹbu-Ode, told me this story in relation to a personal experience of mine, so that I would not feel discouraged. Things had been going amiss; it was one of those kinds of days that is often associated with the workings of Eṣu, the unpredictable trickster/messenger, who in the story was instrumental in transforming Ọrunmila's disgrace into fame and fortune. According to his family history, Ọṣitọla is a seventh-generation diviner as well as a drummer and a member of the Oṣugbo society, formerly the indigenous judiciary in Yoruba communities (M. Drewal and H. Drewal 1983). He and I have been working together since 1982, tape-recording more than one hundred fifty hours of conversations (fig. 3.1). Our talks, mostly in English, but interspersed with key concepts and discussions in Yoruba, covered religious and ritual topics.

Trained in the two hundred and fifty-six sets of divination texts (Odu Ifa), each with uncountable verses (ẹsẹ), Ọṣitọla has a keen memory.[3] In 1986, he remembered details of our discussions from 1982, sometimes reminding me that I was being redundant. When I responded that I was merely cross-checking, he retorted, "no, you are double-crossing." He always looked forward to "wonderful" questions, that is, ones that made him wonder. They were not always easy for me to produce; Ọṣitọla thinks analytically and by his own account used to pester his father and grandfather quizzing them incessantly on the whys and wherefores of various ritual acts. He learned divination as a young boy simply by accompanying them during ritual, and at recess in primary school he used to divine for classmates on the ground. By the age of ten he was already taking leading ritual roles. From his grandmother, who was a priest of the deity Oriṣanla, he learned how to prepare shrines and care for the deities.

Nicknamed Abidifa (A-bi-di-Ifa, "One who teaches the ABC's of Ifa"), Ọṣitọla can go on at great length naming the segments that make up the rituals he performs, describing the action associated with them, and explicating their meanings. In interviews, after exhausting all my questions, he would usually end by telling me what I had failed to ask. This eventually developed into an almost structural feature of our interviews. My most "wonderful" questions by his standards were the ones for which there were no ready answers, the ones that required thought and sometimes left him momentarily blank.

We discovered that the best method of working was simply for him to narrate what he does—step by step—and for me to ask questions for clarification. The Ijẹbu Yoruba term for a discrete ritual segment is *aito*, which is related to the noun *eto*, an order or program, the root word for *letoleto*, implying "in an orderly fashion one after the other." The serial form of performance is evoked in the very terms Yoruba use to characterize it (M. Drewal and H. Drewal 1987). Therefore, not only are participants' experiences of ritual fragmented, but the form itself is segmented.

During our many discussions of various kinds of rituals Ọṣitọla performs, he kept referring to the "journey" as a way of conveying the experiential impact that ritual has on its participants. Finally I asked him explicitly, "are all rituals journeys?" He explained,

the whole life span is wonderful. And even the actors are wonderful, I mean, the human beings. They are the main actors. The two are wonderful.

3.1   Diviner Ḳolawọle Ọṣitọla and his three sons, together with
the author. Ijẹbu area, village of Imodi, 1 November 1986.

One proverb says, when a young child falls, he looks to the front, but if an
elder is falling he will always turn to look back in search of what befell him.
Nowadays, the elders don't look back to see what has befallen them.

It is a sort of wisdom to reflect on past events to make a good decision
on where we should try to go or what should happen. And this makes a
journey. But it seems to me as if everybody is contented, everybody is
satisfied, everybody has already completed their journeys. No more journeys.
Then I get worried. The actors want to end the journey. Or the journey
wants to end. But to my knowledge the journey ends not. That is one of
the things that makes your question wonderful to me because I know you
are one of the actors. And I wondered how you could even ask, are they all
journeys. (Ọṣitọla #86.75)

Ọṣitọla does not use the word "actors" in the Western sense of "players of
roles." Rather, he means people of action. I perceived the significance of his use
of the metaphor of the journey only after I began to realize just how many
Yoruba rituals are actually constructed as journeys.

JOURNEYING IN ORATURE AND RITUAL

Divination verses tell of the journeys of ancient diviners and of deities and
witches, "when they were coming from heaven to earth" (*nigba ti wọn n t'ọrun*

bọ w'aye). The journey (*irin ajo*, or simply *ajo*) is an important organizing meta-phor in Yoruba thought.[4] The verb *rin*, "to walk," when compounded means "to travel" (*rin irin* or *rinrin*). More than simply a movement forward, the act of traveling implies a transformation in the process, a progression.

Rituals in the form of masking displays travel in the sense that trained specialists "bring them into the world" from their otherworldly domain and send them away again through their performances of spectacle (H. Drewal and M. Drewal 1983:2–4). The deities journey into the world, too, by mounting the heads of their priests, who go into states of possession trance (M. Drewal 1986, 1988). Elaborated transitional stages mark the deity's arrival and withdrawal.

Wherever Yoruba religion thrives—Brazil, Cuba, the United States—this practice of journeying through possession trance has been maintained. Cast in a myriad of ways—in narratives and in ritual performances—the journey as a metaphor highlights the experiential, reflexive nature of day-to-day living. No-where is this more explicit than in the oral tradition and performance of Oṣugbo, the traditional society of elders that historically formed the judiciary in communities throughout southern Yorubaland.[5] Oṣitọla recited the following Ifa verse as the foundation of Oṣugbo (taped discussion #86.83):

> A small child works his way off the edge of his
>   sleeping mat.
> A bird soars high above it all.
> They divined for our elderly people,
> When they were preparing to leave heaven to go to the
>   world.
> They said, what are we going to do?
> They asked themselves, where are we going?
> We are going in search of knowledge, truth, and justice.
> In accordance with our destiny,
> At the peak of the hill
> We were delayed.
> We are going to meet success.[6]
> We will arrive on earth knowledgeable.
> We will arrive on earth in beauty.
> We are searching for knowledge continuously.
> Knowledge has no end.

***

> *Ọmọ ilé tí a gbà gbé l'órí ẹní, yí o já bọ.*
> *Òkè l'ẹyẹ fò wún.*
> *A díá fún àwọn àgbàgbà,*
> *Tí wọ́n ti ìkọ̀lè ọ̀run bọ̀ wá ilé ayé.*
> *Wọ́n ní kíni wọ́n ńlọ ṣe?*
> *Ènyìn ọ̀rò, níbo lò ńlọ?*
> *À ńlọ wá ìmọ̀, òtítọ́, àti òdodo.*

Kádàrá àyànmò,[7]
L'órí òke
Àti pètèlè.
À ńlo sí ààfin oba réré.
A ó dé ilè mímò.
A ó sì dé ilè tó l'éwà.
À ń wá ìmò síi l'ójo júmó.
Ìmò kò ló'pin.

Ositola's gloss on this verse was as follows:

"A small child works his way off the edge of his sleeping mat. A bird soars high above it all." These were the words of wisdom spoken to some wise elders when they were leaving on a journey from heaven to the world. The classic meaning is just that a person should not be elevated unless he is prepared to fly above and search more.

Ifa told the elders to make a sacrifice. He told every one of them to carry along a walking stick for themselves, because their journey was far and they would feel tired. They did, and their path was blessed when they grew old.

These people in youth had the power to do things; in middle age the spreading world still had power;[8] then they moved to the elderly age. Their sacrifice was the staff, their assistant.

The elders thought. They started to search. They felt uncomfortable in their positions. They wanted to know more throughout the world. They decided to search for more, more, more. Because they were getting old, they felt worn out. That is why they were assisted by their staffs. Then their minds struck and asked them, "you, where are you going?" *Enyin oro, nibo lo nlo?* It started changing their conscience. Then they remembered what Ifa had told them. On their journey they are searching for truth, wisdom, and knowledge. *A nlo wa imo, otito, ati ododo* in obedience to their *kadara ayanmo,* destiny. In accordance with our destiny, we are searching for true knowledge and the facts. Then their conscience told them to continue with the search.

A person still searches with a staff in his hand after he has labored. Then the elders quickly remembered that their conscience told them that if they search for knowledge and wisdom, it will be through all the rough paths, *ori oke on petele.* That means, if they want to fulfill their destiny, they have to walk the path through the land, the hills, the water, the thorns, the troubles. They have to pass all troubles so that they can fulfill their destiny. And if they can afford to do this, they are sure to land at a holy place. *L'ori oke, ati petele, a nlo si aafin oba rere, a o wa dele mimo, a o si wa a dele to lewa.* That means, if we can continue to search, to search, the end of our journey will be a cooler place where we have a good head, where it is holy, where it is smooth. This story is in Ifa.

Why I am telling this story is that it is related to Oṣugbo. That is their guidance or their foundation. When you are a member and you are upgraded to a point, that is your foundation—that Ifa verse relates to the behavior, the belief, the thinking, and the reasoning of the Oṣugbos. That was why you saw me nodding when we concluded that the journey continues, the search continues.

You know Ogboni means elderly people. You think that you still start, you feel that you still begin. And even at your dying point, you will feel that you will decide you will still continue. You will not be sure whether you have searched enough. And even on your death, after you have found yourself at the resting place, at the cooler place, then you will feel you are leaving the search to be continued with those who will take it from you. They will bid you bye, and say you are expected to continue. That is why you see me so serious that night when we are trying to agree that, oh, the search continues.

This story may not be so interesting, but it is a true picture of our discussion, and it is a true picture of Oṣugbo. It relates to the research of the elders and why elders are still searching. You know nowadays elders get contented, even at [age] forty.

The reason why I am trying to translate or transcribe it or share the view with you to digest is because it is very serious. That is one of the foundations of our family. Their foundation is the search continues. That is one of the motives behind our continued inheritance of Ifa and Ogboni in our family. We want the search to be continued. Even my grandfather wants me to continue; my father wants to continue; I want to continue. Since Oṣijo [the father seven generations back] we want the search to be continued.

The verse is one of the important things my grandfather gave me. And I have been graduating on it. He didn't elaborate it to such an extent, but when I became a staunch member of Oṣugbo and I learned more, I found more, I could get what he was really concerned with deeply from my initiation, going through some rituals, and I found out that, oh, the search continues in fact. In my family circle, it is my life.

Oṣitọla's explanation was an improvised narrative based on a preformulated verse. As he commented, his grandfather "gave" him the verse, but did not elaborate it. Only later—Oṣitọla claimed—after going through rituals did he come to understand his grandfather's deep concerns. The verse served as a precedent for the narrative and to some extent guided it.[9] He contextualized both the verse and the improvised narrative within our conversations, regarding the latter not only as a "true picture" of what it means to be a member of Oṣugbo, but as a "true picture" of our own conversations. By that time, I had in

fact gone through a preliminary initiation into Ọṣugbo at Imodi so that the story
was meaningful for me on two levels. The narrative also reflected Ọṣitọla's
perception of my work as a researcher, which he correlated with the "journeying" of Ọṣugbo elders and Ifa priests.

At Ọṣugbo meetings during the annual festival—I attended six in three
different society lodges (*iledii*) between October 11 and December 1, 1986—
each of the titled elders danced solos from one end of the enclosed space to the
other, giving concrete expression to the idea of the journey. Their performances
were improvised. Each dance was a personal condensation of life's journey (*ajo
l'aye*), performed to the drum language of music called *ẹwẹlẹ*, an ideophonic
word implying an assortment of rhythms considered good for dancing. As an
Ọṣugbo drummer, Ọṣitọla says he changes the rhythms according to the particular dancer's concentration. By approximating the tonal patterns and rhythm of
spoken Yoruba, Ọṣitọla weaves into the music praise epithets (*oriki*) particular
to each dancing elder. For Akọnọrọn—to take one example—the titled elder
who acts as the defense counselor in criminal cases, Ọṣitọla sometimes plays:

> Teacher of the art of speaking
> The one who teaches how to state a case
> Pleads for the innocent

***

> A kọ́ni ní oro
> A kọ́-ni lẹ́jọ́
> Àwí jàre

In and around the praise epithets, Ọṣitọla weaves dance instructions—one-
liners that are mixed and repeated to form a free rhythm, each alluding to life's
journey. One tells the dancing elder in effect to watch where he or she is stepping. It alludes to life's potential pitfalls—"the thorns, the troubles" and the
value of reflecting on the past in order to guide present action:

> Elder, watch the ground

***

> Àgbà wolẹ̀

Improvisationally in step with the *agba* drums, the dancer enacts "checking up"
the ground (fig. 3.2), visibly watching where she or he places the foot. Or, in
another example:

> Carry on [stepping] on the ground

***

> Ǹṣó n'lẹ̀

The lẹ in both verses above refers to the ground or earth, ilẹ. To the latter rhythm the dancer is supposed to step lively and confidently on the earth. How the rhythm is interpreted spatially and stylistically is left to each dancer's discretion. The latter verse, Ọṣitọla explained to me, is an assertion that the elders have authority over the earth; therefore, the drummers direct them to "carry on" with the business at hand. Their authority is rooted in the precolonial, gerontocratic government of Yorubaland.

It was with his experience of this kind of ritual performance described above that Ọṣitọla said he came to understand his grandfather's deep concerns. On the surface, the verbal content of the drummed messages does not say much. It is only in living, or "journeying," that elders begin to read meaning into such esoteric words and actions. My own understanding comes from Ọṣitọla's explanations, and only then after my initiation, which entitled me to enter Oṣugbo lodges to participate in certain performances.

In many kinds of Yoruba ritual, the performance processes embody all of the characteristics of a journey: 1) travel from one place to another, and a return—sometimes actual, sometimes virtual, 2) new experiences, 3) joys and hardships along the route, 4) material for further contemplation and reflection, and 5) presumed growth or progress as a result of the whole experience. Rites of passage that scholars mark in a tripartite movement from separation and liminality to reaggregation (Turner 1977a:94) are in a very real sense journeys. But transition is not merely social, not simply a collective adjustment to internal changes or an adaptation to the external environment.

Like journeys, rites of passage are fundamentally transformations of experience, a deepening and broadening of each individual's understanding in relation to his or her prior experience and knowledge. If this were not so, how would participants *feel* social transition? Or, from another point of view, why is it that social transition cannot often simply be legislated or ordained? Even in our own society, rituals often attend legislated transitions. Thus what constitutes a marriage legally has little to do with what getting married means performatively. The latter in most cases constitutes the greater part of the experience of transition. Both in rituals and in journeys, participants operate at different levels of understanding and also have different capacities for making meaning.

As Ọṣitọla argued for a ritual he conducts:

All people who go to the sacred bush [igbodu] benefit from it. They may be observers; they may be priests; they may be the initiate. Only we concentrate on the initiate most. Yet everybody is involved, particularly the priests, for there is a belief—and it's an agreement between ourselves and Odu [the deity] within the sacred bush—that we are reborning ourselves. Even we priests, we are getting another rebirth. At every ritual, we are becoming new because we have something to reflect upon. We have something to contemplate during the journey, at the journey, after the journey. Our brains become sharper. We become new to the world. We think of everything. We *do* there, and we *see* there. And even more simply we pray for everybody. (Ọṣitọla #86.134)

With each restoration of behavior, even the ritual specialist is transformed and "becomes new to the world." This is also true for me as I experience Yoruba ritual repeatedly. Through a process of observation/participation, conversations with participants, contemplation, and reflection, I too become a ritual traveler in Ọṣitọla's sense, although what I derive from the experience will not necessarily be the same as what anyone else derives from the same experience. This is so not only because of differences in cultural and personal experience, but because of differences in the motives and motivations of the various participants. Most important is the idea that the sojourner may return to the same place physically, but not experientially.

Rituals attend both birth and death and serve as temporal articulation points of ontological transformation analogous to the spatial point of articulation represented by the crossroads. Such rituals are the focus of the remainder of this chapter and the next. As a member of Oṣugbo, Ọṣitọla narrated to me a detailed outline of funeral ritual from the practitioner's point of view, designating the names of the various stages of performance. Ọṣitọla's outline is an individual's normative account of what he knows from personal experience, not a presentation of dogma. Whether or not a funeral *always* happens just this way is not my concern here, although his descriptions of the public portions do correspond to what I have observed.

My intention is threefold: 1) Ọṣitọla's account illustrates how Yoruba practitioners conceptualize, order, and explicate ritual. Both the doing and the talking about the doing derive from the same stock of performance knowledge (Giddens 1986:29). 2) His specialist's view is also revealing about the concept of the ontological journey. This is critical at the end of the chapter for a reevaluation of the notion of cyclical time in Mircea Eliade's sense (1959:77–78).[10] 3) Equally important, Ọṣitọla's conceptual model underscores the centrality of play in Yoruba ritual, a topic I explore throughout the rest of the chapters. It is apparent throughout that Ọṣitọla is conscious that ritual specialists are engaged in acts of interpretation and representation. Although I have not always quoted him verbatim, I have preserved his language, descriptions, and explanations quite literally, restricting my own comments to footnotes.

THE FUNERAL PASSAGE

There are many different kinds of funerals. The circumstances of death, its perceived causes, the age and social as well as religious affiliations of the deceased all are taken into account as a family decides what type of funeral to perform. Here Ọṣitọla narrates the structure and content of the funeral he claims everyone hopes to have—the desired one—except if the deceased is Muslim or Christian.[11] These funerals (*isinku*) are for those who have died of old age. They are not simple matters of burying the corpse; rather, they involve seven days of ritual (etutu) performed to convey the spirit of the deceased to its otherworldly realm, where it remains along with other ancestral spirits. Friends of the deceased's family experience a funeral primarily as a time of dancing and feasting in celebration of the elder's long successful life. For the family, however, a funeral demands great effort and an enormous expense to ensure the continued beneficence of the elder's spirit toward those still on earth. A funeral is a critical time when the deceased's spirit lingers in the world, disembodied. There is also the expectation that the spirit will eventually return in newborn children. A funeral in this way marks an ending as well as a new beginning.

The actual interment of the corpse is conceived only as a preliminary event to the funeral process. The performances that follow are more critical for the family. After the interment, family members gather to decide on a date for the performances that complete the isinku, the funeral. Since the isinku entails great expense, it is incumbent on the family to set a date far enough in the not-too-distant future to give them time to gather sufficient resources. The funeral may therefore occur anywhere from a month to a year, or more, after burial. What follows interment, according to Ọṣitọla, is a seven-day program in which certain days are set aside for celebration: the first, or "main," funeral day of ritual (ọjọ isinku); the third day, for feasting (itaoku); the fourth day, a public celebration or day of play (irenoku, literally "playing on the deceased's behalf"); and a seventh and final celebration day (ijeku).[12] Funerals are in this way elaborated with feasting and public performances, part of the sacrifice to the deceased.

Most of the rituals that revolve around interment are exclusive. They are the prerogative of the Oṣugbo society, whose membership in the past was restricted to those whose parents were dead. Prior to the colonial period, Oṣugbo included the senior members of each family in a community. Because of their age, accumulated knowledge, and power, they comprised the segment of the community that was indeed closest to the ancestors by virtue of their proximity to death.

INTERMENT (IFẸHIN OKU-TILẸ)[13]

"Washing the corpse" (Iweku): A cosmetologist (ọnatoniṣe, "one skilled in the art of restoration"), who is a member of Oṣugbo, prepares the corpse by first sacrificing a cock or a hen, depending on whether the deceased is male or female. In the case of a female, for example, it is said that the voice of the hen follows the deceased to the otherworld.[14] The sacrificial blood, together with a preparation of water and herbs, is used to wash the corpse.

"Rubbing chalk on the deceased's palms" (Ikefunlọwọ) and "Rubbing camwood on the palms" (Ikosunlọwọ): After washing the corpse, the eldest living offspring of the deceased rubs chalk (efun) and then camwood (osun) on the deceased's palms. This means that the child who was nurtured is now nurturing the deceased parent in return. Or, in other words, as a parent brings a child into the world so must the child assist in the parent's passage into the otherworld. As the eldest applies the chalk, the children say to the deceased, "you put chalk in my hand for me" (ikefun lọwọ fun mi).[15]

"Wrapping the corpse of the wise elder" (*Idiku Ologbon*):   Relatives and other supporters of the deceased each bring cloth for the Oṣugbo members to wrap around the corpse. The cloth expresses their gratitude to the deceased for his or her good deeds. The sheer volume of the wrapped corpse is indicative of the social significance of the deceased. The word *ologbon* literally means "a wise person." In this context it refers both to the deceased elder and to a colorful, highly patterned cloth known as *aṣo ologbon*—a trademark of elders (fig. 3.3). The importance of wrapping the deceased in cloth is expressed in the adage "the corpse of the elder should not be thrown away; it is white cloth that I wore from heaven to the world" (*oku ologbon ki s'oko; ala mo fi b'orun w'aye*). The idea is that the elder should leave the world in a similar manner as the child is born into it.[16]

The multipatterned cloth represents the accumulation of the deceased's experiences while on earth. Hence—to quote directly:

> We bury them with these kinds of cloth to make them more concerned. You know they have gotten experiences. They have lived in hot weather— all sorts of weather—they have mixed with all sorts of people. They will be settling differences between people when they quarrel. They have been seeing women with good characters, with bad characters, and men with good characters and bad characters. They have moved with the elders, the youths, the ancestors. Now they have combined many experiences. This cloth contains within itself their many experiences with animals, with human beings, up and down the hills, with dangerous creatures, with non-dangerous creatures. Experiences make you more open to life and death.[17]

"Washing the coffin" (*Iwegi*):   Later in the evening, a representative from both the father's and the mother's sides of the family join the cosmetologist to sacrifice a goat to the coffin, blessing it for the deceased by putting some of the blood in their hands and a little in the coffin. The three of them then wash the coffin inside and out with herbal water: together they dip balls of cotton wool into the water, the left hand washing inside as the right washes outside. Then reversing the process, they cross their arms and use the right hand on the inside and the left on the outside. After working their way around the coffin in this manner three times, the cosmetologist removes the sacrificial goat, whose meat is part of his remuneration for work.

"Laying the back of the deceased on the earth" (*Ifehinkutile*):[18]   This occurs in the evening when it is cool. Starting around eight o'clock, the cosmetologist arranges the body in the coffin in preparation for the next stage of the ritual, when the elders gather and feast with the deceased throughout the night.

"Entertaining with the deceased" (*Ibokuu-yaju*):   When an elder dies, her or his contemporaries, normally the Oṣugbo members, celebrate with the deceased after they have wrapped the corpse. The high-ranking elders go with their drums before it is too dark and send the naive people away—the youth, the untrained, and the uninitiated. They lay the deceased out on a handwoven mat (*ẹni fafa*), and all sit down with him or her to feast. This ritual is conceived as a kind of "send-off party" to bid their comrade farewell. The elders wine, dine, and discuss, reaffirming their camaraderie in the deceased's presence.

As Ọṣitọla put it, "now that the soul is going to join the ancestors, they must present themselves in the same spirit as the deceased and the other ancestors, who may have gathered to receive him, in order to bear witness that they are still loyal. They still love him. Their mind is still open to him." Each time they put the wine to their lips, they also open the cloth and put it to the deceased's lips to express their cooperation. The cosmetologists then dance as the drums are beaten.

This ritual segment tests the honesty and sincerity of Oṣugbo members. Thus those among them who do not show up are assumed to be dishonest,

> because he[19] will not be able to lead himself between life and death. Because he cannot live to the death point, it means he is not supposed to be among them. That is a test, and it is a belief among Yorubas in the olden days that somebody who cannot go through *ibokuu-yaju* has in his mind that he has not been behaving openly. Hence he must be sure to eat and dine with the dead because it is they who join the ancestors. And the ancestors' spirits are supposed to be ruling the community and guiding the community right. Somebody who cannot join somebody who is joining the ancestors is not for the good of the community. He is not open. He may be a sort of liability. He is not a good asset because nobody will be able to believe him.

This ritual is the deceased's initiation by the society of elders into the group of the ancestors.

"Sending away the spirit of the deceased" (*Ikanku*): After the lid of the coffin is closed, the eldest child takes the cosmetologist's brass staff and raps it three times near the corpse's head. The knocking dispatches the soul of the deceased. Finally, the cosmetologist sees to it that the coffin is placed in the grave, completing the interment of the corpse.

THE MAIN FUNERAL DAY (OJỌ ISINKU)

"Collecting money for the deceased" (*Owoetiwẹku*): During the main day of the funeral, family members first of all collect money from all the relatives to buy gin and arrange for food. Formerly bean cakes were most desirable. The relatives contribute money in proportion to their closeness to the deceased. The more distant the relations, the less they are expected to contribute.[20]

"Playing for the funeral" (*Ereisinku*): The first public ceremony is a spectacle of playing and dancing in honor of the deceased. Relatives of the deceased hire music groups and accompany them around the town dancing and singing the praises of the family (fig. 3.4).[21] Family members also try to hire music groups that reflect the stylistic tastes of the deceased. Ọṣitọla told me of the funeral of his father, Ọṣineye, when his father's junior brother attempted to attract musicians from his senior brother's group so that he could personally provide the deceased's favorite musical style. Any style is appropriate as long as the group is mobile, for it is essential to parade throughout the community.

The social importance of the deceased is measured by the amount of *ere*, or "play," going on throughout the town. Forty-three musical groups paraded around for Ọṣitọla's father's funeral. The number of groups became a topic of discussion among townspeople. They asked, "How many groups played for Ọṣineye's funeral?" (*Ere meloo ni wọn ṣe l'ojọ ti Ọṣineye ku?*)

The parades of music and dance independently working their ways through the town are a formal ritual segment (*aito*) that is meaningful beyond the display for its own sake. As Ọṣitọla expressed it,

> they think dancing and enjoying after the death will depict the deceased's achievements on earth, how he or she was able to behave to the community. [. . .] It is not that they are extravagant. They do it for a meaning. If they don't do it, then the deceased who is joining the ancestors will be concerned and unhappy—and be wandering—because he has not been remembered. The deceased will have to answer queries [that is, from the ancestors]. "Why are you not properly initiated, or sent to us? Perhaps you have not performed well, have not achieved well? If you have performed well, why is posterity forgetting you?" The only way for us on earth to judge the deceased is to know how much honor was given to him by his descendants.

"Taking the achievements of the deceased" (*Imoran Oku, Imu ọran oku*):   The main day ends around eight or nine o'clock at night with a more elaborate ceremony to send the deceased's soul to the ancestors. By "taking" the achievements of the deceased, the family this time introduces the soul into heaven. The cosmetologists lead a representative of both the father and mother of the deceased to the grave site. They carry with them a piece of white cloth, a *fafa* mat, and some of the deceased's personal possessions. There they call the soul of the deceased and offer a goat to his or her inner head in a ritual segment known as *ikankuolowo*.

"Invoking the soul of the deceased" (*Ikankuolowo*):   Holding the mat by the corners and dancing to the outskirts of the town to the major crossroads (*orita*), the relatives send the soul to join the other spirits. They do so simply by mutual agreement that the soul is happy to be sent away honorably. On the road, they chant declaratively that the elaborateness of the ceremonies befits the departed ("it befits him," *o ye ọ*). By extension, then, he or she is presumed worthy to dwell with the ancestors. The mat, the piece of cloth, and other materials are divided up so that a portion can be used for the next ritual stage. This ends the main funeral day. After performing the first two parts of the main funeral day, the family feels that they have contributed to the deceased's successful journey to heaven.

THE THIRD DAY OF THE FUNERAL (ITAOKU)

The third day is reserved for feasting; at night there is a sacrifice at the grove of Oro (*igbo Oro*).[22] Children of the deceased and other relatives share their favorite foods with their friends throughout the entire day. During that night the caretaker of the Oro bush sacrifices a ram to the ancestor. Those who hold the title of caretaker (*atejumole*) are among the kingmakers (Agba Oke, or Iwarefa) within the Oṣugbo society.

"Opening the voice of the deceased" (*Ilakuoun [Ila oku oun]*): The new ancestor's voice will be heard for the first time.[23] People say, "Oro is crying." The voice of Oro on that night is presumed to be the spirit of the newly buried deceased coming to endorse the funeral performances of his children and other relatives. After the *atejumole* has opened the deceased's voice, he will ask the deceased to follow the male family members into the town to bless the relatives who have provided an honorable burial. Women must close themselves inside their rooms and lock the doors, for it is strictly forbidden for women to witness Oro. They hear only the sound.

PLAYING ON BEHALF OF THE DECEASED (IRENOKU)

During this fourth day of the funeral, the children and friends parade through the town and feast once again, this time principally to affirm their own success in providing a proper burial, but also to celebrate their ancestor's endorsement of their efforts.[24] It is the second day devoted strictly to dancing and enjoying, a formal ritual segment of play (*aito ku mere muṣe*) that is simultaneously a sacrifice performed willingly and very elaborately at the expense of the deceased's descendants. The children arrange for musicians, just as they do on the main funeral day, only more elaborately. "By dancing around the town, everybody can see from their own places how many plays have been done, how the drummers beat respect, how the children finish the ceremony happily." Again, they also count the number of groups, or plays, on that date as a sign of the seriousness of the descendants. The various groups stop at different places, particularly the compounds of relatives, where it is believed the new ancestor's spirit will stay. "You know the spirit of the father will be going around his children's houses. And he will stop at the marketplace and at important junctions on the outskirts of the town."

SEVENTH FUNERAL DAY FOR THE DECEASED (EJEOKU)

Four days following the play day the children offer the new ancestor pounded yam and fish soup at home (*ibọ oṣi*). After the descendants perform this sacrifice, and another in the Oro grove, the ancestor becomes manifest once more, this time together with Oro music played on *agba* drums, in a ritual segment known as *asipelu*. Thus the deceased comes to receive the sacrifice "in the Oro mood."[25] Oro society members as well as male relatives of the deceased follow the ancestor's voice, which thanks and blesses all the family members. Once again women must close themselves inside their rooms and lock the doors.

This outing of the spirit voice is the final act of transference, the incorporation of the spirit of the deceased into ancestorhood. An incantation affirms, "the deceased who possesses wisdom will not be deaf" (*oku ologbon ki seti*), that is, will attend his or her descendants in the world in return for their attention during the funeral. In celebrating the deceased, friends and relatives of the family pay homage to the ancestors broadly as a collective. As the living send off the deceased, so too the deities prepare the deceased's place in the otherworld. When somebody dies, it is said, "the deities establish the father who sleeps" (*orisa te ni fun, baba o sun*).[26]

In Ositola's account of how funerals should be performed, both play and competition were built into the structure of performance. Not merely a display of wealth for its own sake, the funeral literally constructs the social significance, power, and prestige of the deceased and his or her family at the same time that it constructs for the family and community a representation of the quality of the deceased's existence in the otherworld. The family and the community in this way judge themselves by the spectacle they create, and by extension judge the spirit's acceptance by the ancestors. Strong support for a deceased family member at the same time expresses the power of the corporate group.

VARIATIONS ON THE THEME

In the periods designed for play, especially on the main and the fourth days, funerals for the elderly take on other dimensions, in addition to those described by Ositola, when the deceased has other kinds of affiliations. If, for example, an elderly man was a hunter, blacksmith, drummer, or brasscaster, the funeral will typically include a send-off known as *isipade* or *ipade*, literally, the act of opening the way for the hunter (*a nsi ipa ode*). This ceremony is reportedly conceived to send the spirit of the deceased to join all the other ancestors who during their lifetimes worked specifically with metal implements requiring strong, direct, powerful action—the killing of animals, the forging of iron, the beating of drums (cf. M. Drewal 1989). They include devotees of Ogun, the deity of iron and war, and of Obalufon, the deity of artists.

The members of the funeral party wear old worn-out clothing. If the deceased was a hunter, for example, they carry guns and knives and create havoc around the town. As the drummers play, the spirit of the deceased mounts and possesses the hunter's comrades. The spirits of those in such professions are necessarily brave, fierce, and, above all, active. The participants thus fire their guns, lash and cut themselves, and tear each other's clothes as they engage in mock combat. In the process their clothes become even more ragged.

After parading around the town three times, they then process to a main crossroads on the outskirts. There they remove their clothes and place them at the junction, hanging some on a stake with a crossbar that is reminiscent of a scarecrow (fig. 3.5). This accumulation at the crossroads is the trace (*ipa*) of the hunter, from which the *ipade* derives its name; more literally, *ipa* refers to the translucent trail left by a snail as it moves along the ground. In this way the participants create an impression of the deceased standing at the crossroads. The clothes are also evidences of the tremendous physical energy that the deceased's supporters have expended on his behalf. Their actions also dramatize the ethos of hunters and those who work with metal.

Such special performances woven into the fabric of funeral rites serve to distinguish groups and group affiliations. "You know everybody has his own group in the ancestor world," I was informed. Different affiliations are marked differently. Special funerals are accorded to diviners, as well as to priests of the deities, whose heads have been ritually prepared for possession trance.[27] Likewise, Egungun masks perform as part of the *isinku* of deceased Egungun society members (see chapter 6), Efe and Gelede masks sing and dance for the *isinku* of deceased Gelede society members (H. Drewal and M. Drewal 1983:59–61, 156, 193), and Agemo masks come out during the *isinku* of Agemo society members (see chapter 7). These performances are part of the public displays on the days set aside for play. There are many other variations along these same lines, both public and private.

The funerals of kings are also special, because their rites of installation elevate them to a sacred status. Thus, kings are hailed, "the king with metaphysical power is second only to the gods" (*oba alase, ekeji orisa*). Since Agemo priests are also the headmen of their own communities, their funeral rites combine components of those rites performed for kings, priests of deities, and Agemo society members, including the appearances of Agemo masks.

Multiple affiliations give rise to heterogenous funerals that can incorporate many distinct traditions and styles of performance. In 1978 in a western Yoruba town just outside Ilaro, the funeral of a deceased elder included performances of both the Egungun and Igunnuko masking societies. Igunnuko is an imported tradition, introduced into Yoruba country by Nupe emigrants, who are maintaining their own cultural identities and at the same time being assimilated into Yoruba culture. The deceased's affiliations were multiple, reflecting this heterogeneity.[28] The relationship of one Igunnuko mask to the deceased was explicitly drawn when the mask went to stand on the ancestor's grave just outside the house (fig. 3.6). The two columns that decorate the foot of the grave depict the mask in miniature, while a Muslim writing board with Arabic script is set in relief on the front. Both reflect the deceased's identity as masked performer and Muslim, or at least they reflect the way the family wanted to remember him. The two masking societies to which he belonged worked it out between themselves so that the Igunnuko masks performed in the afternoon, and the Egungun masks performed overnight that same evening.

The competition among families, and even within families, to put on the

largest displays around the town—some say—encourages people in the community to perform better in life with the idea that their funerals will "befit" them.
Since funerals are evaluated, elders fear appearing comparatively insignificant,
especially after it is too late to do anything about it. If the dimension of public
display seems extravagant, even relentless, it is because it is considered a sacrifice. Approval comes back directly from the deceased spirit's voice through the
instrumentality of the elders, whose age, special training, and ritual roles make
them living representations of the ancestors. That is the essence of the elders'
wining and dining the deceased, as Ọṣitọla expressed it. It is the power of public
display to proclaim the enormity of the family's concern throughout the town
and even into the otherworld.

Ọṣitọla did not elaborate the play segments of music and dance since they
are highly variable. Instead, what he stressed was the quantity of the performing
groups. The choice of styles, it was suggested, is based primarily on the perceived
music tastes of the deceased, his or her social affiliations with performing groups
such as Ifa or Agẹmọ, and the tastes of the sponsors. Such funerals incorporate
different styles and traditions of performance.

CYCLICAL TIME AND THE OTHER

Ritual journeys have a synecdochic relationship to the greater ontological
journey of the human spirit in that they are nested in "life's journey" (*ajo l'aye*).
Not conceived as cyclical in the sense of beginning time over or returning to the
world the same each time, journeying is always a progression, a transformation.
The idea of transformation is implicit in a divination text given by Wande
Abimbọla (1976:132), which narrates how three men, before leaving heaven to
come to earth, chose their heads. When two of them, Oriseeku and Orieemere,
compared the success of the third, Afuwape, with their own failures, they
remarked:

> I don't know where the lucky ones chose their heads,
> I would have gone there to choose mine.

Afuwape answers, concluding the verse:

> We chose our heads from the same place,
> But our destinies are not identical.

Every time spirits return to the world, they choose different heads or personalities (*ori inu*), different bodies (*ara*), and different destinies (*ayanmọ*).

One of the projects of the functionalist-structuralist approach, according to
Johannes Fabian (1983:41), was to contrast "Western linear Time and primitive
cyclical Time, or [. . .] modern Time-centeredness and archaic timelessness."
Ritual tends to be placed in the latter category, even so-called secular rituals

(see Moore and Meyerhoff 1977:8). But does this really reflect Yoruba thought?[29]

If in Yoruba thought life on earth is merely a temporary segment in a human spirit's journey, then all time would have to be classified as cyclical, not just ritual time. What Benjamin Ray (1976:41) terms "ordinary linear time" would not exist in Yoruba consciousness, since, conceptually, the human spirit is always coming into the world and returning in one unending cycle. On the other hand, since nothing ever repeats itself, and since from this ontological perspective there is always change and transformation—of body, of personality, of mission, of destiny—then existence in time would be more appropriately conceived in spatial terms as a spiral—neither cyclical, nor linear. There is no time-out-of-time, properly speaking that is, if I have understood the concept as Ọṣitọla expressed it:

> The whole life span of a man or a woman is a journey. That is our belief. *Ajo l'aye* [literally, "journey of life"]. When you are going to start your life, you go through a journey. Even when you are coming to the life, you go through a journey. And if you want to develop on the life, it is a journey. So it is just journey, journey, journey all the while.

Me: When people go on a journey, what does that mean?

Ọṣitọla: I have told you, the whole life span of a human is a journey. What we are doing now is a journey. All movements are journeys. We are progressing, we are moving. (taped discussion #86.77[I])

3.2 The Akọnọrọn of Oṣugbo Imodi watches where he places his foot as he dances. Ijẹbu area, village of Imọsan, 1 December 1986.

3.3 In a dance facing the *agba* drums, the Apena of Oṣugbo Ikan wears a highly patterned "cloth of the elders." The complexity of the designs alludes to the complexities of life itself and the elder's mastery of them. Ijẹbu area, village of Imọsan, 14 October 1986.

3.4 A funeral "play" (*ere*) travels about the town. A member of
the family carries aloft a photograph of the deceased. Ijẹbu
area, village of Imọsan, 13 September 1986.

3.5 The accumulation of
clothes placed at the
crossroads represents the
"trace" (*ipa*) of a
deceased hunter, created
during the *iṣipadẹ* ritual.
Ijẹbu area, village of
Imọsan, 13 September
1986.

3.6 An Igunnuko mask stands on the deceased's grave. In the foreground, two masks in miniature and a Muslim writing board with Arabic script decorate the concrete tombstone. Egbado area, village of Olute, 3 December 1977.

4. New Beginnings

When you are going to start your life, you go through a journey. Even when you are coming to the life, you go through a journey.

Just as a funeral is a rite of separation for the community, but is also conceived as a new spiritual beginning for the individual, the first rituals performed for a newborn infant are incorporations into the material world. Like funerals, these rituals focus on the metaphysical journey between two realms. Whereas funerals are costly public displays in the form of sacred send-off parties, the entry of an infant into the world is a much more subdued, private affair marked by a brief, relatively simple ritual performed by a diviner for the parents to discover the quality of the child's coming. The parents passively and patiently await the diviner's interpretation. The action is more thoughtful and contemplative than physical, quiet rather than loud.

As Ọṣitọla described this metaphysical process:

> You know, the grandfather's body has been molded by Orisanla [Deity of Creation] long before, and has been destroyed. Then his spirit wanders. Orisanla will make another body. The spirit of the father—whose body has been destroyed together with his head—goes to a new body, and then goes to take another head. (taped discussion #82.78)

It is the assumption that, like the deceased's spirit, which lingers for awhile in the world disembodied, the spirit of the newborn babe is still betwixt and between the otherworld and earth. Its spirit has just left its place in heaven (*o yi fara mọ ọrun*). It is still in the process of coming (*o ṣẹ n bọ la ori rẹ*). The infant's first ritual constitutes the third phase of Van Gennep's tripartite initiation process. There is no separation apart from birth itself. The baby arrives in a liminal state, as suggested to Ọṣitọla by the amount of time it spends sleeping and dozing. The ritual concern of the diviner and the parents is incorporation.

In explaining birth, Ọṣitọla made an analogy to my trip to Nigeria:

> As you are here now, your parents are there. When you first arrived in June before we settled down, before you became more Abidifa-ly [that is, more like himself, the speaker], you usually remembered your parents, your

people there, your friends. Your mind had not fully settled with us here.
[. . .] Now you have gradually [gotten] used to us here. You remember
them, but partially.

You have entered into our own world. You have entered into our own
mind. You have entered into our own thinking.

You see that is the work of the *ori inu* [inner head], because it is
coming. It is still with the other ancestors over there. You know the child is
coming on a journey. He has just stepped [into] the world. And he is still a
new man, a new face who *n kọsẹ* [is stepping]. He hasn't settled. (taped
discussion #86.102)

Yoruba salute the parents of a newborn baby, "greetings for the stranger" (*e ku
alejo*). The very concept of the "journey" presupposes the experience of being a
stranger in a strange land.

There is an extremely high infant mortality rate, particularly during the first
three months after birth. Because of the baby's precarious betwixt and between
status, Ọṣitọla performs rituals known as "Stepping into the World" (Ikọsẹ
w'aye) and "Knowing the Head" (Imori). According to him, the former should
be performed between the third and seventh day after birth; the latter in the
third month. During the rituals, diviners propose diverse and extremely personal
courses of action for the parents to take in dealing with the child.

STEPPING INTO THE WORLD

According to Ọṣitọla, the act of stepping the foot is an important segment
(*aito*) of the ritual performed during the week after birth—literally the first
formal step the child takes. The Ifa divination process itself is like every other.[1]
Through interpreting texts, the diviner obtains a sense of the baby's impact on
its family. He constructs for the parents what the immediate future holds in
store. The texts provide clues to the baby's nature, including its name. If, for
example, the baby has come to the world through the intercession of a deity, it
will be named in that deity's honor: Eṣubiyii, "Eṣu gave birth to this one," or
Ogunbiyii, "Ogun gave birth to this one," for example. Also through divination,
the parents may learn that the babe does not want to begin life with "noise" (a
big party) or that the parents should not make any blood sacrifices on the babe's
behalf.

"Stepping into the World" takes place at sunup, when the baby's inner head
is thought to be most alert. As Ọṣitọla began to perform Ikọsẹ w'aye in his
house in Imodi on October 26, 1986, for a seven-day-old boy, I positioned
myself on his right side leaning up against the wall where I could photograph the
action.[2] The atmosphere was relaxed. Everybody present knew me well; they had
grown accustomed to my work. As usual, the entire ritual took only about a half-
hour. The client—in this case the mother—was opposite the diviner with the
baby in her lap. They sat on a mat with the divination tray between them. The

baby's father sat in a chair behind his wife several feet off the mat and looked on, while the mother's mother sat some distance away in a chair.

First, Ọsitọla sprayed gin on the palm nuts to "wake them up" and activate them. Then he offered two kola nuts, touching them to the bottom of the baby's feet and buttocks as he prayed. In this way, he associated the idea of "stepping" with the kola. Splitting them into four sections each and praying, he threw them down in the middle of the divination tray, reading the way they fell as a sign that the baby's spirit had drawn near and accepted the offering.[3]

According to Ọsitọla, the divination tray symbolizes the universe, the entire field of human action and experience, as do the mats that he and the mother sat on with the baby. Marking the number-one ranked divination sign on the tray, Ọsitọla then "centered the baby in the world" by placing his feet and buttocks down squarely in the middle (fig. 4.1). Ikọsẹ w'aye, "Stepping into the World," derives its name from this physical act as well as from the notion that the divination text Ọsitọla elicits will reveal the quality of the baby's entry into the world.

Ọsitọla blew forcefully on the primary instruments of divination—sixteen palm nuts—which he cupped in his hands. Then he "associated" them with the baby by touching them to its feet and buttocks. Before beginning to cast the palm nuts to elicit a set of texts, he sprayed the baby's head and belly with gin to alert its soul and saluted the deities and ancestors by tapping the center of the tray as he invoked each of sixteen sets of divination texts (Odu Ifa) one by one. This act "opened" the tray, covered—as always—with a white wood dust in which diviners mark the signs of the sets of texts they elicit.[4] Sprinkling a bit of the dust on the palm nuts, he "cleaned" them and at the same time purified his own hands. Picking up the palm nuts, he then "beat" them—a technical procedure for divining. Putting them back down again, he then beat himself cursorily to beg their pardon, touching his arm and leg joints and blowing away any danger, first from one hand and then the other. Picking up the palm nuts once again, he grasped them, with his right hand drawing a handful away, leaving two in his left palm.

If two palm nuts remain, the diviner inscribes one vertical mark in the wood dust sprinkled on the divination tray; if one, he inscribes two. After eight casts, one of a corpus of two hundred and fifty-six sets of texts is identified. After three tries of eight casts each, a set of texts is finally isolated based on the rank order of the sets.[5] Once the diviner has isolated the set, he goes on to find a direction within the set, positive or negative, and, further, a path within that direction, and so on. This whole process is performed with great rapidity.

The sign that Ọsitọla elicited through this process was Iwori Ageesa (Age Osa); its direction was positive, indicating prosperity for the baby boy. Ọsitọla took some of the wood dust and put it in the mother's palms before transferring it to a packet that he wrapped up and presented to the parents. Then he instructed the mother to lick each hand, thereby ingesting a portion of the dust, and to rub it on the top of her head. These acts too drew physical associations between the divination sign, the marks in the dust, and the mother's interior

4.1 Oṣitọla "centers the baby in the world" during a divination
ritual known as Ikọse w'aye ("Stepping into the World") by
placing its feet down in the center of the divination tray.
Ijẹbu area, Imodi, 26 October 1986.

and head. The packet of dust, which the parents take home, signifies their
agreement to follow the prescribed course of action that the diviner interprets
based on the baby's personal text. With the wood dust, the parents are supposed
to prepare infusions for the baby.

The casting process concluded, only Oṣitọla's interpretation of the baby's
personal text remained. First he recited a verse. These are often short, poetic,
and elusive; their language is archaic and frequently unintelligible to clients.
Following his recitation, Oṣitọla gave a narrative interpretation (ẹyọ) that took
the form of a parable.[6] Thus:

Ifi [a reed plant personified] consulted Ifa when he was searching for a
place to grow. Ifa advised him to settle near water. But in so doing, he
began to be troubled by enemies; the wind blew him back and forth.
Despite these disturbances, he somehow survived and grew up.

The connection between the baby and the reed plant, Oṣitọla reported, is
"very serious." The baby boy's inner head was said to dwell very near the lagoon,
a symbol of prosperity. If the parents raise the child well, he would be destined

to prosper, for those associated with the lagoon are ordinarily good fishermen, or "catchers," easily able to acquire the bounty of the sea. But it is incumbent on the father not to be wasteful, for wastefulness causes quarrels and unhappiness. To set the baby and the father on the right path toward prosperity right from the beginning, Ọṣitọla instructed the father to go fishing.

At the same time, Ọṣitọla informed the parents that they should prevent the boy from going near bodies of water, where he would be apt to meet his spirit. Nor should he weave or sit down on *ore* mats, which are woven with *ifi* reeds. Like *ifi*, his spirit is destined to benefit from the sea, but he is also subject to being blown about in the wind, an allusion to the turmoil created by his parents' fighting because of the father's alleged wastefulness. Ọṣitọla thus warned the parents not to fight. The unstated implication was that the baby's spirit might become disillusioned and leave; that is, the baby might die.

Based on his interpretation, Ọṣitọla named the baby Ọladele, "Honor-comes-home." In identifying the nature of the baby's soul, Ọṣitọla provided the parents with a program of action and a model of behavior, setting them on a path that they feel will ensure their success in rearing the child. Texts are not perceived to be elicited through chance operations, but rather the particular spirits affecting the baby are thought to come forth to speak through them. Wise parents are expected to reflect on the text and on the action it prescribes in relation to their general situations. From their interpretations and reflections, they gain insight in dealing with the baby as they embark on a course of action, or at least that is the idea as it was expressed to me by Ọṣitọla.

Just as soon as Ọṣitọla finished, a man entered the house. Ọṣitọla greeted him and told everyone that the text of the verse had indicated someone would visit. "Did you see me look around while I was divining?" he asked. The man sat down on the mat with Ọṣitọla and they shared some gin, passing it in their left hands—a sign that they are comrades in an exclusive society, perhaps Ifa, perhaps Ọṣugbo. The man prayed for the baby and also began to interpret the verse of the text similarly to Ọṣitọla, underscoring that the baby did not like fighting.

The following day—I was told later—the father went fishing. As Ifa predicted, he succeeded in catching so many fish that his family could not finish eating them all. Not to be wasteful, he gave fish to his friends. Ọṣitọla's clients in this case were well known to him. The baby's father, who is Muslim, attends most of Ọṣitọla's ritual performances. Thus Ọṣitọla had a sense of the individuals involved prior to the divination session, as well as knowledge of their personal problems. This is not always the case, as with the clients who performed the Imori ritual described below.

A week after the "stepping" ritual, the father held a Muslim naming ceremony at his family compound, to which we were invited. The Muslim cleric in charge at the ceremony made Ọṣitọla an impromptu master of ceremonies even though Ọṣitọla has on occasion openly expressed his resentment of Muslim encroachment on traditional religion. This occasion illustrates the multiple allegiances and identities individuals often assume in social situations.

KNOWING THE HEAD

After "Stepping into the World," the next critical ritual for children is "Knowing the Head" (Imori), ideally performed within the first three months after birth.[7] This time the objective is to learn the nature of the inner head (*ori inu*)—or personality—that the animating spirit or soul (*emi*) brought to the world, so the parents can help the child coordinate the two. As time goes on, the inner head comes to dominate the soul, and the two become fused into a unified personality.[8] If not,

> when the head knows that his person will gain if he goes to Lagos, then—because he has not been following his head properly—his soul will just follow another path and take the body, go. You know the soul controls the body, but the head controls the soul. And the inner head decides what the body should do. (Ọṣitọla #82.78)

To unify the child's personality, the parents must first of all know from where the soul comes. There are three possibilities: the father's side of the family, the mother's, or a deity's. The latter soul is "free" in that it is newly created.

At three months, a child is still not fully of this world. Thus,

> he has not been used to the world as we, the elders. So he has no knowledge of the world. He has not had much contact with people. His dealings have been with those in heaven. He has just arrived, so he is still more heavenly than worldly. We have to perform his own rituals very anciently, very nearly heavenly. He is a new man. Nobody knows him. He is from heaven. He may be the father; he may be the mother's mother.[9] But he is still coming from heaven. We don't know what he is doing here. Until we know what the child is doing here, we can't treat him like ourselves. We treat him like a stranger who has not been used to this place. Until he is used to this place, he can't have the knowledge.
>
> Mark you, you have just arrived now. You may like to eat spaghetti [or] the backs of the beans more than to eat *eba* [cassava porridge] until you have spent years. In ten years, you can eat *eba*. We can't give you *eba*. We have to be treating you Americanly, and—partially—you see, that is the case. (Ọṣitọla #82.104)

Ọṣitọla's observation was about the difference in our foods—not strictly what we served each other and ate—and the discomforts of transitions.[10]

On the night before an Imori ritual conducted by Ọṣitọla on October 27, 1986, the parents jointly put black and white thread on each wrist, elbow, ankle, knee, and neck of the child, a sign to alert the child's spirit to prepare for the ritual. When a child is irritable, cries a lot, and does not sleep, the parents know, according to Ọṣitọla, that its ancestral spirit is pinching its body, anxious to gain recognition.

Like "Stepping into the World," this ritual occurred at daybreak when the child, a little girl around three years old, was fresh and attentive. Ọṣitọla began in the front of his house by making a small sacrifice of palm wine and palm oil at the shrine of ancestral diviners (oju orere), throwing kola to determine that it was accepted.

The parents of the girl brought other sacrifices. In the past, a father reportedly brought a male yam and a smoked rat; the mother, a female yam and a smoked mudfish. Today, parents do not necessarily separate out these items. Sometimes only the mother attends the ceremony, especially if the husband is Muslim or Christian. The rat, a bush animal—Ọṣitọla suggested—evokes the agility of males as active hunters, while the fish implies the coolness and patience of females.[11] Ọṣitọla placed the items brought by each parent on different sides of his divination tray—the male ones on his right, the female ones on his left. By extension, these items stand for the two sides of the family from which the girl's spirit is apt to come.

Ọṣitọla began by offering gin and kola nuts to the deity of divination, Ọrunmila, just as he had done in "Stepping into the World." After marking the divination board with the first sign of the set of texts, Ọṣitọla picked up the girl from her mother's lap, touching her head first to the floor and then at the center of the divination tray as "an introduction" to the world, for in Imori it is now time to associate her head with the world. With Ọṣitọla's aid, the girl in effect prostrated for the deities and ancestors, something, he explained, she should be doing throughout her life.

After spraying the girl with gin to "wake up" her inner head, Ọṣitọla then struck the center of the divination tray with a tapper, invoking the sixteen sets of divination verses. But before he began to divine he was interrupted when a neighbor from across the street entered. It was Apena, one of the senior chiefs in the Ọṣugbo society. Apena greeted everyone, shared some gin, and prayed for the girl. All this happened very quickly, however, because Ọṣitọla, seemingly a bit annoyed, pressed on not to waste time. To get good results, he explained later, Imori should be performed sedately and without distractions as soon as the sun rises.

Before beginning to divine, Ọṣitọla poured water on the ground as a libation and all shared it around. First the girl drank and gulped down the water so quickly that Ọṣitọla had to pull the container back. This engendered laughter, since normally a person takes only a small sip. Ọṣitọla then sipped, followed by the mother, the father, and myself. Next he served gin all around. The girl took a big gulp of gin too and proceeded to cough.

With two tiny, thin sticks that stand for each side of the family, Ọṣitọla stirred the dust on the tray and prayed.[12] Speaking to the small sticks, Ọṣitọla then asserted quietly that "Jẹmilawọ and Abudu [the mother and father] have been blessed by a child, oh. If it is from the father's side, let Ifa tell us oh. And if it is from the mother's side, let Ifa tell us oh. If it is from neither side, but from a deity, then Ifa should tell us." After praying for the girl's long happy life and success, he touched the sticks to the palm nuts, the girl's forehead, and the ground and then related them upward in space toward the spirits, three times in a row to draw a visible correlation between the sticks and each of the three sides.

Diviners cast Ifa nine times altogether, in three series of three for the three sides of possible origin. As in "Stepping into the World," the seniority of the sets of verses determines which side takes precedent. But one side must take the senior position three times in a row, otherwise the process continues until a clear pattern develops.[13]

Afterward, Ọṣitọla goes on to identify the specific ancestor or deity that the child represents.[14] During this process, the child is expected to go to sleep, a sign that the spirit of the ancestor or deity, as the case may be, has taken possession. If the child does not sleep, it suggests that the child's inner head is not yielding to the soul. Such a child, it is feared, will be continually troubled by the soul, who will not allow him or her to rest peacefully.

Divining once more, Ọṣitọla then learned more about the girl's inner head, drawing forth a set of verses and then isolating a more precise direction within it using objects called *ibo* that represent ten different directions, half positive, half negative. The five favorable paths are: 1) long life (*aiku*), represented by a stone, 2) progeny (*ule*), represented by a seed, 3) triumph over enemies (*iṣegun*), represented by a bone, 4) wealth (*aje*), represented by a cowry, and 5) combined overall achievement (*aredẹwa*), represented by a seashell. These favorable paths indicate core Yoruba values. On the negative side, the same objects represent the major hardships of life: untimely death, barrenness, oppression, poverty, and combined overall failure. By isolating a direction within the set of verses, Ọṣitọla could also identify particular sacrifices that the parents were supposed to make. But they were to return at a later date for this.

Meanwhile, Ọṣitọla prepared a packet of "title-holder's leaves" certifying that the girl had performed the Imori ritual.[15] In three leaves, he put bits of all the ingredients and sacrifices used during the ritual—yams, rat, fish, oil, some of the wood dust.[16] Marking the sixteen sets of texts on the tray one by one, Ọṣitọla sprinkled wood dust from each sign over the other ingredients and concluded by rubbing some on the girl's head. Before wrapping up everything in a packet, he touched each ingredient first to the palm nuts and then to the girl's forehead and mouth. Finally, he wrapped the packet tightly in the same thread that was put around the baby's arm and leg joints and neck so that all of the ingredients that represent the ritual accomplishment blended together.

Placing the packet in a porcelain plate, Ọṣitọla then placed the plate in the center of the divination tray. Turning it first clockwise and then counterclockwise, he asked, "the child has come to the world, or the child has not come to the world?"[17] The parents responded three times affirming that indeed "the child has come to the world." Rotating in the dish, the packet is said to be "enjoying all around the world," as it is hoped that the girl will do. Ọṣitọla handed the bowl with the packet to the mother and prayed for the girl's long life and prosperity, sprinkling some wood dust in the plate. The dust then became the material representation of the prayer. Periodically, the mother is supposed to make an infusion from the contents of the packet for her child to drink.

Ọṣitọla ordinarily chants the verse and interprets it for the clients. If he is familiar with the verse elicited during the child's "Stepping into the World," then he will weigh the two together to see if and how they may relate. Between 1982 and 1986, I witnessed several "Knowing the Head" rituals. The interpretations Ọṣitọla gave to the parents were quite diverse. The three-year-old girl I just described was well beyond the age considered ideal for the ritual. Her head never yielded to the ancestor's spirit; thus the girl did not sleep. Through divination, Ọṣitọla determined that the girl was the reincarnation of her mother's mother. When he cast once more to determine the nature of the girl's inner head, the path led to the negative side of Ọyẹku meji, a powerful set of texts already considered tough because it is full of death and destruction. As Ọṣitọla expressed it to me, "darkness went inside darkness."

The girl, he determined, was "born to die" (abiku). An abiku is a child whose soul is considered "irresponsible" because it never completes a full life cycle. The child dies young and its spirit lingers nearby, continually plaguing the mother with rebirths and sudden deaths. Once identified, diviners perform special rituals of verbal abuse to mercilessly shame such children into remaining in the world.

When this text was drawn forth Ọṣitọla fell silent. He did not chant as he usually does, because, as he explained later, it is not customary to invoke such bad things. All he needed to do was to identify the girl. Thereafter, the parents reportedly went to greet him regularly, but up until the time I left, about a month and a half later, they had not followed through with the recommended rituals.

It is hard to say how being identified as abiku influences a child. In 1975, I met an abiku woman in Ilaro known as Iya Sikiru. She and her husband regularly consulted a priest who deals with abiku problems. As it was described to me, Iya Sikiru was unable to lead a prosperous life, which made her a liability in her family. Her business ventures usually failed. Most Yoruba women are traders by profession; to fail at something so crucial to women's identities was taken to be serious. Iya Sikiru had been selling bean cakes for a loss at the roadside. When I suggested to her uncle—the vice-principal of the local high school—that she might do better selling her wares to students on the school compound, he refused to consider the possibility, reminding me she is abiku. She would cause trouble, he told me, getting into fights and embarrassing him. He clearly drew a correlation between her temperament and her identity as abiku.

CONVERSING WITH VERSE

On a separate occasion, Ọṣitọla and another diviner named Ọmọṣeṣe conducted "Knowing the Head" for two children simultaneously. Making no attempt to synchronize words or actions, each diviner went at his own pace. The overall feeling was chaotic, yet each was proceeding systematically. Ọṣitọla claimed it is important to perform "Knowing the Head" for both children at once so that each can begin when the head is sharp and the spirit nearby. Spirits, it is felt, should not be kept waiting. The recitations and the interpretations, however, were staggered.[18]

As Ọṣitọla chanted a verse from Ọsan Eṣu, Ọmọsẹsẹ, the second diviner, echoed him line for line in word and gesture. The parable he improvised based on the verse was about Vulture (Igunugun) (Ọṣitọla #82.113):

> The diviners of a woman named Ede told her she would have a child only after making sacrifices. Even then, they told her, her child would be lost one day, but would eventually be found. When she performed her sacrifices, she was instructed never to grow annoyed.
>
> One day, Vulture and Ede had a disagreement, and he ran far from home. Ede set out in search of him. Meanwhile, Eṣu inquired if she had offered sacrifices. Assured she had, he made plans to lure Vulture back home. Transforming himself into a dog, he tracked Vulture, catching his attention with sacrifices, attracting him nearer and nearer. As Vulture approached, Eṣu made a trail of food, gradually drawing him back to his hometown. In this way, Vulture was eventually led into his mother's house. Ede sang, "Little by little, Vulture returned home."[19] People told her, "you see, that is how Vulture, who should have been lost and not been seen again, eventually returned home. It was with Eṣu's help that Vulture was redirected home."

Ọṣitọla warned the father of the child that his son was a "troublemaker" (*onijogbon*) and that there would be a time when he would mature and run away from home. He told him further to perform a sacrifice so that when this happened Eṣu would attract him back home and he would not be lost forever. "I told him he would have to exercise patience because the mother of Vulture had a grievance that caused him to run away."

Immediately after his interpretation, Ọṣitọla sent the father outside to sacrifice palm oil at the site of Eṣu's shrine. As the father cooled Eṣu with palm oil, so too Ọṣitọla attempted to impress upon the father the necessity for coolness, or patience, in dealing with his children. Ọṣitọla's interpretation also anticipated a hot-tempered child. Once again, Ọṣitọla attempted to set the parents' attitude toward the child, suggesting a course of action to direct the child's journey through life.

The idea of the ontological journey is given expression in both "Stepping into the World" and "Knowing the Head," as well as in funerals. If funerals comment on the significance of the deceased during his past life and his various group affiliations through elaborate public spectacles of dancing and drumming, rituals that attend birth construct the personality of the child and set the parents on a course of future action in line with that construction. During the first year of a child's life, Ọṣitọla's interpretations are directed more toward the parents and their understanding and treatment of the child, and affect the child only indirectly.

In the rituals described above, Ọṣitọla's most significant role is as an interpreter of esoteric verses that construct children's identities. As he expressed it, "nobody will ever know what the verse is saying in listening to it unless the explainer explains more" (#86.67). He went on to characterize the interpretative process as a "conversation" between the verse and his own personal experience. Beyond that, he was unwilling to discuss the matter, saying if I wanted to learn to be a diviner I had to start from the beginning and go through the proper training.

Ọṣitọla's "conversation" is an improvisation. It takes the form of a parable, which he creates extemporaneously based on the relationship he perceives between the esoteric verse—itself reformulated in rhythm and phrasing with each repetition—and his reading of the clients, what he prefers to call his experience. That is what I understand him to mean by a "conversation," although he never admitted—and yet never denied when I inquired—that his intuitive evaluations of the clients figure into his interpretation.

The parents are supposed to use the prescribed courses of action reflected in Ọṣitọla's narrative in much the same way scholars have traditionally used theoretical paradigms to distance themselves from their subjects of study in order to gain perspective. And like those paradigms too, the models for action reflect the perspectives of their subscribers, telling as much about the attitudes and situations of the parents as they do about the child. As Barbara Kirshenblatt-Gimblett (1976) has shown, a parable's meaning is essentially what particular participants attribute to it in a specific context.

As a distancing device, the model provided by Ọṣitọla's interpretation constructs a distinctive personality, or inner head (ori inu), for the child even before he or she is old enough to exhibit it. Although I have been unable to follow up on the implications this process has for personality formation, I suspect it would affect more or less how the parents relate to the child, which in turn surely has some impact on the child's perception of self. At the same time, the prescribed actions and identities are temporary, dealing only with the child's immediate future as a stage in life's journey.

How personalities are formed is best left to a psychologist. For my own purposes, what these divination rituals reveal strongly is that Yoruba not only have a very clear concept of individual differences, they cultivate and respect them. Divination parables not only posit courses of action, they suggest by extension the quality of action—whether forceful or gentle, hot or cool, direct or indirect, and so forth. The Yoruba concept of individuality is critical for understanding human agency as performers, competing interests, play, and improvisation. Indeed, to compromise one's inner head is to court failure and misfortune in life. This will become more apparent in the following chapter on "Establishing the Self."

As boys grow to an age of understanding—around seven years old—diviners perform further rituals to construct their identities, and in so doing attempt to transform their consciousness. To accomplish this, Ọṣitọla together with his entire group of diviners lead young boys through a ritual dialectic on autonomy and dependence, bestowing on them personal paradigms for living, in this way initiating their independent pursuits of self-identity. Through this ritual, boys are differentiated and their future roles as performers in specific kinds of rituals are often established.

5. Establishing the Self

Concede to each person his or her own particular character.

Yoruba adage quoted in Abịodun (1983:15)[1]

A woman giving birth to two, three children will not expect them to behave the same way. One man's food is another man's poison. One man's behavior may be contrary to another man's behavior. For instance, one may prefer to talk, talk, talk, talk, talk, talk, as Abidifa prefers. One may not prefer so much talk, as Ọmọṣẹṣẹ does not prefer. Everybody comes to the world for a mission, for a purpose. We can't just all come to the world for the same purpose.

Kọlawọle Ọṣitọla[2]

Many types of ritual focus on the individual as their central concern. In the fourteen-day long series of rituals known as Itefa, "The Establishment of the Self," diviners set out to interpret the precise nature of the individual's inner head.[3] The ritual is not geared to an entire community, nor is its focus on a collective. Itefa rituals are explicitly concerned with the identity of the individual and with his social relationships only by implication.

In Itefa, what Ọṣitọla and other diviners hope to accomplish beyond the initial identification of an initiate's personality is to provide him with an ever-expanding corpus of texts that serves as models for self-examination and self-interpretation. Since individuals ideally accumulate texts that comprise *their* personal corpus of models over their lifetimes, and at various points weigh those texts in relation to others that may turn up in subsequent divinations, they embark on a lifelong program of searching, reflexivity, and interpretation. This program serves, according to Ọṣitọla, as their guidance in life.

To establish the initiate's self, diviners conceptualize and perform Itefa as a journey with travel from one place to another, and a return; new experiences; joys and hardships along the route; and material for further contemplation and reflection.[4] As in funerals, the first, third, seventh, and in this case fourteenth days of the Itefa I attended were marked by special ritual segments (*aito*). In brief, day one through to the night of day two were journeys to and from a sacred grove, when the initiates learned their personal sets of Ifa divination texts supposed to guide their lives. On the third day back home, the diviners checked their progress through divination. This was also a day of feasting, dancing, and playing. The seventh day repeated the action of the third day of "checking."

Finally, the fourteenth day marked the reaggregation of the transformed novice back into his ordinary, everyday routine.

In the three Itẹfa I attended, the ritual segments of the third through the fourteenth day were flexible. They were variously abbreviated, condensed, elaborated, or eliminated in accordance with the financial conditions of the initiate's family and his psychological state. Diviners also inserted special sacrifices and even invented novel ritual acts based on their interpretations of each initiate's special texts. Itẹfa's segmented, discontinuous form permitted these various kinds of manipulations. During one Itẹfa in July 1986, for example, Ọṣitọla instructed one twenty-year-old initiate and his wife to burn their bed pillows as a ritual act. The gathering for the burning of the foam pillows was a spectacle in itself (fig. 5.1).[5]

THE RITUAL CONSTRUCTION OF SELF[6]

One of the diviners' explicit intentions in performing Itẹfa rituals is to prepare the initiate's personal set of divination palm nuts, which will be used initially to divine his personal texts and subsequently throughout his life whenever he consults a diviner. As the diviners "worked on" the initiate during Itẹfa rituals, they simultaneously worked on his palm nuts to "build them up," imbuing them with the power to overcome life's difficulties. This personal set of divination palm nuts represents the male initiate's rebirth, his personal destiny, and, by extension, Ọrunmila, the deity of divination.

On the nights before the journeys began, the diviners focused the attention of the sojourners on the work at hand in a formal preparatory ritual (*idiifa*). They accomplished this by invoking the sojourners' inner heads. The diviners displayed all of the sacrificial items and other materials brought by the initiate and his family at the diviners' request to be used during the following fourteen days. Each diviner held up each item one by one for all to see and then touched it to the forehead of the sojourner. Associating the two physically in this way, the diviner simultaneously chanted the items' names and invoked the sojourner's inner head (fig. 5.2).

The idea was for family and friends of the sojourner, as well as the deities and spirits, to bear witness (*jerii*) that the necessary provisions had been made openly and willingly. These preliminaries served to bind the spirits, deities, ancestors, and particularly the human beings together in a pact or contract to see the coming fourteen days through to their completion. The formal preparations anticipated what was to come and were situated liminally between everyday life and the ritual proper. Ọṣitọla often referred to them in English simply as "the prelim."

The journeys began at dark the following day with a warmup in front of Ọṣitọla's house, when his group of diviners chanted texts and explicated the original journey and what it accomplished. As the story went, when Ọrunmila failed to educate his three children properly, they carried him to the bush and threw him away, something that the sojourning party would also do, but with one major difference in light of the original mishap. The sons would now receive an education on their trip to the bush and therefore would not discard their father (Oṣitọla #82.38[11]; see also Oṣitọla 1988:34). Since the incantations were cast in archaic language described as "deep words" (ọrọ ijinle), the uninitiated could not understand them. But, Oṣitọla explained (1988:35), as the verse is explicated, "all the participants are listening and have ample time so that they might reflect for themselves." After a couple of hours the journey began.

The sojourning groups were made up of the ritual specialists—the diviners and their students (ọmọ awo)—the initiate, his mother and/or wife—depending on his age—and other family members and friends. Their numbers vary greatly at any given time according to the number of initiates and their family members: there were anywhere from thirty to fifty people in the Itẹfa I attended. Although the group's physical destination was only Oṣitọla's backyard not more than fifty yards away, the diviners imbued the trip with a feeling of distance. They took a circuitous route stopping at significant places along the way to chant incantations alluding to the spiritual and physical hardships of life in order to "clear their path" (fig. 5.3). The group carried all their supplies on top of their heads—one of the hardships of the journey.

In Oṣitọla's backyard is a grove made of tin sheeting, an enclosure for the deity Odu (igbodu = igbo Odu, "Odu's bush"), a sacred, exclusive space that the diviners constructed themselves (fig. 5.4). Before the initiates could enter the grove, there was a prolonged sequence of actions outside in full view of everyone. They included a divination on the road to determine if the palm nuts were strong enough to survive the rituals (idafa ọna); a two-hour, or longer, dance segment of stepping on the buried palm nuts (ọrọkiti), part of their buildup; and an elaborate sequence of incantations at "the gate" (ẹnu ọna) in order to "take permission" to enter (ikaago) (fig. 5.5). The initiates were as if entering the ancient city of Ile-Ifẹ—according to oral tradition the sacred origin of all humankind, the only ancestral city with which Yoruba collectively identify. This was followed by a ritual washing of the palm nuts by women (iwẹfa); another dance to celebrate the participants' successful arrival at another stage in the ritual process (iyi ifa); an elaborated entry into the sacred grove, when the initiate and the mother or wife proceed down the path on their knees carrying an iron staff on top of their heads (imosun)—a further hardship (fig. 5.6); and finally a sequence of jumping through fire (finona), an affirmation of the initiate's resiliency; together with a sacrifice to Death at a site prepared for the iron staff (ibosun). At last, the initiates entered the sacred grove (imawogbodu), and they did so blindfolded (fig. 5.7).

Only the diviners, their initiated students, and the initiates themselves were allowed to enter the sacred space. This began their period of physical separation from their family and friends, who remained in close proximity outside and kept a vigil in the "women's market" (ọja obinrin), that portion of the backyard where women can wander freely in contrast to the restricted space of the grove.[7] As Oṣitọla (1988:36) explained, even if you were allowed to see inside the *igbodu*, you would see only the impotent part of it. The knowledge is the potentiality, the knowledge you must sustain, the knowledge you must learn—not the materials. If the materials are exposed to everybody, they may just bastardize it, as when school children do Orisa [the Deities'] dancing as theatre, trying to bastardize all the traditions by taking it [tradition] just for the fun of it. But when you are unable to see it [*igbodu*], then it [this inability] will give you a sense of reasoning. It will become a challenge to you so that you will want to go through the ceremony in order to be prepared to know more about what we do there. So we don't just allow people to see it.

   If you were to see it, you would know it is a strange place. It is not common. It is not the gate to Mecca or to the barracks, but to the holy land *igbodu*. I have my own *igbodu*. You can prepare your own *igbodu* at your place as well.

The knowledge of which Ositola speaks is the knowledge of representation, *how* the materials are brought together and used to create a desired effect. The diviner's power is this knowledge, and—as Ositola affirms—not the materials themselves.

   On the inside of the grove, initiates experience many "wonders" that were kept secret from the uninitiated. Part of the importance of making a portion of the journey secret was to preserve the intensity and impact of experiencing it for the first time.[8] During this period of separation, males were given rebirth. In the wee hours of the morning as the sun rose, the initiate and his family learned through divination the set of texts that "brought him to the world," that defined his personality and potential in life. Once a person begins to learn his personal texts, he will understand how to conduct his life to maximize his chance for success. The diviners' identification and interpretations of each initiate's personal texts foregrounded the individual and provided guidelines for living. Those who do not perform Itefa risk "behaving against their luck, against their way of living."

   By the evening of the second day, the initiates emerged from the grove with heads shaved and painted white, wearing white cloth and the red tail feather of the African grey parrot on their foreheads (fig. 5.8). The white cloth is the color of the birth caul, and thus the color worn by all human beings when coming into the world anew. In painting the initiate's head with "star chalk" (*efun irawo*), the diviners made a visual analogy between the newly defined personality of the individual and a shining star.

   The group journeyed home again as elaborately as it had journeyed to the *igbodu*. Once back in Ositola's house the initiates were confined to specially prepared mats (*iten*), where they slept and ate for the next twelve days. There, too, all the subsequent divinations were performed.[9]

   On the third day (*ita* Ifa), the diviners checked their progress through divination. Like the third day of a funeral, the greater part of the day was taken for feasting, dancing, and playing. Between the third and seventh days, the initiates formally saluted the deities first thing every morning, rested, and ate. On the seventh day (*ijefa*) they again made sacrifices, feasted, and danced. The four-

5.1 Ọṣitọla and other diviners gather with an initiate and his wife for the burning of the foam bedpillows during an Itẹfa ritual. Ijẹbu area, Imodi, 14 July 1986.

5.2 The diviners perform the "prelim" for the four novices on the eve of an Itẹfa journey. Ijẹbu area, Imodi, 1 November 1986.

5.3 Itẹfa participants journey to Odu's grove carrying all their loads for the ritual performance. Ijẹbu area, Imodi, 2 November 1986.

5.4 Odu's grove is made of concrete blocks and tin sheeting with a mat covering the entrance. Ijẹbu area, Imodi, 14 July 1986.

5.5 With a diviner in the lead, the group of participants takes permission to enter "the ancient city of Ile-Ifẹ." Ijẹbu area, Imodi, 3 November 1986.

5.6 Ọṣitọla helps his son carry the iron divination staff on his head as he walks down the path to Odu's grove on his knees. Ijẹbu area, Imodi, 3 November 1986.

5.7 The initiates are blindfolded before being taken inside the grove of Odu. Ijẹbu area, Imodi, 3 November 1986.

5.8 Ọṣitọla's second son leaves Odu's grove all in white and with his head shaved and painted white. An Egungun mask follows carrying this son's palm nuts. Ijẹbu area, Imodi, 3 November 1986.

5.9 On the fourteenth day after going to Odu's grove, the
     initiates dress up as "new men." Ijẹbu area, Imodi, 15
     November 1986.

5.10 Containers of palm nuts that belong to male family
      members line the walls of an Ifa shrine. Ijẹbu area, Imodi,
      23 July 1982.

teenth day (*ijenla*)[10] the novices were reincorporated into their ordinary daily routine. They became "new" (*titun*), discarding their ritual dress and putting on everyday clothes and hats (fig. 5.9). Then they enacted weeding, and for not working hard enough were whipped with single, quick, sharp lashes across their legs or backs at irregular, unexpected intervals; they were forced to climb a tree; and finally they pretended to sell cloth in the market—all, Ọṣitọla explained, were lessons in perseverance (*iroju*) for success in the real world. At the end of the day, the diviners prepared each initiate's personal Eṣu shrine for the trickster deity, which "works" together with the prepared palm nuts of divination. How this was done was also determined through divination so that no two Eṣus were the same. Even in these seemingly set actions, there was great maneuverability. As in funerals, formally framed play segments were inserted.

Intended for six- to seven-year-old males whose ways of life have not yet taken shape, Itẹfa is also performed for adult males whose lives have been "shattered and scattered like a broken calabash." This metaphor conveys the adult's lack of a strong sense of self, indeed a lack of personal wholeness. The goal of Itẹfa is to begin the synthesizing process between the individual's inner head, or personality, and social life. This was represented by the chalk on the initiate's reborn head, a shining star, a focal point which reads "he is together"—neither broken nor scattered.[11] For adults, then, Itẹfa is considered remedial, and their problems are often critical by the time they decide they need to perform it.

SHATTERED, SCATTERED LIVES

My first Itẹfa experience in May 1982 involved a young married taxi driver in his early twenties. Every time I saw him during the days leading up to the ritual, he was slumped down in his chair, still and silent. Walking across the room put him out of breath as if he had just done something extremely strenuous. He seemed not to care. I wondered if he could survive the series of rituals. I worried too if perhaps he needed to be in a hospital, or at the very least in the care of a medical doctor. On the journey to the sacred grove, he struggled to fulfill his ritual acts. In his condition, these became extraordinary hardships. When Ọṣitọla's right-hand man, Ọmọṣẹṣẹ, performed the divination on the road to test the serviceability of his palm nuts, Ọṣitọla commented to me that the initiate's head was very stubborn and the diviners would have to work harder. I do not know what took place inside the sacred grove other than divining the nature of the initiate's inner head, but when he emerged in ritual dress, head shaved and painted, he had indeed been transformed. He no longer appeared weak. He was even alert.

Later on, Ọṣitọla confided that the initiate was an alcoholic. His personal texts had identified that; one of his taboos turned out to be alcohol. Ọṣitọla then admitted he had intentionally given the initiate plenty of food and water from the very beginning, acknowledging that alcoholism had prevented him from eating properly. When I returned to Nigeria in 1986, the young man was again driving a taxi as well as attending others' Itẹfa rituals and the annual Ifa festival. Ọṣitọla confirmed that he was doing well and prospering. And his wife had a child.

PLAYING THE TROPES[12]

One of the most interesting things about Itẹfa is that the same series of ritual segments works both for children and adults. The openness of the ritual form enables diviners to tailor it to the initiate's immediate needs. Reportedly, Itẹfa ritual segments are themselves based on experiences from the lives of the deity of divination (Ọrunmila) and other ancient diviners, as documented in the corpus of oral verses, or texts. The verses, often chanted during rituals, relay these experiences, which then serve as precedents for the series of actions comprising Itẹfa. Both the male and his mother, or wife, as the case may be, perform many of these acts simultaneously. When re-created, these acts bring the presumed past to bear on the present situation. As models for present practice, they are regarded as tried and true formulas for negotiating the desired results for the initiate through what Stanley J. Tambiah (1985:72, 77) has referred to as the transformative power of analogical thought and action.

At one level, Itẹfa is about the relationships of men to women. Diviners, who are male, take over women's prerogative by giving males a rebirth. According to one of the myths that served as a precedent, it was the wife of the deity of divination who taught her husband how to perform Itẹfa. She divulged her secret power to him, telling him that if he gave her proper respect she would use that power to help him. Through this wife Odu, Ọrunmila got his "sixteen children," that is, the sixteen major divination signs known as Odu Ifa. Odu is represented in ritual by a closed calabash, usually concealed inside a larger container, which a woman carries during rituals (Ọṣitọla 1988:35) (see fig. 5.3). Odu's essential secret is the knowledge of birth.

On November 3, 1986, not long before four young boys performing Itẹfa entered the sacred grove, women danced with their ritually treated palm nuts, which had been submerged in a herbal bath inside a calabash. The form and style of the dance were not as significant in this context as the act itself. The dancer often performs a simple, repetitive stepping pattern requiring no particular skill. This dance, Ọṣitọla claimed, "brings happiness into the heart of the palm nuts."

As the women danced, the diviners invoked women's spiritual support by singing a series of incantations. The first asserted that "it was a woman who gave birth to a king before he could become sacred," that is, the deputy of the gods. The second added, from a woman's womb come all the important people in the world. The third called attention to the pact between mother and child by reminding the mother of her days breast-feeding, or nurturing, her child. The fourth song cursed any evil intentions on the part of women. It alleged that the diviners had offered them all the required sacrifices; therefore, if any of them cause trouble, let them go the way of the sacrifice (that is, let them die). And the final incantation, sung to ensure that their sacrifices would be accepted and the ceremony would be successful, reminded women of the pact between the deity of divination and his wife, who is the source of female power. To demonstrate men's respect, one of the diviners prostrated himself at the feet of each of the dancing women.

The diviners invoked the spiritual support of women by acknowledging their power and appealing to their motherly roles, especially to the close physical and emotional bond between mother and child. The palm nuts are to the calabash that the dancing woman carries what the unborn child is to his mother's womb, and indeed it is this relationship that the diviners appeal to during the women's dance. Afterward, each initiate danced with his own palm nuts in a ritual segment called "the owner of the deity has come," that is, the owner of the palm nuts. The inner head of the individual was elevated to the status of a personal deity; the palm nuts are its shrine. According to Ọṣitọla, the dancing woman represented both the mother and the Ifa devotee's potential wives. The transfer of the palm nuts from the mother/wife to the male initiate is at once analogous to the diviners taking charge of the processes of rebirth and an assertion of the autonomy of the initiate.

As a sign that the dancing had finished successfully, Ọṣitọla sprinkled the heads of the others—the diviners, the women, and the initiates—with the herbal water that contained the palm nuts. He thus drew a physical relationship between the participants and the palm nuts through a process of incorporation. Then he "split Ifa" (*ilafa*), a performance segment also called "hippopotamus swimming, or splitting, the river," *erinminlado* (*erinmi n la odo*). He put his hand in the water to make ripples as he prayed, giving thanks for the safe return of the initiate from his journey through the water just as, according to an oral text that served as the precedent for this segment, Ọrunmila, the deity of divination, returned successfully from his journey to visit the goddess of the sea, Olokun.[13] Conceptually, the palm nuts and the initiate are united.

The metaphors piled up and played off each other to create a new synthesis: the palm nuts were to the herb bath what the initiate was to his mother's womb what the hippopotamus is to the river (or a:b::c:d::e:f). This latter image referred broadly to water as the source of all life, wealth, and prosperity. The earth's water mass is personified in Ijẹbu Yoruba cosmology as Olokun, the deity of the sea, who by extension owns all waters. Hippopotamus in Yoruba is "the elephant of the water," *erinmi* (*erin omi*), an image that monumentalizes a rather minuscule action. These verbal and kinetic manipulations in effect attached the physical origins of the newborn child to the spiritual origins of all life, wealth, and prosperity and then brought them into relationship with the initiate's rebirth. It is not by chance that among the Yoruba rivers and streams tend to be associated with female deities.

This mini journey through water was nested within the larger context of the ritual journey and was represented by the dance and later on by the motion of the diviner's hand in the water. As Ọṣitọla conveyed it, he "puts his hands in the water as if something is going through the water as a hippopotamus goes through the river without a hitch." There was a further contiguity in the ease with which the passage was, and would be, achieved—"without a hitch," in Ọṣitọla's words—the ease of the hand through water, the ease of the hippopotamus through the river, the ease of the new baby's idealized passage through his mother's water, as well as the ease with which the palm nuts soak in the herbal bath in relation to the ease of the woman's dance. This idea is conveyed explicitly in the name of the final ritual segment of the *iyi ifa*, known as *tutu nini*, which characterizes water as a "cool" medium for "cooling down." It is "very cool, like the bottom of the ocean." With this, Ọṣitọla took the palm nuts inside the enclosed sacred space where Odu's shrine had been erected to "work" on them further.

The ritual transformations occurred through sets of metonymic displacements performed by Ọṣitọla, each set based on a container/contained structure.[14] This structure was sustained throughout the ritual and carried over into the initiate's daily life. Thus, when an initiate is young, his mother provides his first container to hold his palm nuts. Like Odu's shrine, this container should be a calabash. During the preliminary portion of the ritual, which initiates the preparation of the divination palm nuts, the mother replaces the calabash with a clay pot. Then, for the next stage of the ceremony, she replaces the clay pot with a wooden or porcelain one. Finally, when the child grows up and marries, his wife should replace the third container with one specified through divination. Whenever these series of rituals are performed for an adult male, his wife provides all the various containers for the different ritual stages.

As these containers are discarded, according to Ọṣitọla, they are buried inside Odu's sacred grove, just as the afterbirth is buried in the bush, or in the backyard, after the birth of a child. The changes in containers that hold the palm nuts reflect their maturity, that they have been "built up" through successive rituals. At the same time, they reflect the devotee's maturity and his changing relationships with the women closest to him—first, as a dependent infant, with his mother, and later with his wife. There is a progression in the sequence of containers from calabash, to clay, to carved wood or porcelain. The various types of palm nut containers that line the back and side walls of a family's shrine room, as well as those set out on display during annual festivals, reflect the different stages of maturity of male family members (fig. 5.10). While the palm nuts represent the devotee himself—and by extension his male deity Ọrunmila—the containers represent his mother and ultimately his wives—as well as the wives of his deity.

The initiates did not understand the sophistication of the analogical thought that the series of words and acts embody. At first, they did not even fully understand the implications of their personal texts. There was no common intellectual or emotional meaning for all the participants in this ritual. They experienced only unfathomable difficulties and "wonders." But, as Ọṣitọla noted, the journey does not end there. Itẹfa is to be re-experienced for further contemplation.

Once the child has been initiated into Ifa practice, he is from that time on permitted to join the group of diviners inside the restricted grove during the transitional period of others' initiations. From a different perspective, he then experiences again what he has already gone through. Ọṣiṭọla himself—as much as he understands and explains about the ritual process—continues to analyze and interpret what he does, asserting that any diviner who claims knowledge of everything is spurious because, if there is anything that a wise person knows for certain, it is that there is always more to learn and understand. People participate in ritual with different degrees of understanding and different capacities for making meaning.

Ọṣiṭọla's play of tropes took on another dimension when, during the Itẹfa of the alcoholic taxi driver, he requested me to dance with the palm nuts on the initiate's behalf, a tactic I suspect he employed deliberately to influence the initiate's attitude toward the proceedings. I was a stranger, previously unknown to the initiate. My primary interest was Ọṣiṭọla's performance; the initiate could have been anybody. But in a peculiar sort of way my determination to see the whole thing through to the end, staying up all night, being attentive, and even dancing with the initiate's palm nuts served as encouragement from Ọṣiṭọla's point of view. It was clear that I considered what was taking place to be important. And as Ọṣiṭọla had already acknowledged, the initiate's head was "stubborn."

My participation was particularly persuasive because I was under no obligation to be there. My identity as American was also significant. Americans are presumed to be successful and prosperous, states of well-being that those performing Itẹfa hope to achieve in their own lives. And, in comparison to those performing Itẹfa, foreigners in Nigeria are relatively prosperous. When Ọṣiṭọla said the diviners had to work harder, that was extended to me. Ọṣiṭọla engaged me so that I might be a model of perseverance for the initiate at a critical time. My dancing figured into Ọṣiṭọla's play of tropes. Yoruba ritual specialists manipulate ritual in this way; the paratactical structure is conducive to it.

ON YORUBA INTERPRETATION

The Yoruba notion of interpretation in divination practice (ẹyọ Ifa), its personalization, and the way it ultimately shapes further performance can to some extent be evoked in an account of an Itẹfa ceremony conducted between the 1st and the 15th of November, 1986, for four children, three of whom were Ọṣiṭọla's sons, the other also the son of a diviner. Commonality was evident throughout the boys' collective participation in the ritual, although most Itẹfa are performed singly. This Itẹfa followed the model outlined above. At a certain point, however, commonality receded. The diviners revealed and interpreted each boy's personal texts, differentiating their personalities.

As Ọṣiṭọla put it,

to know the final meaning [of the divination], you have to know the
direction and some stories related to it. That is only the A of it. There are
other things we do in reciting the verse in that direction, which sometimes

is personal to the diviner. Because—you know—everybody works with some knowledge, and possibly power too. There is some power which directs the reciter from within. But the aspect that I can explain is the direction. (Ọṣitọla #86.142)

This inner life—the "power" to which Ọṣitọla refers—the workings of the mind, the actual work of interpreting, is inaccessible. Ọṣitọla's representations of his conclusions drawn, on the other hand, are accessible, but only momentarily because they are mere steps in a lengthier process.

> Our concern is taking care of the child. You see we don't finish Itẹfa in a single instance. We do it just to know how to establish [the individual]. It is the initial information on somebody. And that enables us to know how we shall prepare the individual further based on our interpretation according to the changing world. [. . .]
> One of the things in reciting a verse that occurs during an Itẹfa for somebody is that finding a meaning to it is a continuous exercise. For instance, I still need to discuss it [the verse] with some senior diviners other than my colleagues. And I am sure they will still have to educate me more on some of the facts that I don't know. Nobody can claim single knowledge of all the sets of verses. We still need to discuss it further with other people. But to know the direction, it is this that can be explained.
> Even I want to tell you, Yemi himself [one of the initiates] will still continue to find meanings to his life, to his verses. In the first instance, it is only a direction. I still find meanings to my own verses. We don't relent. It is our guidance. We have to be looking at it thoroughly.
> Tomorrow somebody might come from Cuba and tell me a meaning of the Olosun meji [his own personal set of verses] and advise me on it. If it is sacrificial, I still have to do it. If it is not sacrificial, I have to abide by the advice—by the words of wisdom. It is continuous; it is to know a direction.
> But other diviners will continue to give meaning to your particular set of verses all along, all along, as it develops. It may be the next century before I get more meaningful interpretations to my own verses. (Ọṣitọla #86.142)

The dialogue between one's divination texts and one's personal experience is lifelong. There is no concept of "a meaning," or "the meaning," of a personal set of texts. Thus when I suggested to Ọṣitọla that he might be "partial"—that is, biased—if he interpreted his own children's texts, he replied no. Quite the contrary, "not to interpret them would be partial" [that is, incomplete]. Indeed, the more meaning a person reads into his personal texts the better he knows himself. Ọṣitọla thus interpreted his children's verses, although he was not permitted to cast the palm nuts to elicit them. Instead, he was the diviner for the fourth child and, as a result, served dual roles in the ritual as father and diviner. On the issue of meaning, Ọṣitọla commented:

When you are asking about your verses [that is, from other diviners], you ask generally. When you ask generally then you extract what it has to do with you—its relationship.

At the same time, you don't eliminate or abandon whatever meaning may be related to you. But you have to go in your own particular direction. What Ọyẹku meji has to say to one person is different from what Ọyẹku meji has to say to another person.

For instance, Ogbe atẹ is the sign for Wale; Ogbe atẹ is also the sign for Ọdẹlẹyẹ. But what Ogbe atẹ has to tell both of them is different. So you go to your section. But when you are asking your sign, it is not necessary to tell a diviner "this is what my verses have said." But it will be your own confidential fact. When somebody recites for you, you just say, that's alright. Not all they will say will be to your own way of life, but different, different people may say what they like, and then you relate it to yourself.

For instance, when I am asking from other diviners about my children's signs, I will just mention the sign. It is my own concern to collate, or relate, whichever verse I like. (Ọsitọla #86.142)

Not only were the four children's signs different, but the same sign for two different people will have different meanings.

Once the diviners have arrived at a set of texts and find a direction within it, they recite the appropriate verses according to their expertise. The full group of diviners interpret the sign, beginning with the least experienced so that he has a chance to contribute what little he knows before the more masterful ones take over. Etiquette in Ọsitọla's group dictates that the most experienced diviner recites last and gives the concluding meaning or the summation. It is possible for a diviner not to know any verses within a particular set, or to know many but not ones that relate to the particular path that has been called for through the divining process. Women may also interpret the sign.[15]

The meaning of the sign reportedly operates on two levels: First, the verses of a particular sign or set (*ẹsẹ* Ifa) suggest sacrifices to satisfy the moment. Thus,

the sacrifice we make at the sacred bush is the beginning of one's life. The journey does not finish there. That is not the end of everything for that man. We don't say, because he has done a sacrifice, that is all he can offer in his lifetime. He can still progress. Ifa says, do such-and-such this time, just for the moment, for the time being, in order to start life properly. The first sacrifice that we do at the sacred bush is [in order] to start life properly. Nobody can live all his life just within one hour one day. (Ọsitọla #86.142)

The diviners find out, using the initiate's palm nuts, whether the sacrifices in all the verses recited by the various diviners should be combined and offered as a group or whether there is a hierarchy operating beginning with the most expensive to the cheapest. In the latter case, some of the sacrifices can be eliminated, yet the offering will still satisfy the requirements of the group of texts. The belief is that once the divination palm nuts have been ritually associated with the individual, then when cast they will reveal what his inner head prefers.

Whatever Ifa reveals is thought to be in the best interest of the individual. Oṣitọla drew the appropriate analogy this way:

> If a host asks his guests what they will be pleased to receive to be entertained, and they agree to take Guilder beer, is it not to his own satisfaction and to the guests' satisfaction as well? Because the guests have pleased him by accepting his offer. That is why he asked what they liked. And by giving, he is benefiting and the guests are benefiting. He has satisfied the guests to please himself. (Oṣitọla #86.142)

The sacrifices are a multidirectional system of exchange. In pleasing the spirits, the individual pleases himself as well as the entire group, which shares the food cooked with the meat, while the spirits are conceived to take the blood.

The second, and most enduring level of meaning is in the interpretation of the verses themselves—quite apart from the sacrifices they propose. Sacrifices satisfy only the moment, but the parables told based on the verses linger for reflection. Thus,

> the story is related to the sacrifice. Once you have done the sacrifices to please the spiritual powers, you have to reflect on the story. All of the interpretations are given to you for reflection, to continue to think upon, to continue to work upon, to prepare yourself. You have merely done the sacrifices to please the spirits so they will allow you to go your way.
>
> When somebody comes here, we entertain him. That is not the end of the relationship. We still reflect on his coming and what we have done, the motive behind the coming, and what will happen in the future for having invited him. That is not the end. It is not the sacrifice alone that entertains him. (Oṣitọla #86.142)

The recitations and interpretations at sunrise on the second day of Itẹfa are not as crucial as the notion that the individual from that time on will pursue knowledge of his personal verses. The divination sign and the parables that result remain for reflection and reinterpretation throughout life. Men accumulate texts, adding to their personal store of knowledge. Whichever of the signs or sets appears thereafter in subsequent consultations will be weighed in relation to the personal one divined during Itẹfa. At the same time, the signs that were divined during "Stepping into the World" and "Knowing the Head" rituals are now canceled.

Moreover, the outcomes of the divining process are unpredictable, the interpretations often inventive, uneven, and quirky. They are situated responses to the "changing world." Parables are told with varying amounts of detail. Even the number of verses and parables associated with each child during Itẹfa varies, primarily because the knowledge of the diviners themselves varies. Whichever sign turns up in the divining process, the diviners all interpret it independently. The depth and breadth of their results vary greatly from case to case.

The interpretations of the verses, given below, provided by the father of three of the boys represent a particular moment in time, November 30, 1986. They cannot be anything more than that because of the emphasis diviners place on the processual nature of interpretation itself. Thus, how the verses are narrativized on a particular day will not necessarily reflect how they will be understood on any other day. This is because the parable and its meaning are context-specific (Kirshenblatt-Gimblett 1976). The parable the diviner improvises based on the verse is cast in relation to the individual's situation at a particular moment; the parable is, in Ọṣiṭọla's sense, a "conversation" between the verse and the individual for whom it is recited.

On the Bright Side of Darkness: The Envied One

Ọyẹku meji was the Odu divined for Ọṣiṭọla's eldest son, age eight at the time.[16] Its direction indicated overall achievement. Ọṣiṭọla narrated a parable about a child named Sunrise, who came to the world protected:

He lived a full, complete life, and he was bright and prosperous and loved. He had everything in life.

Words of wisdom were spoken to Sunrise in his early life [i.e., when he was rising]. They said he would complete his journey, that his journey would be bright; everybody would like his brightness. And he would also be powerful. But if he wanted to ensure this success, his parents must make a sacrifice on his behalf. They should sacrifice a bunch of brooms, a bundle of white cloth (*ala*), and a sheep.

Sunrise gathered the items and was told, as you are rising, as your life becomes bright, there will be some enemies who will be jealous, who will try to dim your brightness.[17] They will use their power of dangerous inner eyes (*oju buruku inu*) to stare at you. But, if you can satisfy the divine mediator, Eṣu, then he will assist you to prevent those dangerous eyes from dimming your brightness.

Sunrise's parents, named Eṣuwata, made the sacrifice on his behalf.[18] They prepared Sunrise for his journey right from his rise. When he arrived at his destination, everything went well. People understood his light. Everybody admired him (*Ojo yii san an*), for they did better as a result.

But, as he moved higher in the sky, as Ifa predicted, some people attempted to dim his light by staring at him with their dangerous eyes. Immediately, Eṣu, the divine mediator, who was by Sunrise's side, inquired from wise men, "things are now topsy-turvy, what happened? What is the matter with these troublesome people?" The wise elders responded, "it is Sunrise they want to trouble." But Sunrise had been well prepared, he had been well established, he had performed the necessary sacrifices. Eṣu asked, "where is the evidence of the sacrifices?" The wise men showed him the bunch of brooms prepared with medicines, instructing him to put the brooms on Sunrise's forehead so that no one can see his inner head well.

Because Eṣu blessed the brooms, when anyone stared at Sunrise they saw only the brooms, which scratched and hurt their eyes.[19] It is the broom straws scattered in the sunrise that injure people's eyes and prevent them from looking into it; it is the broom straws that prevent people from dimming Sunrise's brightness. The broom blinds the evil inner eyes of onlookers.[20] Extraordinary eyes cannot penetrate a prepared person. If they dare disturb the child, they will be blinded.

The last two lines take the form of a curse.

Oṣitọla only hinted at how he understood this parable:

> You see, the interpretation of Ifa just provides us a model to follow, not just exactly what should be done. You can perform in the changing world manner. You don't have to do exactly what Ifa did historically. Our own knowledge, our own power, our own aṣẹ [power of accomplishment] may not be as powerful as the one they used for the broom in the past. And, again, it may be more powerful than that. And it may not be in [the manner of] that broomish preparation. We have to look at what to do. How can we do it? For instance, we are not in a world where we can give [name of child] a broom to be carrying all the time. Then we have to do it in the changing world fashion.
>
> What shall be given to him as protection? It may not necessarily be material things like a necklace, or wristwatch, or any such thing. It may be some sort of food he can eat. It may be some sort of soap he can take a bath in, and nobody will know that he has been prepared.
>
> We can also make use of incantations. It depends on the changing world and our research. You have got the examples. You know what has been done. You can relate it. (Oṣitọla #86.138)

In addition to understanding how the parable related to his son's life, Oṣitọla also had to figure out how the suggested remedies to the problems sketched out in the oral texts applied to "the changing world." The part of the interpretation that had to do with the immediate action to be taken was confidential for the reason that, if potential detractors were to gain access to the secret, they could counteract its potency and render the action ineffective.

In the road of "overall success," Oyẹku meji posited a bright child both intellectually and physically, who would be embarking on a journey in a jealous, vengeful world.[21] In 1986, Oṣitọla's eldest son was an extremely intelligent, quiet, but intense child, with very beautiful refined features and large bright eyes with thick lashes (fig. 5.11). It is not difficult to understand the meaning of the story of Sunrise in relation to the boy or the jealousy his very existence would be expected to incite. The parable constructs the son's brilliance in multiple senses.

At the same time, Ọyẹku meji is considered a harsh sign because it speaks generally about the threats of death and destruction. It is the same sign that appeared during the Imori ritual for the girl "born to die," when darkness went inside darkness. To understand Ọyẹku meji as general overall success in the midst of threats of death is to prepare the Itefa initiate to operate cautiously and to be sensitive to the implications of making others jealous.

THE ASTUTE SOVEREIGN

Ogbe atẹ (Ogbe irẹtẹ) was the sign that brought the second of Ọsitọla's sons to the world; its path indicated long life and health (*aiku*).[22] As Ọsitọla told it,

> three ancient diviners cast Ifa for one of Ọlofin's children called Sisan, advising him to make a sacrifice in order to live long. The Adapa, the senior diviner, said he should sacrifice a sheep, the Adamoje said it should be a pig, but it was the Amututu who told them that, although Ifa said this boy would live a long life, the first thing they should offer on his behalf at the earliest is snail fluid.[23]

As a result, Ọsitọla sacrificed a snail on the second son's palm nuts.

Ogbe atẹ also called for a cat's skull. Ọsitọla recited simply, *ori ologbo a gbo gbo, ma rin o*, which means "the head of the cat is durable, it will last a full lifetime." With this, Ọsitọla added a cat's skull to this son's container of pre-pared palm nuts.

A lengthier verse also referred to Ọlofin, "The-Owner-of-the-Palace," in effect a king. Thus,

> the words of wisdom for Ọlofin indicated he would live a long life. However, he should be prepared to do something extra in order to make his long life meaningful. To give life meaning, he should perform, "placing the *ayo* game down on the sacred mats" *[ilẹtẹn ayo]*. If he performed this, Ifa promised that Ọlofin would then add something meaningful to the world and to his community.
>
> Ọlofin complied and began to play *ayo* at his palace. Wherever people play *ayo*, others will gather around and join in. Where people gather, they will be joking and exchanging views. They will be relating their knowledge, telling what they can do for the world. By sharing other people's knowledge, Ọlofin was able to rule well, to act. He seized the opportunity to gain from others in order to add his own quota to the world.[24]

When people play games in public, they attract the attention of passers-by who then become active spectators in the process. Ọsitọla continued,

> when you play games, you gather all sorts of information, or facts, which will be useful for you. You embrace people, and they come around you. If a

5.11 Portrait of Ọṣitọla's eldest son, the would-be "envied one." Ijẹbu area, Imodi, 15 November 1986.

5.12 Two initiates play an *ayo* game, a ritual segment that was inserted into the Itẹfa performance based on the interpretation of one of the initiates' personal texts. Ijẹbu area, Imodi, 8 November 1986.

person is able to gather people, then he can collate what he learns from them, or connect it with his own experience, to make progress in his life or to make his life meaningful. That is what Ọlọfin gains from playing *ayo*, so they gave it to him to play. The gathering and exchanging of views will be beneficial to Ọlọfin.

Games engage people in dialogues. In this case, long life in and of itself was not considered meaningful enough even though that was the road designated within the Odu.

Because of this parable, an additional ritual segment was inserted into the proceedings of the seventh day. Thus, the children and the diviners took turns playing a newly purchased game (fig. 5.12). It was no ordinary competition, however. The action designated "playing" the game, but there was no actual game played to completion. There was no winner or loser. But then the story was not concerned with winning and losing. After a cursory game, the board and the seeds used in playing became sacrifices. Ọsịtọla placed his son's prepared palm nuts into the spaces in the game board cut out to hold the seeds, adding to them the cat's skull mentioned previously. On top of this, he poured the blood of a freshly decapitated duck and then added its head to the rest. He concluded by folding up the game board and putting it on his shrine, thus synthesizing in one material representation the remains of the ritual acts that were suggested by the oral texts as a group.

A fourth text was recited for Ọsịtọla's son by a visiting diviner. Since Ọsịtọla was not familiar with this verse, he only explained the sense he derived from it without full narration. The visiting diviner said that the ancestors came to establish the son's feet firmly on earth. And they wanted to continue to assist him. Therefore the parents should acquire a physical representation of the ancestor so that it will "be at the boy's back" to assist him in his life and prevent any disturbances. He reported further that the representative of the ancestor wanted to appear on that very day inside the sacred grove in order to assist this son right from the beginning. "Nobody can cross the road for the ancestors.[25] That is the meaning Arifayọ recited, and it is in the long-life line of Ogbe atẹ. That is why we agreed with him and the ceremony was done."

What happened was that the diviners sent for an Egungun masked performer, who entered the inner shrine during the period of the boys' seclusion so that he could "be around" the second child. As a result of this story, the Egungun became one of the many "wonders" that the children experienced while in the interior of the sacred grove. But it was more than the children "could bear," according to Ọsịtọla, and for a while there was apparently turmoil inside the sacred grove. Reportedly, only the child whose sign called for the ancestral mask showed no signs of fear. This was taken as a validation of the text. A few days later I observed the second son teasing his brothers, imitating their expressions of fright when they confronted the masker.

Ordinarily when the group of sojourners returns home from the sacred grove, the initiate's mother—or a female friend of the mother if there is more than one son being initiated—lines up behind the son to carry his container of palm nuts in procession. It was so on this occasion except that the Egungun followed the second child to carry his palm nuts (see fig. 5.8). In addition to these ritual variations, Ọṣitọla and his wife agreed to prepare a costume for their son some-time in the near future, which he is supposed to wear during local Egungun performances (see chapter 6). As a result of Itẹfa, boys often become performers in specific other ritual traditions. Since there had been no Egungun in the family before to anyone's knowledge, this son's participation in it would forge ex-tralineal alliances.

As a group, the diviners knew more verses from Ogbe atẹ than they knew from those sets divined for the other three boys. And this fact influenced the ritual processes for differentiating the four children. Many of the actions taken as a result of reading the Odu were not evident in the rituals either because they were secret or because they did not involve spectacle. But both the *ayo* game and the Egungun were striking additions to Itẹfa performance that served to identify and differentiate the children. The Egungun indeed alienated the other three.

At the time of the Itẹfa, the second son was a thin, wiry boy, but very strong physically and extremely inquisitive, talkative, and active (fig. 5.13). For him, sitting still playing *ayo* would be a true sacrifice. He is an explorer with an insatiable curiosity, going into people's pockets before they realize what is hap-pening. The other children are also curious, but do not express it with such overt eagerness.

The path of longevity in Ogbe atẹ constructed a long peaceful life of game playing and the ancestors' support, a life free from the kinds of dangerous threats confronting the eldest child. Like Ọlọfin, the second son would make a contribution to the world by drawing people around him, engaging them, listen-ing to their ideas, exchanging views, and then using them to make things hap-pen. He would also become a masked performer, another kind of player, but no less engaging.

THE BOLD ACHIEVER

The sign of the third son was Otura irẹtẹ; its direction indicated all-around success. According to Ọṣitọla's interpretation, this child will add more to the works/accomplishments and reputations of his parents.

Ifa said that Smallness [Kekere] was a child in Ọrunmila's house. Ọrunmila moved in the company of the witches, but he took them very seriously. One day they decided to pose a problem for him. Meanwhile, Smallness made up his mind that these witches were ordinary human beings. This trickster child took it upon himself to grab their weapons, meeting their force with his own. And to everybody's astonishment, he rendered them harmless.

Ifa is saying that the boy will be acting even while everybody else is

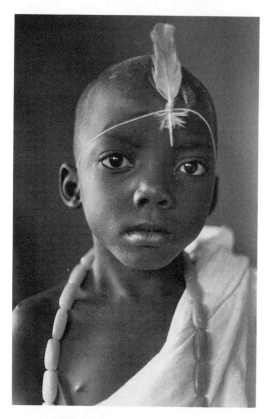

5.13 Portrait of Ọṣitọla's second son, the would-be "astute sovereign." Ijẹbu area, Imodi, 15 November 1986.

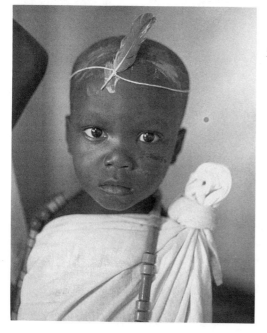

5.14 Portrait of Ọṣitọla's youngest son, the would-be "bold achiever." Ijẹbu area, Imodi, 15 November 1986.

retreating, when other people are saying it is dangerous. And with that, he will achieve a lot for his action. What Ifa tells of him is that he is an action person. Ifa said he will do more than his father. We are hopeful. Ifa said he will do more than his predecessors. But we have to establish his inner head strongly because he will dare to go anywhere no matter the result. So we have to prepare him for this life because he is bold and active.

The diviners interpreted this story from Otura irẹtẹ in the following way. Ọṣitọla in his role as father was advised to perform a special ritual in the forest on the fourteenth day of Itẹfa. The diviners called it "the destruction of his house in the otherworld" (iwole ọrun). Ọṣitọla's assistants went to the bush and built a shed (ikọle ọrun) using large branches and leaves, which they said represented his "house in the otherworld" (ile orun). As soon as it was completed, Ọṣitọla led a tethered sheep down the path deep into the forest. Entering the shed, he sat with the sheep momentarily on the ground inside as the diviners chanted. He then ran out suddenly as his assistants picked up the sheep and plunged it down on top of the shed, thoroughly demolishing it. The demolition of his otherworldly house was said to prevent Death from interfering with Ọṣitọla, so that he would have ample time on earth to establish his children properly in their own lives.[26] The diviners accomplished this through metaphoric contiguity. Thus the idea of "the house in heaven" was brought into comparison with the constructed shed in the bush, which the diviners successfully destroyed, by implication doing damage to the idea. This ritual segment was taken to be critical particularly because of the youngest son's boldness, which by extension may bring repercussions on his father.

Even-tempered, jovial, and playful, the youngest of Ọṣitọla's children was only three years old at the time of the Itẹfa (fig. 5.14). Often entertaining himself and experimenting creatively with things, he turned containers into hats and cardboard boxes into shoes. Not self-conscious about trying new things, whether attempting to weave a mat, play the ayo game, or talk, he jumped in without hesitation and always appeared undaunted even when people laughed. His devil-may-care way of operating suggested his trickster potential, an ability to insert himself into situations and transform them.[27]

INDIVIDUALITY, REFLEXIVITY, AND EXPERIENCE

The divination texts interpreted during Itẹfa posit for the children distinct personalities, life situations, and their interrelationships with others, thus setting up expectations and broad courses of action. Through this process, boys may be steered into other ritual performances, just as Ọṣitọla's son was directed to perform as an Egungun masker. Diviners do not reject individuality, but rather provide the children with reflexive models for self-examination in coping with social complexities. To compromise the inner head of the individual is to interfere with his destiny.[28]

The fourteen-day rite of passage is a decisive point of articulation in an unending interpretive process. As Ọṣitọla so aptly expressed it,

> nobody stops at fourteen days. We stop only the dancing and the eating. We prepare the celebrants for the journey. Then after we take them, we know who this head is.
>
> After all, when your child is born, he is crawling, crawling, crawling. At one stage we hold his hand to make him walk. We can't just stop. We will continue to train him.
>
> That is why we prepare him for another stage of life. We dress him up. We have established him to a stage; the suffering continues. But gear up for work. Nobody stops. Who stops him? We give him a cutlass to weed, work. Work ethic! Then if he doesn't want to work, then he has to learn to work by force. We teach him. Work, climb, go to the sea, go to the sky, go to the moon, *kiakia* [with haste]. So that is another stage, we don't mind. Because if we don't make him work, he will just keep crawling, crawling, crawling on the *itẹn* [mat]. Nobody stops at seven days. Who stops? I don't stop. (Ọṣitọla #86.143)

The journey to the sacred grove of Odu presents the initiates with new experiences, with lessons about the hardships and joys in life, and with a wealth of material for further reflection.

The experimental part of Itẹfa ritual, its creativity, was not confined to its structure or its process or to any liminal phase of performance. Rather, its creativity lay in the talents of performers to improvise, to play the tropes, to interpret, and to manipulate the action skillfully and persuasively. All these operations were ongoing throughout the performance.

Ọṣitọla emphasized thought, reflexivity, and interpretation—all of which were invoked in the rituals he conducted. Individuals must know themselves in order to succeed and prosper in a highly competitive society composed of potential allies as well as enemies.[29] In a society of highly differentiated, operationally strong selves, people's relationships often get worked out through play. It emerged in chapter 3 as a structural feature of funerals and in this chapter in the improvisations and interpretations of diviners. In the next chapter, I explore playing as a mode of action in a kind of ritual that Yoruba also call spectacle.

6.

Ritual Play *about* Play: Performing Miracles in Honor of the Ancestors

> The performance process is a continuous rejecting and replacing. Long-running shows—and certainly rituals are these—are not dead repetitions but continuous erasings and superimposings. The overall shape of the show stays the same, but pieces of business are always coming and going. This process of collecting and discarding, of selecting, organizing, and showing, is what rehearsals are all about. And it's not such a rational, logical-linear process as writing about it makes it seem. It's not so much a thoughtout system of trial and error as it is a playing around with themes, actions, gestures, fantasies, words: whatever's being worked on. From all the doing, some things are done again and again; they are perceived in retrospect as "working," and they are "kept." They are, as it were, thrown forward in time to be used in the "finished performance."
>
> Richard Schechner (1985:120)

In Yoruba ritual, the whole workshop/rehearsal/finished performance complex to which Schechner refers is compressed into one event. The improvised ritual *is* workshop, rehearsal, and finished performance all at the same time. It is the occasion when masters continue to refine their skills and when neophytes learn in plain sight of everyone (fig. 6.1). That is part of the attraction.

The mere existence of a ritual structure, or strategy; rules for its operation; an in-body technique capable of manifesting it; and origin myths to validate it do not reveal how individual performers manipulate those structures, rules, techniques, and myths. Such manipulations constitute what de Certeau (1984:xviii) calls "trajectories obeying their own logic." He goes on to argue that, "although they are composed with the vocabularies of established languages [. . .] and although they remain subordinated to the prescribed syntactical forms [. . .] the trajectories trace out the ruses of other interests and desires that are neither determined nor captured by the systems in which they develop." Well versed in the ritual form and in the practical techniques for achieving it, trained specialists like Ọṣitọla perform tactical operations on their ritual structure, on the process, on context, on oral tradition, on ritual dress, on rhythmic and kinetic patterns, and on a combination of all of them.

Where improvisational skill is most evident is in fragmented, open, and explicitly competitive performances, where performers match skill with skill and attempt to transcend it, where each participant vies for attention, contributing to the steady stream of events, both initiating action and responding to other competitors. The multilogics of this kind of performance provide great creative amplitude. In this chapter I explore this idea in a masking spectacle known as Egungun, which honors the spirits of ancestors.

Egungun masks are regarded as physical representations of ancestral spirits. As such, they perform during the play segments of funerals for society members as well as during annual or biennial Egungun festivals held in communities throughout Yorubaland. Performance dates are set through divination and announced publicly. Spectators gather in the open air, often at central locations, when they hear the drummers begin to play. Attendance is optional, and audiences are diverse in age, sex, and social status, at once including locals, visitors, and strangers. The size of audiences varies, too, depending on whether the performance is for a funeral or for the annual festival, whether it occurs in a city or in a small village.

As representations of spirits, the masks do not portray dead individuals *per se,* with one exception.[1] Neither do they bear the names of human beings. As representations of spirits, they are given special praise epithets such as Owolẹwa ("Riches-Bring-Beauty") and Ayelabọla ("The-World-Bestows-Honor"). Others, like Kulodo (fig. 2.3), bear praise epithets that are shared by all the members of the lineage, who are known as "children of Kulodo" (ọmọ Kulodo).[2] Whatever it is, the name usually celebrates the spirit by representing its sacred origins and, by extension, the sacred origins of the owner and his or her lineage.

Egungun performances reshape perceptions of the world and give concrete form to ontological concepts. Ritual specialists bring that which is normally inaccessible, unseen, or imagined, into the phenomenal world where it can be observed and contemplated. Through a practical mastery of performance techniques, the maskers manipulate the perceptual world, the world as it is experienced daily; they play upon, embellish, and transform reality. The *as if* becomes *is* as illusion becomes its own reality, or, more appropriately, illusion reveals an otherwise undisclosed reality. The performers possess *aṣẹ,* the power to bring things into existence.

As they do in Itẹfa, myths serve as documents of precedent in Egungun ritual. These narrative accounts construct the circumstances of the "original" performance. The Yoruba assumption is that these narratives have the power to draw on past experience in order to critique and guide a future experience (LaPin 1977:135). In Egungun, the experience that myth directs is the restoration of performance.

AT PLAY WITH MYTH

Egungun masked performances transform and re-present myth through the fragmentation of its narrative structure much in the same way as divination

rituals do. The performances are paratactical—made up of equal, but themati-
cally and stylistically disconnected, segments strung together temporally. Reference to myth in ritual is, in the words of Ọṣitọla,

> like uprooting a tree from the root, from the beginning. It's like laying a
> solid foundation of that particular stage of the ceremony. Every stage of a
> ceremony, we try to start from the background, from the foundation. So we
> don't just start from anywhere. And when you start from the foundation,
> then everything, the *aṣẹ* of the ceremony, will *act* properly. (#82.44)

Each ritual segment, then, is grounded in its own independent origin. When
actualized, segments may serve to evoke narrative wholes. As a Yoruba adage
explains, "it is necessary only to give half of a speech to the well-bred person;
inside him it becomes whole" (Owomoyela 1979).

When reenacted, the precedents documented in myth are carried into the
present and are brought to bear on the current situation much in the same way
as legal precedents direct court action.[3] The notion is that patterns from the
past, when restored through performance, establish the terms on which the
desired consequences can be negotiated. They are conceived to do so not because they participate somehow in primordial time, but because they are perceived to be tried and true formulas developed over time by wise people with
previous experience in such matters. These formulas then become models for
present practice that permit a wide range for interpretation and representation.
To illustrate, I provide an Egungun origin myth below and then examine its
relationship to performance.

An Egungun Origin Myth

Through a series of twists and turns, the burial of a dead father is transformed into a funeral rite of entertaining masked performances. The mythical
relationship between dead fathers and their sons is actualized in Egungun
masks. This relationship was made visually explicit in the house of some
Egungun devotees in the town of Ilaro, where a wall mural placed over their
forebear's grave depicted the series of masks owned by the family (fig. 6.2).
According to one version of a myth published by Joel Adedeji (1970:72–73),
when a king—a hunchback—died, his three sons had no money for a proper
burial. The first son saw his father's corpse and fled. The second dressed the
corpse up only to leave it behind. The third, after trying to sell the body in the
market (for use in medicines), finally abandoned it in the bush.

Years later, when the eldest son succeeded his father, a neighboring king
presented him with a wife named Iya Mọṣẹ. For many years, Iya Mọṣẹ did not
give birth to any children, so she and her husband consulted diviners independently. Whereas Iya Mọṣẹ's diviner told her that she would give birth to a son,
the king was informed that his failure to perform the proper funeral rites caused
his problem and that he would be unable to father a child until he had com-

pleted his own father's burial. The king was in a dilemma, for by that time his
late father's corpse had decomposed.

One day at a nearby stream, a gorilla raped Iya Mọsẹ and she became pregnant. Ashamed, she fled to the King of Oponda, where she hid until she bore
the child, who turned out to be a hybrid—half human and half monkey. Iya
Mọsẹ left secretly, throwing this hybrid child into the bush before returning to
her husband. The baby did not die, however, and was later rescued. Eventually
Iya Mọsẹ revealed the story of the birth to her husband. He returned to consult
his diviner, who predicted that the child would grow up to be Amu'ludun (literally, "One-Who-Brings-Sweetness" to the community). The diviner advised further that the funerary rites of the king's father should be performed in the bush,
where his spirit would materialize in a costume, and that the hybrid child should
be mounted on the performer's back to impersonate the father's hunchback.
This hybrid child was called Ijimere—the Yoruba word for the red savannah
Patas Guenon monkey.

The narrative goes on to chronicle the origins and ritual roles of several
Egungun titles. It also sets up a ritual relationship between sons and dead
fathers through the art of masking. In actual practice, it is the sons and daughters who provide the cloth for the costumes in which the spirit of the deceased
ancestor becomes manifest.[4] And, finally, the myth ties funeral rites to the
theme of entertainment (that is, the masked performer is "to cheer up the
community"). The relationships among characters outlined in myth have by
analogy implications for the ritual participants' current relationships. In
Egungun ritual, performers interpret and re-present elements of the narrative in
playful ways, giving them a transitory concreteness.

MYTH, MASKS, AND PERFORMANCE

Egungun masks play subtlely on the attributes of the red savannah Patas
Guenon monkey in stylized ways that remove the image from any realistic representation. This is particularly evident in *alabala*-type masks (figs. 6.3, 6.4),
which are among the first ones members acquire when joining Egungun societies
among Ẹgbado and Awori Yoruba. Like the Patas monkey, *alabala* masks are
tall, predominantly red, and have horizontal black and white bands across their
faces and top knots on their heads. A mantle of long cloth at the back of the
costume can trail on the ground like a long tail or can be gathered up around
the back of the neck like the monkey's fur ruff, in either case suggesting one of
the monkey's two physical features. Also like the Patas monkey, who walks on
the ground upright on its hind legs, the masked performers appear in troupes
and are playful, agile, and acrobatic.[5]

Presenting themselves as hybrids, they are not human *but*—to use
Schechner's double negative (1985:110)—they are not not human; not monkey, but not not monkey. There is a play on the play, that is, on the relationship
between the performer and his role. The mask itself is a reflexive comment on
the performer's role as masker. Thus, when the performer and the role come

together the "not me, not not me" status of the performer gets subverted in the not not human/not not monkey—a double negative doubled—built into the mask's identity. The Yoruba way of implying the play on the play is simply to smile and say "it's a spirit," deferring meaning still further. It is also a way of saying, therefore, "it can be anything it likes," that is, take any form or color or personality.

Other types of masks refer to the Patas Guenon monkey in other ways. While *alabala* masks as a category allude to the monkey's physical features and behavior in highly stylized ways, another mask that appeared at the 1977 Egungun festival in Isalẹ Eko, Lagos, on October 15 recontextualized actual monkey skulls. The monkey and the deceased forefather represented by mask were brought together in a very concrete way, suggesting the relationship between them contained in the myth. Yet another mask in Itesi quarter, Abẹokuta, April 1978, instead of incorporating an actual skull substituted carved wooden monkey skulls interspersed with those of hornbills. The head of the hornbill is often used in medicines, when participants carry heavy loads on their heads just as the hornbill carries his horn. It was used for this purpose, for example, in Itẹfa ritual on the journey to Odu's sacred grove when Ọsitọla's eldest son carried a hornbill skull packed with his loads carried on his head (see fig. 5.3). By analogy, the special power of the hornbill, with the visibly weighty horn on his bill, was transferred to the Itẹfa initiate as well as to the masker carrying the heavy, wooden mask on top of his head.

In these various examples are three distinct kinds of representations of the monkey, all of which bear some relationship to each other and to origin myths about the performance.[6] They have similarities, and they have differences. Various oral and visual images refer to each other in a play of signifying references, signifieds always in the process of becoming signifiers (Derrida 1984:7). The hornbill on the other hand has its own distinct reference metaphorically, which relates to the job of masking but not to Egungun myth or to the monkey.

A fourth masker who performed at Imasai on December 23, 1977, alluded more literally to the segment of the myth that described the gorilla raping the wife of the king (fig. 6.5). Gorilla (*Inọki*) had naturalistically carved wooden testicles and a penis painted red on the tip. He sneaked up behind unsuspecting women in the performing space, raising his penis as if he were going to rape them. Meanwhile the drums sounded an ideophonic *sabala-sabala-sa-o*, which represented aurally Gorilla's fucking gestures. The mimetic action paralleled a segment of the narrative, but the outcome was renegotiated as women screamed and ran away from his lewd advances to the amusement of other spectators. The ruse worked because at no time during Yoruba performances I have witnessed was everybody's attention uniformly focused. Thus it is possible for such masks to catch people unaware. That is part of the play. The interest of the spectators was not so much in the repetition of a stock formal segment as it was in the process of the negotiation, in the play of the moment.

Another mask at the same performance—a dancing mat called Alagẹmọ—had a dual reference. A monkey image painted on the surface recalled the monkey's centrality in myths about the origin of Egungun (fig. 6.6); however, the form of the mask itself had been appropriated from an entirely different Yoruba masking complex called Agẹmọ (chapter 7). The ritual precedent for the Agẹmọ mask is relayed in myths associated with a group of powerful chiefs, who took the symbol of the chameleon (*agẹmọ*) as their emblem of office. While the ritual precedent for the Agẹmọ mask's use in an Agẹmọ context is considered to be documented in oral tradition, its precedent for use in an Egungun context is Agẹmọ performance. Only the monkey motif added to the mask's surface relates specifically to Egungun.

Ritual specialists identify precedents from myths—such as the one above about Egungun—then bend its themes, shape them, and remold them through present practice. The performance has a wonderful double dynamic. Just as the masks themselves refer backward in time, to ancestral spirits, to a presumed past, they simultaneously renegotiate the present.

REFLEXIVE PLAY

The dancing mat and Gorilla were part of a flexible repertoire of "miracles" (*idan*) performed in the context of Egungun Apidan, "Performance of Miracles." Because Apidan are autonomous, self-contained segments within Egungun festivals and the play segments of funerals, they can also serve to mark other special occasions—like the anniversary celebration of an installation of a king or the opening of a factory. From a Yoruba point of view, what better homage could a family hope to pay the ancestors than to perform at the opening of a factory, a symbol of progress and potential prosperity for the entire community. The secular setting contributes meaning to the event, but does not totally construct it.

Although the entire performance is play in Yoruba terms, involving drumming and dancing, it also includes invocations to the deities and blood sacrifices, usually performed at Egungun shrines on the morning of the masks' public appearance. Indeed, Egungun masks themselves are shrines in motion, composed of the ingredients that constitute the stationary shrines inside devotees' compounds. Apidan performance highlights the essential interrelatedness between play and ritual in Yoruba thought.[7] It is an entertaining reflexive discourse on the act of transformation itself. The principal mask, the "miracle worker" (*onidan*, literally "owner-of-miracles"), is a magician, a master of the art of transformation (*parada*) (figs. 6.7–6.11). He is simultaneously a dancing womb, and his dress parodies a Muslim woman in Purdah (Taiwo #s 75.4a and 75. 14b).[8]

Like other Egungun masks, miracle workers have personal identities and reputations based on their skills as performers. In the town of Ilaro on November 15, 1975, a miracle worker named Ajofunoyinbo ("We-Dance-for-the-White-Man") stood on top of an inverted mortar, invoking the forces at work in the universe to win their support.[9] After a lengthy invocation and three songs, the drummers went into their staccato dance rhythms, and Ajofunoyinbo stepped down off the mortar whirling, his cloth spreading out in a massive cone shape. Descending smoothly, he spread his cloth out over the earth in a large circle as his body spiralled. Rising, he alternately whirled and paraded, raising his legs high as he stepped around the arena to bow down and greet the elders (fig. 6.7). As the drums then beat an extremely rapid cadence, the miracle worker bent forward, transforming before the audience's eyes by turning his outer garment inside out (yi aṣọ pada). Finally, Ajofunoyinbo peeled off his outer garment, changing to the hybrid monkey form (fig. 6.8).

Masters of this mask have discovered numerous techniques for turning their cloths, from bending over low to the ground and peeling over their backs to flipping it high in the air as they run forward (figs. 6.9, 6.10). In changing their cloths, they sometimes pull one on under another (fig. 6.11). Ajofunoyinbo's mastery was in the skill with which he handled his cloth, transforming before the spectators' eyes without exposing his human form underneath. The audience is to perceive only what the performer wants it to see, that is, an elusive being continually changing form and color in plain sight of everyone.

If a miracle worker dances well, the drummers may change to irregular rhythms known as ẹgọ (Agbelelu, master *bata* drummer, #75. 13b). Ordinarily, the drummers emulate the pitch patterns and rhythms of spoken Yoruba, enabling the drums to speak proverbs and aphorisms. But in the irregular rhythms of ẹgọ, phrases are divided and subdivided, and words are repeated so that the lead drum is often referred to as the "stutterer." While the dance of miracle worker, with his big circular garment, is more a virtuoso display of cloth and its manipulation, miracle worker transformed into the hybrid monkey concentrates on the intricacies of stepping to complex, irregular rhythms (fig. 6.4).

Such transformations signal another stage in the performance. From underneath his big circular, womb-like garment, the miracle worker Ajofunoyinbo began to "give birth" to a whole series of "miracles" that caricatured the "world." This was not played out in any literal way, but was something understood by most participant/observers. As Egungun specialist Raimi Akaki Taiwo of Ilaro commented about an *onidan* named Ayelabọla ["World-Bestows-Honor"]:

> Now you see that Ayelabọla, before it comes to play everything—as I can see—there is a big abdomen. In the morning when it comes out, it means that it has conceived. But in the evening when the dance is made, then that one will be removed. It means that he bore all things inside the abdomen, like snake. [. . .] From Ayelabọla—from inside his cloth—that crocodile, snake, wife and husband, drunkard, and some other performances that we saw yesterday—from inside that big garment of Ayelabọla—they all came out. (#75.4a)

Conceptually, it is through miracle worker's giant womb, his caullike garment that the miracles come into the world. But like the stylized Patas monkey, the performer alluded to, but in no way mimed or literally re-presented, the theme.

Both in giving birth to miracles and in turning his cloth inside out, the miracle worker played on gender and the biological prerogatives of women. The idea was only a point of departure. By inverting his womb, exposing the inside, miracle worker presented an ironic play on a familiar Egungun incantation that stresses, "the eyes of the blacksmith cannot see underneath the ground of his shed. [. . .] The eyes of the potter cannot see the inside of clay," nor for that matter can the mother see inside her womb (recorded in Ilaro, November 1977). The miracle worker in that sense transcended that which not even women can do in giving birth to children.

In the performances I attended, the miracles the performers gave birth to commented on the world. They presented humorous reflexive images of existence. Just as miracle workers inverted their wombs, turning the inside into the outside, so too the miracles from underneath their cloths presented to the world a comical mirror image of itself. It was as if the spirit realm materialized to show the phenomenal world to itself. Among the images presented were playful and ferocious animals. Animals "at play" mimed copulation; others chased children. Human caricatures were also popular: at an Imaṣai performance a husband and his three well-dressed wives eventually got into a fight, with the wives first fighting with each other and then ganging up on the husband; a mother-to-be, in retying her wrapper around her waist, exposed her pregnant belly at Ibara Quarter, Abẹokuta (fig. 6.12); a palmwine drunkard staggered around, stumbled, fell, and begged spectators for money at Ilaro. If the performance is for a funeral, the relatives of the deceased attend and spend money on the performers.

Another popular character was the prostitute. One at Ilaro went about seductively stroking her two fanglike teeth. The suggestion was that she was somehow inhuman, more like an animal in behavior. Other characters, such as a priest of Eṣu or a mother of twins, often made playful reference to the performers' own families. Those "miracles" that represented priests of Yoruba deities often performed the actual dances associated with a particular deity. Warriors, forest spirits, and foreigners were among other favorite characters. Using a combination of dance and mime, the performers improvised, bringing each character to life.

Although the characters were stereotypical, there are infinite possibilities for rendering them so as to alter how they are read and perceived. The characters that made up Apidan performances varied greatly from troupe to troupe, as did the orders of their appearances. But Egungun society members insisted that the last character to perform should be Bride (Iyawo) (fig. 6.13). The Bride was the only miracle to appear consistently time after time in the Apidan performances I observed in western Yorubaland. All the other masks were variables to be manipulated—to be inserted, deleted, and reordered.

Bride represents the miracle worker's ultimate transformation, and that is why she closes the performance. Bride is miracle worker *before* he gives birth, and thus the performance inverts the normal sequence of things—that is, instead of the new bride becoming pregnant and giving birth to children, she gives birth first, then becomes the bride. Another form of play, this inversion is consistent with other inversions in the performance, for example, miracle worker's act of inverting his own cloth. The relationship between the miracle worker and Bride is often drawn visually by having the two masks dressed in the same cloth, which is sewn differently.

Egungun society members explained the sequencing in two ways: 1) that by the end of the performance Bride is old and can no longer give birth (an ironic use of the word bride)[10] and 2) that Bride is a young, newly married woman, who will be pregnant by the next performance and ready to give birth again. In this latter sense, Bride establishes a sense of continuity between performances, for in the subsequent performance the miracle worker always begins again as a pregnant womb and continues to bear his children before turning again into Bride. Thus Bride is an ending and at the same time presages a new beginning, the continuity of the performance process.[11]

Through a reshuffling and recombination of segments, Apidan performance can evoke or, more precisely, invoke and actualize numerous myths, rituals, and other contexts simultaneously. It is heterological. Equally important, Apidan performance can also incorporate new material within its structure. If popular and adopted widely, the new material itself eventually becomes conventional, as it has in the case of the Agẹmọ mat mask whose painted monkey image refers simultaneously to Egungun myth and to Agẹmọ ritual.

Such performances constitute a blurred genre in Geertz's sense (1983). Thus they have been a source of frustration for scholars struggling to locate them within a continuum from the sacred to the secular—from ritual to theater.[12] Apidan performance defies strict categorization, for it is ritual play *about* play and transformation. The source of ambiguity lies in its exploration of reality. It is a reflexive discourse on the subjunctive and the indicative. The central message is that things are not always what they appear and that illusion is its own reality.

In the city of Abẹokuta, where a professional warrior class developed during the nineteenth-century civil wars (Ajayi and Smith 1964; Ajayi 1965), masks regarded as very rough and dangerous storm through the town and disrupt Apidan performances unexpectedly, causing the alarmed dispersal of the audience. Retainers hold them back physically, but now and then one breaks loose and must be restrained, while pedestrians scatter in all directions. One warrior mask, with wild, unkempt hair and imported combat boots, had a face in front as well as behind so that onlookers could not tell immediately whether he was coming or going. His most outstanding feature was his horrible stench, reportedly the result of having soaked his tunic in human blood for some weeks prior to the performance.

Warrior masks are turned loose to run rampant throughout the town from their separate households (fig. 6.14).[13] Since they are not confined to one visibly unified playing area as are the Apidan masks, their appearances at various places in the town are sudden and unexpected. They are followed by small armies of young men who grab all sorts of things in their paths and throw them—metal buckets, chairs, sticks—and who sometimes tear down sheds or other obstacles. The townspeople stampede to escape confrontation and flying objects. People are knocked down, stepped on, and everyone in general gets more or less shaken up. The scene re-creates the disruptions of war that characterized the nineteenth century. This re-creation terrorizes people for the duration of the performance, even though spectators know it is not real warfare.

Part of the drama of the warrior masks is their sudden intrusions into public spaces where people work and live. People know that it is the time when warrior masks are out and about, but the precise moment of confrontation is unexpected. During this period, young men from warrior families and the maskers prepare themselves with medicines. In so doing, they work themselves up for the performance. As each ingredient is added the young men go into a kind of trance state and charge through the community with cutlasses and other weapons.

During a 1978 Egungun festival in Abẹokuta, on the afternoon of an Apidan performance one young warrior with glazed, bloodshot eyes ran up between two houses and suddenly appeared in the area where I was standing. He was mounted by the spirit of a deceased warrior.[14] Blood streamed down the side of his mouth. People scattered, including myself, but the young man seemed oblivious and pursued a direct path with a sense of purpose and determination. The confrontation was frightening. I was not certain whether he was genuinely injured, was simply playing a role, or both. The performers have been brought up in the warrior tradition and perform on cue. Why was it the impulse of the bystanders caught off guard to run and get out of his way if they were watching only make-believe? Were all of us caught up in a ruse of the sort that my acquaintance pulled on the police? Whatever the case, these kinds of improvisational interventions into ritual time and space formally transform the structure of each performance and how it is experienced.

In 1982, just before the Nigerian national elections, it was rumored that the minority opposition political party in one southern town was going to use the outing of the warrior masks to riot. The pliable nature of the performance lends itself to this kind of political protest, which the traditional ruler of the town was determined to avoid.[15] He thus canceled the entire festival midway through in order to stop this particular performance that was supposed to be part of it.

IMPROVISATIONAL INTERVENTION:
A CASE STUDY

Improvisational interventions similar to those above are part of the dynamics of Yoruba ritual. Such interventions run a whole gamut from total disruption, fighting, and even the cancellation of ritual to heightened pleasure, giving participants enormous self-satisfaction. On November 9, 1975, in the Ẹgbado community of Ijado, a woman intervened in an Apidan performance in which she had no formal or structural role. This performance was part of a funeral rite for her husband. In commanding the spectators' attention, the woman successfully inserted herself into the action and commandeered the ritual, embellishing it to the extent of becoming its main attraction.

Iya Ṣango, as she is called, is a well-known performer in her own right, a priestess of the deity of thunder and war, Ṣango (M. Drewal 1986). As the miracle worker Ajobiewe (One-Who-Dances-Like-a-[Fluttering]-Leaf) swept off his inverted mortar, Iya Ṣango took off her wrapper and shoved it toward him like a bullfighter taunting a bull. Ajobiewe turned and walked away.

Iya Ṣango then spread her wrapper out on the ground. Women from her husband's family were supposed to put down money, an expressive gesture in compensation for the loss of her husband. Spreading cloth to receive money is conventional; *how* she went about it was not. With exaggerated gestures, Iya Ṣango dropped her cloth on the ground, punctuating its landing with a small jump up. Moving to the side with high kicks calculated to correspond to the drumming for the miracle worker—who was dancing simultaneously—she wove mannered stepping into the task of putting down the cloth, achieving a synthesis of two separate actions and intentions in one double-voiced process.

While Iya Ṣango danced, women came forward and dropped their money. Suddenly, a chicken unexpectedly crossed her path. Instantaneously she leaned down, grabbed it with one hand, and slung it around her waist. Flapping its wings, the chicken got loose, fluttered across her back, and escaped on the opposite side. At this point, Iya Ṣango reclined on the cloth on one elbow and conspicuously counted her money. All this was going on while the miracle worker danced, in a kind of multichanneled operation.

After miracle worker's transformation into the stylized Patas monkey mask, two dancing mats scooted across the performance space, hesitating to spin and plunk down, to quiver, to fold in and expand, and finally to glide off; the stylized monkey mask danced simultaneously just in front of the drummers. Meanwhile Iya Ṣango squatted in front of the lead drummer, scissoring her knees out and in, then jumped up unexpectedly and dashed off into the audience.

Two masked children, their cloth dangling at their backs, performed mannered stepping patterns, carefully placing one foot down in front of the other with little mincing steps, traveling forward in that position before lifting and placing the opposite leg down. In rushed another miracle called Pop Eyes (Olojukujuru). Wielding a whip, he charged me as I was filming him and then dropped back when I failed to respond. Pop Eyes continually shifted his weight, lunging forward and back from a wide sagittal stance, giving the impression of an agitated readiness to attack. He combined this action with leaps straight up into the air, throwing one leg up and both arms out before landing (fig. 6.15).

Such masks have taught me to be responsive and to become part of the show. On more than one occasion, I have evaded Gorilla and darted off to get out of the way of Leopard and Hyena to laughter and even cheers. In this way, the performers made me part of their show and made my task as photographer work to their immediate advantage. They also appreciated that I was willing to play this out.

Other masks followed: another hybrid monkey, accompanied by two children's masks, and then one satirizing Hausa men, often the meat-sellers in Yoruba markets. The Hausa character wore a white, northern-style garment (*riga*) and had a puffy distorted face and red fingers, mouth, and teeth that appeared bloody. The insinuation, according to an Egungun society member who used to sell meat for a Hausa man, was that Hausa meat-sellers are so uncouth as to nibble on the raw meat they are selling.

The Hausa mask danced a vigorous, but simple, repetitive pattern. As he spun around, Iya Ṣango joined him and they twirled side by side. Suddenly, the Hausa masker went off toward the drums, but Iya Ṣango grabbed his arm and pulled him around, engaging him in a dance face to face, at the end thrusting her red head tie—thrice—provocatively between her spread legs, using large emphatic arm gestures in time to the drumming. As the Hausa mask turned and walked off, she pursued him close behind bumping against his backside. Straddling the drumhead again, she bumped her pelvis forward, at the same time looking over her shoulder and gesturing with her hand at the base of her buttocks for the Hausa meat-seller to mount her from behind. The Hausa mask put his hands up over his eyes as the audience cheered. Meanwhile, Iya Ṣango walked off into the audience.

Engaging the Hausa mask once more face to face (fig. 6.16), Iya Ṣango this time flipped the front hem of her petticoat toward him as she danced, always relating rhythmically to the drumming, and in a final punctuation of the drumbeat she flung her petticoat all the way up in his face. Then she stalked him in a circle with her torso stretched forward horizontally to the ground. With her open palm, fingers extended, she pressed her hand in his direction in a cursing gesture. Both the Hausa meat-seller and Iya Ṣango then ran toward each other, stopped short, and bumped their hips once simultaneously. The drummers continued to guide the dancers rhythmically, but the actions they inscribed on those rhythms were worked out spontaneously on the spot. The dancers were familiar with the drumming style, and likewise the drummers were familiar with both dancers. As the Hausa mask walked passed Iya Ṣango to go off, she again turned and trailed him close behind with another bump of the pelvis. But he was unaware, and the crowd roared with laughter.

The Hausa mask was followed by a scruffy Dahomean warrior (Idahọmi) with boils on his face, a condition associated with the malnutrition suffered by warriors stationed in war camps in alien territories during the nineteenth-century Yoruba/Fọn wars. The Dahomean lumbered around the performance space in time to the drums, but never appeared very threatening—just ugly— and he soon exited with little audience reaction.

As soon as he left, some adults put a young aspiring Egungun performer forward to dance; he was not more than six years old and unmasked. Holding the bottom corners of his shirt out with his fingertips, he concentrated on his Egungun stepping style, lifting his legs high and placing them back down again with a sense of calculated precision. Performances often serve as the training ground for the young, and part of their attraction is in watching young performers develop their technique and style from one time to the next.

Iya Ṣango took another opportunity to intervene in the performance, this time competing with a Bariba mask, satirizing another northern neighbor of the Yoruba. Instead of engaging the mask, she engaged the drummers again, dancing right in front of them with wrapper in hand, swinging it wildly all around in the air. Flipping her hips percussively side to side, she approached and straddled the drumhead once more. Then she bumped her pelvis forward as she gestured downward percussively with her right hand as if striking the drumhead. To punctuate the ends of rhythmic phrases, she reached behind, abruptly slapping her own buttocks. And in a final flourish, she threw her petticoat up and over the drummer's head. The spectators cheered, clearly responding more to her performance than to that of the Bariba mask going on simultaneously. Bride then concluded the performance with a lengthy dance that parodied female style— gentle, smooth, understated—which Iya Ṣango did not interrupt.

This particular performance focused on foreigners residing on Yoruba borderlands, particularly those who have had a major social or economic impact in Yoruba country.[16] Iya Ṣango's improvisational interventions, however, dominated. She commandeered the performance successfully, foregrounding herself and usurping the prominence of the masks. This worked in part because the miracles she chose to engage or subvert were themselves objects of Yoruba ridicule. Already constructed as derisive characters, they lent themselves to further play.

What Iya Ṣango did was to take advantage of their statuses as comic figures, a tactical maneuver that turned their performance into her own. She effectively subverted the comic discourse on foreigners, creating another one on top. Playing the situation, she transformed the lead drum into a phallus and an undesirable foreigner into an ironic object of her own desire. And she did so aggressively, in marked contrast to the parody of female style performed by Bride.

In the acquisition of techniques for the body, performers master codes. But as a resource, acquired techniques need not be deployed uncritically. Iya Ṣango used her training and technique in Ṣango dance to comment on and transform Apidan performance. And if audience reaction was any indication, she was highly successful. The relationships between the maskers, the musicians, the spectators, and other participants were multiple, reciprocal, and continually shifting. Participants engaged each other freely, adding their own comments and responses. The dynamics emerged organically as each action turned on a previous action, or even interrupted it.

It is impossible to know the deeper implications of Iya Ṣango's performance. Did the fact that the Apidan was performed in honor of her late husband create other, more personal meanings? It seems clear that she took license in this situation because she was performing on her husband's behalf, playing for the play segment of his funeral. In any case, the form of Egungun Apidan is open, allowing multiple and simultaneous dialogues to be played out rhetorically on the spot.

Egungun performers refer to precedents from the past by making analogies to myth and then add to them new material (Europeans kissing, Gorilla sneaking up on the researcher trying to document the performance) and new insights (the problems of polygamy in an inflated economy, for example). The performance is in some measure planned in advance, as was the program of miracles representing foreigners, but finally all of it is renegotiated in improvisational practice. Each ritual segment is fluid; Iya Ṣango's performance was a perfect example.

In Yoruba ritual, materials received from the past can be repeated—either elaborated, condensed, extended and expanded—or deleted entirely, all at the performers' whims. This was equally true for Itẹfa as it was for Egungun. Scholars have acknowledged processes of situational adjustment and the factor of indeterminacy in society; however, they contrast this with ritual. Thus, Sally Moore (1975:219) has written that rituals represent "fixed social reality" and "stability and continuity acted out and re-enacted." She continued, "by dint of repetition they deny the passage of time, the nature of change, and the implicit extent of potential indeterminacy in social relations" (Moore 1975:221). What Moore failed to take into account is the indeterminacy of improvisation as praxis in ritual, that is, the transformational capacity of repetition itself.

Special attention to the discrete segments of the whole in Apidan produced an overall form that was multifocal, often characterized by shifts in themes and perspectives: from a dancing mat to a Hausa meat-seller to a youth practicing his stepping style. Each element of the whole communicated in its own ways and referred to a different kind of subject: monkeys, pregnant wombs, Muslim women in Purdah, specific lineages, aspiring dancers, foreigners, warfare, and so on.[17] And masks appearing together, or following each other sequentially in time, were often stylistically diverse—from naturalistic human caricatures to more abstracted dancing wombs and hybrid monkeys. The outer features of such rituals include segmentation, discontinuity, simultaneity, spontaneity, free rhythm, intertextuality, and density and play of meanings. Apidan performances varied greatly, based upon the degree of improvisation and elaboration by individual masked and unmasked performers, the number and kinds of maskers, the order in which they appeared, the social importance of a particular patron, the financial conditions of the owners of the various masks, and the extent and quality of audience participation.

It was not necessary for Yoruba spectators to know a myth, or myths, in order to experience and appreciate the performance, nor was it necessary for them to have witnessed the performance to comprehend a myth. The performances thus operated in a field between presumed pasts that are, from a Yoruba perspective, documented in myth and the performers' and spectators' involvements in the moment. The masks themselves, then, not only mediated the spirit world and the phenomenal world, the past and the present, but they mediated oral texts—themselves flexible through repeated performances—and the current social context, transforming a verbal, narrative form into a fragmented, multichanneled, multidimensional one of masks, songs, drumming, and dance. If a Yoruba storyteller manages "an unruly present by means of a precedent from the past," according to Peel (1984:118), then the ritual performer is more an up-to-the-minute interpreter of the present in the face of that presumed past.

Sometimes spectators spoke of the person inside the mask, commenting on his performance. At other times, they operated as if the mask was really a spirit. Even at this level, there was a great deal of play back and forth in people shifting their assumptions. Thus, in conversation with Egungun society member Taiwo:

He commented:	*Alabala* [the hybrid monkey form] is a girl, but when she's married to her husband—I'm telling you the representation of the matter—then it becomes a woman. When she becomes a woman, you know she must give birth to children. If a woman begins to produce children, she becomes *onidan* [miracle worker] then. From there, you get male and female. Out of them, you will see maybe a farmer, maybe a mechanic, maybe an engineer, maybe a doctor, and so on and so forth like that.
Me:	Maybe an animal?
Taiwo:	So a woman can bear an animal, can give birth to an animal? I am asking you a question!
Me:	No.
Taiwo:	A woman cannot?
Me:	No.
Taiwo:	Oh ho! But Egungun is not a human being and that is why he can give birth to anything. (Taiwo #75.11a)

People carried on entire conversations operating from one point of view or the other. They agreed to operate on similar assumptions just as Ọṣitọla and I mutually agreed that the question he had asked was really my question.

Everybody knows that the spirit images are human beings, but at the same time they protect the secret of the mask, which is really no secret at all. As Karin Barber (1981b:739) has pointed out, this way of operating does not mean that people do not really believe in the power of the ancestors. Rather, ritual specialists bring the idea of the spirit into a tangible existence. If men as maskers were performing an illusion, then women as spectators were engaged in performing the belief that their illusion was reality. If, on the other hand, action transforms consciousness and is indeed efficacious, then there was no such thing as suspension of disbelief. Rather, the spectator looked through multiple levels of reality and moved back and forth between them at will. There was no puncture in illusion; there was no puncture in reality. There was only a reorientation of working assumptions.

As play, ritual spectacles operate as another mode of being, which—like any other mode of being—people shift into and out of depending on the context and the circumstances. The play on transformation deliberately confounds the *as if* and the *is*. It attempts to jolt spectators into being conscious of being conscious. That is what Apidan asks of its spectators. It is precisely in this sense that spectacle dwells conceptually at the juncture of two planes of existence— the world and the otherworld, at the nexus of the physical and the spiritual, the phenomenal and the ethereal, the visible and the invisible. And just as it is informed by tradition, it is also experimental.

6.1 Young Egungun dance before a *bata* drummer. Ẹgbado area, village of Ijado, 10 December 1977.

6.2 A wall mural painted over the father's grave depicts the Egungun masks owned by the family. Ẹgbado area, city of Ilaro, 16 December 1977.

6.3   A hybrid monkey form of mask known as Alabala dances,
with the tail of the cloth flying loose at the back like the tail
of the Patas Guenon monkey. Ẹgbado area, village of Ijado,
10 December 1977.

6.4   A hybrid monkey mask wraps
the tail of his cloth around
his shoulders like a fur ruff.
Ẹgbado area, city of Ilaro, 12
November 1977.

6.5 A "miracle" representing Gorilla refers to a character that features significantly in Egungun origin myths. Egbado area, town of Imaṣai, 23 December 1977.

6.6 A "miracle" called Alagẹmọ is a form that was appropriated from the Agẹmọ masked performance of Ijẹbuland, but with a monkey painted on the surface in reference to Egungun. Egbado area, Imaṣai, 23 December 1977.

6.7 A "miracle worker" mask named We-Dance-for-the-White-Man kneels to greet the elderly women in the Egungun society. Ẹgbado area, Ilaro, 15 November 1975.

6.8 "Miracle worker" changes his cloth, leaving the large circular womb-like garment behind on the ground as other maskers look on. Ẹgbado area, Ilaro, 15 November 1975.

6.9 Another "miracle worker" named Ọya in the process of turning his cloth inside out. Ẹgbado area, Ilaro, 12 November 1977.

6.10 Back view of We-Dance-for-the-White-Man flipping his cloth to turn it inside out. Ẹgbado area, Ilaro, 15 November 1975.

6.11 "Miracle worker" named Ọya prepares to pull on a second cloth underneath the first. Ẹgbado area, Ilaro, 12 November 1977.

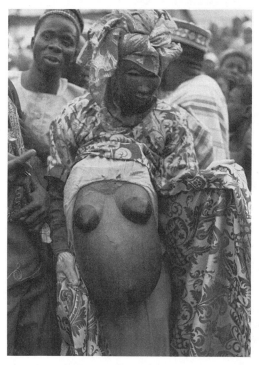

6.12 Pregnant Woman exposes her abdomen in retying her wrapper. Ẹgba/Ẹgbado area, Ibara Quarter, Abẹokuta, 7 January 1978.

6.13 Bride dances gently to conclude the performance of miracles. Ẹgbado area, village of Ijado, 9 November 1975.

6.14 Warrior mask runs rampant through the town followed by an army of young men. Ẹgba/Ẹgbado area, city of Abẹokuta, 23 April 1978.

6.15 Pop Eyes dances. Ẹgbado, village of Ijado, 9 November 1975.

6.16 Iya Ṣango approaches Hausa Meat Seller, who has a puffy distorted face and bloody teeth and fingers. Ẹgbado, village of Ijado, 9 November 1975.

7. The Collective in Conflict, or, the Play of Personalities

"Acting like Eṣu complements Agẹmọ."[1]

This popular expression highlights the trickster-like behavior participants shift into when experiencing Agẹmọ—another masked performance with a very different style and flavor from Egungun. Announced publicly in the news media, annual Agẹmọ festivals attracted thousands of people from all walks of life—the wealthy, the poor; locals and out-of-towners; young and old. Spectators were treated to plays of competing interests—trickster personalities like Iya Ṣango's times more than sixteen, all converging in the same performance. Rather than one long social drama in Turner's sense, Agẹmọ ritual performances consisted of a multiplicity of minidramas. The action surged back and forth between poles of joking and fighting, so that to get involved in Agẹmọ was indeed to become a trickster. The polarity is reflected in Agẹmọ titles. Thus Ija, the title of one priest living in Imọsan, means "Fight," while Ṣerefusi, the one living in Igbile, means "Playful-Beyond-Measure."[2]

Agẹmọ performances included formal segments of drumming and dancing as well as informal intrusions into ritual time and space at the whims of individual participants. Once again, improvisation was the mode of production. In keeping with the trickster deity's personality, participant/observers had to be quick and agile, fickle and flexible, ready to joke one moment and fight the next. Agẹmọ demanded it of those who wanted to "see," or truly experience, the ethos of the performance.[3] Everybody got caught up and pulled along in the performative flow of events.

IDEOLOGICAL CONFLICT

The Agemo priests are traditionally the intellectuals of Ijebuland and they are usually found contemplating the principles of life and death and the inscrutable force which controls them. They appear to be close to the source of cosmic power or energy but they cannot tap it at will. They tend to feel acutely the paradox of their position, namely, the gulf between their conviction that this is a world that should thrive on co-operation and the negation of this very

principle in their own organization. In their village isolation, the Agemo priests
spend much of their time meditating on this paradox.

Oyin Ogunba (1985:294)

In the festivals I attended, there was no existential communitas expressed
among Agemo participants except as factionalism. If ritual hinges on the exchange of symbols of commonality (Schwartz 1978:429), then it seems ironic
that conflict and controversy were endemic, that the style of the exchange
should be rough and tumble in character. But, as Schwartz points out, commonality makes communication about difference possible.

There was almost no tradition upon which all Agemo priests agreed.
There are, everybody said, sixteen titled Agemo priests; in reality there were
more. The stories presented to explain this discrepancy were as numerous as
those that explain the history of the Agemo institution itself. And although
the priests could describe in enormous detail how Agemo ritual should be
performed, it never happened just that way. The king of Ijebuland, the
Awujale, has not played his formal ritual role for nearly twenty years because
of his conversion to Islam, but Agemo, priests and others never failed to
include him in their descriptions of festival events. The office was in a sense
present symbolically even in the absence of the king. Or rather, he was present in spite of himself. What each priest tended to narrate was his personal
role in Agemo performance; all others by comparison became secondary so
that what I ended up with were as many different versions of the practice as
there were official participants.

At a fundamental level, Agemo practice fomented conflict. Thus Agemo
priests were known traditionally for their abilities to curse, which they hurled
against each other as well as against women. As the son of one Agemo priest
said of his father's relationship with another priest who lives in close proximity,
"they are close friends, but at festival time they become enemies."

The notion of ritual as journey persists. More specifically, Agemo involved
pilgrimage and the relationship between a center and its periphery. Agemo
priests encircle the capital at Ijebu-Ode, living in outlying communities that are
anywhere from six to fifteen miles away (Map 2) (Ogunba 1965:178). Most of
the myths that serve as precedents for Agemo performance attempt to explain
how they got there. In one story I was told, the historic king of all Yoruba
peoples, the Ooni of Ife, ordered his son, together with sixteen priests, to go out
and found the Ijebu kingdom.[4] These sixteen priests were renowned for their
knowledge of powerful medicines. When the founder settled down, he became
the king of Ijebuland, known as Awujale. He dispersed the priests to the periphery of his kingdom and ordered them to meet only once a year during the
Agemo festival, when the priests and the Awujale would come together to bless
each other. In light of this story, it is curious that Agemo was not mentioned in
the official migration histories of Ijebuland that were published on the occasion
of the present Awujale's Silver Jubilee (Anonymous 1985a; Anonymous
1985b).

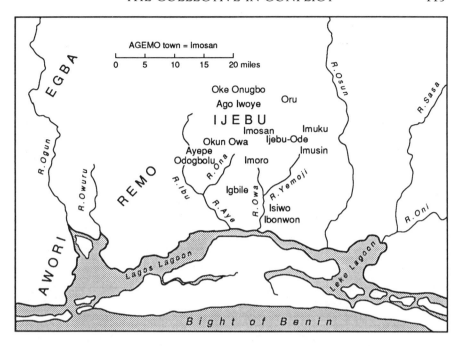

Another story claimed that, when the Awujalẹ first arrived in Ijẹbuland, he met these sixteen priests already settled at the center.[5] Since they owned their own crowns, that is, since they were kings in their own right, the Awujalẹ banished them to the outlying territories, where they must remain except on the occasion of the annual Agẹmo festival. Other stories suggested that, because of their knowledge of powerful medicine, the Agẹmo priests were summoned by the Awujalẹ, or his wife, from far away to perform fertility rites for the land and its people (Ọṣitọla, personal communication, 3 July 1982). Because of the increasing numbers of human sacrifices the priests demanded for their rites, townspeople protested. Thus the Awujalẹ was forced to banish them to the periphery of his territory, allowing them to return only once annually to bless him during the festival.[6]

Running throughout these conflicting accounts is the political tension between the center of Ijẹbu Yoruba administrative authority, represented by the Awujalẹ, and the periphery, the domain of the Agẹmo priests, who are also chiefs in their own communities. The stories explain both the dispersement of the priests and their pilgrimage back at festival time. This is Turner's pilgrimage process in reverse, although he acknowledges the waxing and waning of centers and peripheries as new waves of migrations redistribute people and their relationships to sacred centers (Turner 1974a: 227). The variations in the stories basically hinge on the order of events and on a concern with seniority—who arrived on the site first—presumably because the order of arrival establishes ultimate authority.

THE PILGRIMAGE

Nobody witnesses an Agẹmọ festival in its entirety, not even the Agẹmọ priests themselves. At festival time both in 1982 and 1986, the Agẹmọ priests prepared their gear in their individual communities, which surround Ijẹbu-Ode. Then they and their male entourages pilgrimaged on foot, carrying their heavy loads to a sacred bush grove just outside the town of Imọsan, three miles from Ijẹbu-Ode, the administrative center. The loads reportedly contain medicines and provisions for encamping in the sacred grove, as well as the regalia of the priests—their stools, costumes, and masks. Attendants reportedly carried their priests' loads on their heads down the original bush paths that in the past supposedly linked the center with the outlying towns. That is what everybody said. In fact, Henry Drewal and John Pemberton saw members of an Agẹmọ entourage riding in cars, although some groups were more conservative. Each priest had a different route, which combined stops along the way at various places to pray and bless communities and to rest and receive sustenance. The journeys began about midday and took the entire afternoon into the evening.

THE POSITION OF WOMEN

Whenever Agẹmọ priests are processing on the road with their loads, there is a curfew on all women, who must shut themselves inside and close all windows and doors, just as women do during funerals when the voice of the deceased is invoked (chapter 3). For obvious reasons, I have never marched in an Agẹmọ procession, although women participated inside their enclosures, chanting along with the men and praying as the loads passed. Those less concerned watched television. Once, I caught an unexpected glimpse of an entourage from a distance at the local festival of the Ajagaloru of Oru when the car I was in rounded the corner behind a group carrying their loads—this moments before I dived to the floor of the car. A rather pragmatic move it was on my part since I was in the company of the Onugbo of Oke Onugbo, one of the Alagẹmọs. The group's pace was pressing and forceful. When women disappear from the streets, over half of the visible population vanishes, and there is an eerie feeling of an abandoned town—an absence of a presence.

On the road, the Agẹmọ entourages reportedly threaten women with curses should any of them see the priests en route. They call out, for example:[7]

> Agẹmọ is coming!
> Women, do not look!
> A fleeting look,
> A fleeting death!
> Death in the world,
> Swift like a shadow!
> Who is this?
> What do you want?

A curse or a prayer,
Or to eat and not be filled?
Epilepsy or leprosy,
Or to become an invalid?
If you see me,
And I don't see you,
May your eyes become tobacco tins!

***

E kee e!
Obìnrin mà ìwò ó!
Wọ wò fèrè,
Wọ kú fèrè!
Ikú ayé,
Òjìjì fírífírí!
L'ẹwẹ́ wá a?
K'ẹ ma gbà?
Èpè àbí ìre,
Àbí ajé iyò?
Wóró wóró tàbí ètè,
K'àbíkó gb'órúpò má wọ run'rẹ?
Ko rí mi,
Kí mi rí ẹ,
K'ójú 'rẹ májì b'ágolo tábà!

One of the reasons that women must be kept at a distance is that menses is thought to pollute the priests' powerful medicine, rendering it impotent.

There is a popular story of a confrontation between the priests and women that re-presents one important aspect of Agẹmọ conflict. As Oyin Ogunba (1985:301) has reported,

> a story is told of an Agemo priest who was passing through Ijebu-Ode one year in the early 1930s, during an Agemo festival. The Apostolic Church was then in the heat of Christian evangelism and converts were encouraged to openly disrespect the practitioners of traditional religion. On this fateful day, the church was holding a revival service and women members were deliberately called out to look at what used to be regarded as secret. The Agemo priest became angry and uttered an *epe* [curse] and proclaimed that the church would collapse before his return from Imosan, the following week. According to the oral tradition, the church did collapse. Whatever the merit of this story (and it has not been corroborated outside the Agemo fold) it is an indication of what the ordinary man thinks or used to think about the mysterious nature of the power of the Agemo priests.

And it was not only Agẹmọ devotees who told this story. I have heard it from highly educated citizens of Ijẹbu who profess Christianity.

In fact there was an incident between Agẹmọ pilgrims and an Apostolic Church on June 21, 1939.[8] In a letter sent to the then colonial resident through the Awujalẹ, the Pastor-in-Charge of the church complained that an Agẹmọ priest had entered the church during a woman's Bible class and had thrown poisonous medicines on the floor. He complained further that although the medicines had been collected by the police, who took notes on the incident, the Awujalẹ had been too busy to hear their report. By the 30th of June, when they had still not yet received any judgment from the Awujalẹ, the Pastor wrote to the Resident asking him to take note of the following "facts."

1. "It is a Rule in the Constitution of our Church that a member (male or female) must not look at any kind of Heathenish or Idolatrous Processions.

2. "In the present case, Sir, none of our women Church Members have ventured out of the Church to look at the Agemo Procession.

3. "The statement published in the 'PILOT' of the 27th instant that 'our women rushed out from the Church to see the Agemo Procession' is quite incorrect.

4. "We would like the Oba Awujale [King] and Your Worship to maintain in the Province, the liberty which every Christian enjoys in other lands [. . .]

5. "We really can never postpone our religious duties for the mere reason that the Agemo Festival is being celebrated, and we are prepared to die for our Faith rather than to submit to such a great act of impiety.

6. "The Agemo Priests have no right to fight any one, male or female, and if they feel that some women looked at them their only redress—according to native law and custom—was to utter curses, so that such women may die and thereby serve as a warning to others.

7. "My Church, Sir, have no objection to the Agemo Priests uttering curses as much as they like against the women-folk, but they resent very much their entering the Church deliberately in order to curse women worshippers, contrary to native law and custom."

Finally, in the name of "RELIGIOUS TOLERANCE," the Pastor begged the Resident and the Awujalẹ to consider seriously that a) the Agẹmọ priests should be warned never to enter their church or to molest them in any way and b) they should restrict themselves to cursing women, according to established custom.

This incident not only underscores the importance of the curse in constructing Agẹmọ ethos, but it illustrates the kinds of conflicts that emerge in Agẹmọ performance and the force of their subsequent representation. The curses themselves are part of the performance of power. Interestingly, however, apart from the priests' curses against each other, it is women who pose the greatest threat to Agẹmọ power. Peter Morton-Williams (1960b:38) has suggested that, when men as a group project onto women a threatening power, they construct a sense of solidarity among themselves. If this is the operative ideology, then it is effective only at the level of the individual entourage—of which there are up to sixteen.[9]

Women from Agẹmọ families viewed themselves quite differently than did women outside Agẹmọ. For them, closing themselves in demonstrates solidarity with their father or husband, as the case may be, since they have the ultimate power to undo his works. These women seemed to enjoy the excitement of the event and sat inside either joking among themselves or chanting along with the men parading by outside. Sitting inside with the senior wife of an Agẹmọ priest while her husband's procession was in progress, I asked her why they do not want women to see Agẹmọ on the road. She exclaimed in Yoruba, "because they will go blind!" At that point, the junior wife, who was about my age, quite literally fell out of her chair laughing. That was all part of the play. Women usually do not like to discuss the impact of their menses. Because of the power of the medicines the Agẹmọ priests were thought to have carried to their encampment, women also prayed rigorously for what they wanted just as the group outside passed nearby. What the curfew on women effectively does is to remove them temporarily from the discourse of power that is in play on the outside.

THE POSITION OF THE PRIEST OF THE GROVE

In 1986, while the majority of the Agẹmọ priests were on the road, Posa, the priest who is considered the owner of the sacred grove, stayed home in the town of Imọsan and awaited their arrivals. Posa is also the headman (Baalẹ) of the community. Since he had also prepared his loads to carry to the grove just down the road, he too was considered to have intensified power, so that, on the day the others were traveling on foot, members of Posa's community sought his help with their family problems. I stayed with Posa and participated in the rituals at his house during the day. He settled disputes and made personal sacrifices to his Agẹmọ shrine and ancestors, and we all feasted on meat stews made from the sacrificial animals. On that day, too, all the heads of Posa's children were shaved and all of the branches of a sacred tree in front of his house were cut. That same day, Egungun masks from nearby towns performed in Imọsan, each making a stop in front of Posa's house to receive money. The Agẹmọ priests called them "beggars" because they piggy-backed the Agẹmọ festival to tap into the cash flow it generates.

Agẹmọ devotees in Imọsan made sacrifices to their personal deities in the privacy of their homes. Ọmọsẹsẹ, Posa's junior brother as well as a diviner in Ọsitọla's group, sacrificed to the spirit of twins (*ibeji*) as the father of deceased twin children. In 1986, a pair of Egungun maskers representing twins passed Ọmọsẹsẹ's house purely by happenstance, he said. As he sacrificed to his shrine inside the house, the Egungun, parodying women with padded bosoms and hips, elaborate plaited coiffures, gold jewelry, and pocketbooks, danced outside in front, accompanied by their roving musicians (fig. 7.1). I, too, arrived on the scene, by chance spotting the Egungun heading for my friend's front yard, all of us converging on the spot simultaneously. These kinds of fragmented encounters and juxtapositions are typical in Imọsan on this day. They establish a festive atmosphere throughout the entire town.

POSITIONALITY AND PERSPECTIVE
IN FESTIVAL PERFORMANCE

Simultaneity and multifocality characterized the festival. As Posa sacrificed, feasted, and partied at home and Egungun masks of any and every variety circulated around town singing and dancing, the Awujalẹ was supposed to be performing three dances at the Apebi, a site in Ijẹbu-Ode some three kilometers away where he was installed as king (Ogunba 1985:295–296). Instead, however, his palace servants danced in his place; the Awujalẹ has not performed openly at the festival since the late 1960s. Meanwhile, the other Agẹmọ priests made their ways to Imọsan on various roads all passing through Ijẹbu-Ode.

Upon their arrival at the bush grove, the Agẹmọ priests encamped. Before they could do so, however, they awaited the arrival of Posa, the owner of the land, who must enter first. Members of Posa's entourage reported to me that during the 1986 festival he made the pilgrims wait outside the sacred grove on the road in the dark by deliberately delaying his arrival. He also prayed for rain on that day to make their journeys unbearable. The bush grove setting, I am told, has very much the feeling of a war camp.[10] Each Agẹmọ priest had his own separate place within the grove where he sat to receive visitors and stored his regalia. According to the late Nopa, this is the period when the priests begin to curse each other to test their powers (Kukọyi, Agẹmọ priest, #82.95).

That evening the host, Posa, masked and welcomed the pilgrims. This performance was exclusive; done privately within the grove in the middle of the night, a performance in the back region (Goffman 1959:145). There, one masked priest danced for all the others. Posa's dance, some said, pays homage to Oloko, the ancient patron of the cult, literally the "Owner-of-the-sacred-stone" (*oko*).[11] Except for Posa's private showing, the priests otherwise never saw each other perform during the festival.

Afterward, the Agẹmọ priests reportedly washed the deity (*wẹwẹ orisa*) in a herbal preparation of two hundred and one leaves, each with its own invocation that sets its special power into action.[12] Only two of the priests, Adie and Ẹwujagbori, may enter the inner shrine to wash the representation of the deity housed in the back region of the back region. To enter, the priests have to dress as women, with their hair plaited in female style. Adie, who keeps his hair plaited and wrapped the year round, declared that he has a "reserved head" (Bakare, Agẹmọ priest, #86.14) (fig. 7.2). The idea is that his head, having been specially prepared, is *not* for carrying loads—either as a pilgrim or as a masker—roles that the other priests perform. Another popular account, however, had him losing his loads in a flood during an annual pilgrimage once upon a time.[13]

The public performance took place around noon. The priests were sequestered in their camps inside the grove, each awaiting his time to perform. They performed in order of seniority, according to their length of time in office.[14] On that day, the main road on the outskirts of the grove at Imọsan filled with concessions. Traders, mostly women, set up canopies, tables, and chairs and sold beer and soft drinks. The road was transformed into one long row of bars. Boys and young men strolled up and down hawking calendars, T-shirts, and hats, all made up just for the occasion to commemorate that year's festival. Groups of people processed down the road, some with banners. Bands of musicians strolled back and forth among the bar patrons, playing and singing praises of individuals seated drinking beer. People passing by broke into dance. With the flow of alcohol, people began to shift swiftly into their trickster moods to experience the festival.

As I photographed the activity up and down the main road, men warned me not to enter the grove. Meanwhile, a group of men took over the road and paraded with loudly playing musicians at their backs. In the lead were two transvestites wearing wigs, make-up, and padding that built up breasts, hips, and buttocks (fig. 7.3, front right). In a kind of ironic comment on the exclusivity maintained during the festival, they charged with great flair right through the gate into the sacred grove and down the path where women were not permitted to go. Nobody seemed particularly concerned. Later, during the performance, the same group charged into the grove once more, transvestites in the lead, and the women cheered them on.

The Edelumoro of Imoro in his role as "The-One-in-Front" (Ojuwa) performed first. Ojuwa's role is to "clear the way," or "sweep," for the other masked performers.[15] He was the only masker to come out onto the road, where his attendants made a sacrifice for the Awujale in the presence of some of his representatives. This event also signaled the women on the main road that they were now permitted to enter the public performance space just outside the opening into the grove.

The Ojuwa is also the priest charged with distributing the meat of the sacrificial cow to the other Agemo priests, a role reportedly laden with conflict since there are always disputes over who should get what portion and how much—this is the case even though they have supposedly agreed on the rules for distribution. It became an issue only after 1892 when the British prohibited human sacrifices and the Agemo priests subsequently substituted a cow (Ogunba 1985:300).

Once the Ojuwa has returned to the grove, the most senior Agemo priest, the one who has been in office the longest, should be masked and ready to appear publicly. In 1986, it was Ija, "Fighter." There was a sense of pressing urgency about exits and entrances. No time is supposed to lapse between performers. As one mask returned to the grove the next in line to perform passed him going out so that the two meet about twenty feet inside the Agemo encampment (H. Drewal, personal communication, 4 July 1982). They move close and confront each other without touching and, as attendants hold medicine horns and rattles up next to their masks for protection, they hurl curses—something like, "you will not return next year," that is, "you will die in the coming year." Hardly before one mask could return to the grove, outriders for the next rushed out into the performance space.

Mostly made up of young boys from the priest's hometown, relatives, and other friends, these rowdy groups preceded their masked priest, wielding freshly cut tree branches as whips and inducing a sense of excitement, in this way warming up the spectators (fig. 7.4). Those who do not clear the way in the midst of an onrush are apt to be trampled. Boys lashed each other with the whips, bystanders unavoidably got involved, and fights erupted in pockets throughout the crowd. Women from the priests' households emerged from the crowd to sing their "father's" praises and to dance. Other women were restricted to a certain area well beyond the entrance to the encampment. Some got so involved that they wandered innocently, or perhaps not, too close. Men charged and cursed them.

The more chaos and noise, the more the ethos of Agẹmọ is felt. In the 1982 public performance, the rain poured down, turning the whole area into a field of mud. Few people were daunted. The Agẹmọ priests reportedly prayed for rain so as to test each other's stamina. In a large crowd of several thousand people with only a vaguely defined performing space, it was difficult to foretell from which side a fight would erupt, or a bunch of ruffians would charge, or young men would break out lashing each other with long slender whips that sting and break the skin (fig. 7.5).

Most spectators see only the headpiece of the mask floating by at a distance, so far away that it is impossible to make out its form or content. What they experience physically are the ripples of pulling and tugging that flow through the crowd as each performing entourage charges through the space pushing the people on the fringes back into the mass of spectators. To be part of the scene and sustain it required agility. One had to be able to get out of the way at a moment's notice and not fall down; to resist curses, even to send them back; to play; to sing the praises of the priest you support one moment and be prepared to fight the next; to insert yourself into the action, by force if necessary; to stand your ground, or, confronted by a surging mass of people to go with the flow or beat it.

The following day, the priests left Imọsan *en masse,* but not together, and proceeded to Ijẹbu-Ode, the administrative headquarters where the Awujalẹ resides. All but Posa went, for he is not permitted to spend the night in the capital. On either the fourth or ninth day after the dance at Imọsan—the length of time is determined through divination—the "leader" of the Agẹmọ priests, the Tami, used to meet the Awujalẹ at a neutral space known as Ọjọfa. The Awujalẹ was also masked in the sense that he always wore his veiled beaded crown in public. The two met under a cloth canopy, parting their veils to expose themselves face to face, and they prayed for each other and the kingdom. Tami first of all prayed for the Awujalẹ by placing his brass staff in the king's open palms, wishing him and the whole of Ijẹbuland long life and prosperity. Afterward the Awujalẹ reciprocated by praying for the Agẹmọ priests and the Ijẹbu people in like manner. Apart from this annual occasion, the Awujalẹ and the Agẹmọ priests are not supposed to meet.[16] Ever since the Awujalẹ stopped appearing at Agẹmọ festivals, Tami has performed his duties with the Awujalẹ's palace servants, whose job it was traditionally to train kings in ritual performance. Their offices are hereditary.

Upon leaving Ọjọfa, Tami and his entourage are supposed to parade to another sacred site in Ijẹbu-Ode known as Isasa, where the priests are to perform another public display just as they did at Imọsan. The priests dance that very afternoon, following the same order of seniority, except for Tami, who completed his own work at Ọjọfa. By some reports, Tami used to own the land at Isasa and his family donated it to the Agẹmọ priests as a sacred encampment and shrine site when they were dispersed from Ijẹbu-Ode. It is for this reason, some said, that Tami was made the head of Agẹmọ. As with other traditions, this one was also disputed by many of the priests.

As soon as the entire performance has been repeated at Isasa and the most junior Agẹmọ priest—the one who took office last—has performed, the rest should have already packed up their loads and be ready to move out. In order not to delay the priests in their treks back home, women began to disappear from the crowd by the time the last two or three masked priests were ready to perform.

At the two Agẹmọ festivals I attended, there was a sense of urgency as the end drew near. Dierdre LaPin (personal communication, 1986) told me of an Agẹmọ festival she attended in the 1970s when a policeman ran up and threw a blanket over her head, telling her to hide, or she would "kick the bucket." It was her first Agẹmọ experience, and nobody had bothered to warn her of the consequences of being caught out on the street when the Agẹmọ priests moved out of the sacred grove. In 1982, I was pushed down in the floor in the back seat of a Volkswagen beetle surrounded by four males trying to protect me in case the Agẹmọ paraded from the grove in our direction. The point was, if anybody in one of the priest's entourages were to spot me, they would be obliged to curse me. And that would mean I too risked "kicking the bucket."

The tension between women and the masks surfaces most explicitly in the public performances outside the encampment. It is the women who are enclosed while the men are on the road, but it is the men who are then enclosed in the grove the remainder of the time, while women are free to move about. In the former, men are in public space; in the latter, they are in private space. The threat to Agẹmọ potency occurs in public space. From this angle, it is difficult to judge just who is being isolated from whom.

For several months following the pilgrimage to Imọsan and Ijẹbu-Ode, the Agẹmọ priests hold their own local Agẹmọ festivals in their own towns, where they alone perform. I was fortunate to attend three of these in 1986, in the towns of Igbilẹ, Oru, and Ago-Iwoye. At such times, the priests who happen to be on good terms visit each other's festivals. Agẹmọ is also performed at the funerals of deceased members of the society as a means of transferring the deceased's spirit to its otherworldly domain (see chapter 3).[17]

ELEPHANT AND CHAMELEON

Within the performance process outlined above, individuals took the opportunity to intrude, to intervene, to turn situations to their own advantage. Their
maneuvers were expressions of personal power, the power of Agẹmọ, indeed the
power of the chameleon after which it is named. Chameleons are a common
motif in priests' carved headpieces, also called crowns (fig. 7.6). Like Agẹmọ
priests, chameleons transform, match power for power, open their mouths almost twice the size of their heads and vocalize loudly with a hissing sound, and
nullify opponents by rendering them harmless. The chameleon's power can apparently match any power on earth except that of menstrual blood.

The impressive hissing sound that chameleons emit is analogous to the act
of cursing that is so prominent in Agẹmọ. According to Agẹmọ priest Idẹbi, a
chameleon's mouth must be kept closed, because if the chameleon should spit
in someone's eyes that person would be blinded (Osilaja #s 86.22 and 86.23).
The relationship between cursing and blindness was also alluded to by Ṣerefusi's
senior wife, who told me women go blind if they see an Agẹmọ entourage on the
road. When Agẹmọ priests want to curse (ṣ'epe), they reportedly first of all spit
on their medicinally treated staffs and utter the fatal words to bring death to the
victim (Sanni, Agẹmọ priest, #86.20).

Agẹmọ is also the name given to a lunar month that occurs in late June/early
July, when the Agẹmọ festival is scheduled. During this month, chameleons are
visibly plentiful, and it is said that their tails—ordinarily curled under in a
spiral—now straighten out. It is taboo to kill chameleons at this time. And in
any case, priests said, medicines prepared with them would be impotent. In
contrast, it is during the Agẹmọ month that the priests are their most powerful.
It is the time when they sacrifice to their shrines and ancestors as well as the
time when people consult them to solve problems. Just as the chameleon takes
on the colors of his environment, the Agẹmọ priests take on the power of the
chameleon, leaving it impotent for that lunar month.

Agẹmọ's ability to transform is encoded in popular stories about the masked
society that recount how a character named Chameleon defeated his enemies by
taking on and thereby matching their powers. The chameleon's protective color-
ation, enabling it to change colors to match its environment, is represented in
the variegated colors of the dried and dyed grasses that make up the mask's
costume.

If the chameleon is a metaphor for Agẹmọ priests' powers of transformation,
the elephant alludes to the grandeur of their presence. Agẹmọ priests compared
the legs of the masked figures with those of elephants; the fiber hung from
underneath the skirt down to the bottom of the feet, indeed visually evoking the
thick round foot of the elephant (fig. 7.7). Agẹmọ priests also claimed the ideal
stepping style in performance is relatively slow, calculated, and heavy—movement qualities associated with the elephant's walk—dignified, ponderous,
weighty. The elephant's substance is also manifest in the thick, heavy ivory

bracelets that serve as one of the Agẹmọ priests' trademarks. Whatever else elephant and chameleon evoke as metaphors, they allude to the quality of power that is expressed through Agẹmọ spectacle.

THE PLAY OF PERSONALITIES

The conflict endemic in Agẹmọ performance is expressed formally in curs-ing. Yet it also emerges in public displays with the pushing and shoving, when tempers flare and fights break out. Whenever the Agẹmọ priests gather, they make more or less subtle attempts to undo each other. The example was given earlier of how Posa kept the other priests waiting outside the grove by deliber-ately delaying his arrival and how he prayed for rain to discomfort them on their pilgrimage. Ever since 1892, when the British moved in and forbade human sacrifice, the distribution of the cow that took its place has reportedly been an ongoing source of conflict. It is considered ill-mannered to ask an Agẹmọ priest which part of the cow he receives. According to one variation of the oral tradi-tion, the amount of human sacrifice itself was a point of contention from very early on, with the result that the Awujalẹ was forced to scatter the Agẹmọ priests at the periphery of his territory to avoid repercussions.

There is another popular story about one priest, the Orimolusi of Ijẹbu-Igbo, who was expelled permanently from the society for losing his loads in a flood during his pilgrimage. A similar story is told of Adie, one of the transvestite priests, who because he too lost his loads in a flood is not allowed to perform with a mask, but he denies it.

The church incident reported earlier is a case in which the popular version constructed a more monumental tragedy than actually happened, attributing enormous power to the Agẹmọ priests. Like the elephant, the stories about Agẹmọ achieve a certain monumentality. Thus an Agẹmọ priest cursed the church and it collapsed. The spectacle and the stories about the spectacle are all part of the same discourse on power. What did happen was a fight, some arrests, a police investigation, and a formal protest to the colonial government. The outcome of the complaint is unknown; however, an incident that occurred in 1986 is suggestive.

In mid-August after the July pilgrimage, during the Ajagaloru's Agẹmọ festi-val in Oru, about fifteen miles north of Ijẹbu-Ode, a dispute within a particular faction led some of the participants to withdraw so that there were no dancing mat masks (Ẹleni) to perform that year. Then, while the Agẹmọ procession was on the road carrying their loads to the shrine, the driver of a new car with a woman seated in the back tried to pass and outrun the entourage. The Agẹmọ group chased the car and some young men broke out its back windshield. In Nigeria's current economic situation, spare parts are in short supply and very costly so that this added another dimension to an already serious act. The woman went immediately to complain to the king of that community. He re-ported to me later that the woman and her driver had no recourse because by traditional law and custom she should not have been out on the street. By being there, she subjected herself to harassment, thereby causing her own problem. The king said further that she could take the case to court, but he did not think she would do so, since she had little chance of winning.

In 1970, according to Ogunba (1985:302–303), a dispute with the Awujalẹ caused the Agẹmọ priests to cancel the festival entirely. Reportedly, the Awujalẹ wanted them to shift the dates of the festival to the weekend for his own convenience. They refused, saying that it was taboo to perform on certain market days and then accused him of attempting to turn the festival into a political event for his own benefit.

In the 1982 festival, during a period of civilian rule, local politicians took the opportunity of using the appearance of Tami at Ọjọfa as a political demonstration. The Awujalẹ at that time was under suspension, reportedly visiting his dentist in London. The elected governor of Ogun State positioned himself more or less in the Awujalẹ's place in order to receive the Agẹmọ blessings. As he paraded into the square with his own entourage, the crowd of spectators raised their hands signaling a V for victory in support of the late Ọbafẹmi Awolọwọ, a native son well-known in Nigerian politics. The demonstration for Awolọwọ was at the same time an indirect protest against the Awujalẹ, who had sided with the opposition represented by the Muslim north.

By festival time in 1986, there had been two coups in Nigeria, and the Awujalẹ had been exonerated and reinstalled. This time a dispute erupted between Tami, the so-called "leader" of Agẹmọ, and Posa, the "owner" of the sacred grove, the first pilgrimage site. No one disputed that it was Tami's job to meet the Awujalẹ at Ọjọfa. What they contested heatedly was that he was their leader, indeed that he was anything more than their representative to the king. Because of Tami's political maneuvers, or so some people thought, Posa announced that, if Tami showed his face in Imọsan, Posa would have his head. He would then report to the Awujalẹ, he asserted, that Agẹmọ killed Tami. This is in keeping with the tenets of traditional authorities such as Oṣugbo, Oro, and Agẹmọ, who had punitive power in the past. Posa's assertion implied that he was merely exercising his traditional authority. People would say that ancestral spirits, not human beings, killed evildoers.

The dispute between Tami and Posa began long before my arrival in Nigeria on this trip. Posa had developed a swollen leg that made it difficult for him to walk, a problem attributed to Tami's bad medicines working against him. As a well-known Agẹmọ curse goes, "swellings will rise on your body like ripe corn kernels," *wọn t'ẹgbẹ y'ọmọ bi agbado*. Posa complained that Tami, wanting to control Agẹmọ, abused his authority by claiming leadership.

Meanwhile Tami reportedly wanted to by-pass the rites at Imọsan because his life would be in danger, and he went to the Awujalẹ for support. The Awujalẹ was apparently persuaded that the priests should go directly to Ijẹbu-Ode without making their pilgrimage to Imọsan. The majority of the Agẹmọ priests refused on the grounds that it was against tradition and that Imọsan was the sacred site for the performance. While Posa continued to assert that Tami would not dare set foot in Imosan, most of the other priests steadfastly proclaimed, "well, we won't know until the time."

Neither Tami nor his Agemo colleague Magodo, who lives only a few miles away from him, showed up at Imosan. Since it is Magodo's responsibility to perform the dancing mat mask, it did not appear in the festival that year. Then, when a tree fell in the Imosan grove shortly after the Agemo priests had departed, people attributed the occurrence variously to Posa and Tami. Posa and his group believed that Tami had caused the tree to fall, but that Posa's power had prevented it from falling until after everyone had left. Others perceived that it was Posa who made the tree fall just to demonstrate his enormous power to the other priests.

Some priests held out hope that Tami would eventually show up in Ijebu-Ode in time to perform his privileged role at Ojofa. The ones I spoke to seemed willing to allow him to perform at Ijebu-Ode even if he had not shown up at Imosan. In the end he did not show up, so the priests held a meeting to determine how to proceed.[18] They decided that Posa, as the owner of the sacred land at Imosan—Agemo's spiritual center—should be the one to go to Ojofa and bless the Ijebu kingdom. The very choice to support Posa as a legitimate alternative in effect aligned the majority against Tami. Posa's mask appeared at Ojofa on that occasion reinforced with extra medicine carried very visibly in front by Omosese, his junior brother who is also a member of Ositola's divination group.

Ija apparently rejected the initial proposal of Posa as the one to dance at Ojofa, on the basis that he himself was the most senior among them, the one charged with dancing first after the Ojuwa cleared the way. He did not succeed in getting the necessary support and was clearly still annoyed by the matter when I visited him a couple of weeks later. At that time, he gave his own version of oral tradition that acclaimed his own forefather as the first Agemo priest in Ijebuland and the first settler on the land.[19]

I never got Tami's version of the story, for that would have broken the trust I had developed with the other Agemo priests. Sometime later Idebi asked me pointedly if I had gone to Tami. I replied, no, that I did not think it appropriate since Tami had refused to take part in the festival. Idebi leaned forward toward me, looked me straight in the eyes, and with great intensity exclaimed, "you are very wise!"

Agemo performances differ from the rituals of conflict between formally defined social and political groups as described by Edward Norbeck (1976:212–213). They are not mere enactments, staged battles, or controlled expressions of hostility. Rather, in Agemo performance, priests and others engage in power plays that engender real conflict and hostility among individual authorities who are opposed to each other on various grounds. Furthermore, the conflict is not confined to a ritual frame. It spills over into the priests' everyday lives.

Agemo performance reflects the pull and tug of individual personalities, expressing conflict within the collective. As a political as well as religious grouping, Agemo is exclusive and tends to stress power divisions and classificatory distinctions within and between discrete groups (Turner 1974a:185), emphasizing factionalism and the conflict of sectional interests. Agẹmọ pilgrimage and the seclusion of the priests in the sacred bush constructs normative communitas only on one level. And there is a certain sense of solidarity among Agẹmọ priests in relation to outsiders that is expressed in guarded secrecy surrounding what takes place inside the sacred grove, particularly on the first night when Posa dances, and in their isolation from women. All of this is undermined at another level, however, by the conflict of strong personalities that is at the very heart of the Agẹmọ ethos.

Conflict among pilgrims has been documented elsewhere. During pilgrimage in the Cuzco area of southern Peru in the central Andes, M. J. Sallnow (1981) has shown, hierarchy is temporarily annulled and, in contradistinction to communitas, new social processes of competition and factionalism emerge. He concluded that such processes are the consequence of the universalism that the shrines themselves proclaim. But this is not the case in Agẹmọ, since each priest has his own shrine and sacred grove in his own community, which sanctions difference.

In trying to make sense out of the conflict, Ogunba (1965:181) argued that the first Awujalẹ, as an invading authority, encouraged the confusion of leadership and divisiveness within the Agẹmọ institution as a sort of divide and conquer strategy. At the same time, he noted that the role of the Awujalẹ in the proceedings is not much more than that of a "blissful," distant patron (Ogunba 1985:297–298). Until recently, he provided all the sacrifices that the pilgrims made at the sacred shrines, and he served them a feast before they returned to their respective towns.[20] Even with his responsibility to entertain the pilgrims, the events remain largely beyond his control.

Attributions of center and periphery, which form the basis of Turner's model of pilgrimage, depend on the individual's orientation. Pilgrimage indeed means a shift in orientation, or rather in a reorientation of one's center. According to Ogunba (1965:181), "an Ijebu man belongs first and foremost to his own town or village and only secondarily to the Ijebu state." Thus, the sacred center for all but two Agẹmọ priests is indeed at the periphery of their homeland. The two who dwell at Imọsan, in the sense that they already live at the central sacred site, are not technically pilgrims. Posa is considered the owner of the sacred site; Ẹwujagbori is the priest whose job it is to make the sacrifices at the shrine located on the site. A third priest, Ija, lives in close proximity to this site, but has no authority there. According to him, he and his people immigrated to Posa's town for protection during wartime (Odunsi, Agẹmọ priest, #86.21). Since he is close by, his pilgrimage does not constitute as much of a hardship as it does for the others. And indeed there is little hardship today for those who choose to ride in cars.

At the same time that Imọsan is the collective sacred center for the priests, it is only three miles away from the administrative center. Or, in other words, the sacred center is closer to the administrative center of Ijẹbuland than it is to the hometowns of the majority of Agẹmọ priests. In essence, most Agẹmọ priests can claim three distinct centers. They each have a personal spiritual and administrative center at home, since each controls his own Agẹmọ site (agbala), complete with a shrine and chieftaincy title. Each also holds his own annual festival and performs in his mask, referred to as his crown.

Second, except for Posa and Ẹwujagbori, the priests have a spiritual center abroad—Imọsan—to which they make a pilgrimage once each year. Thus Posa and Ẹwujagbori's spiritual center is everyone else's "center out there"—to use Turner's phrase.

Third, all Agẹmọ priests have an administrative center abroad, which is in close proximity to the second pilgrimage site at Isasa in Ijẹbu-Ode. In the past, the administrative center headed by the Awujalẹ bound all of the outlying areas into a loose confederacy. The historical reason for such a confederacy appears to have been the control of trade throughout the territory. The title "Owner-of-the-Market," Olọja, held by all the priests, suggests the link with trade. Before embarking on their pilgrimages to Imọsan, each priest makes a sacrifice in his own market.[21] And indeed, the Ijẹbu as a people have been thought traditionally to be traders.

There is some suggestion of site sacralization in the markets as well. The ancestral mother of the priest Nopa is buried in his market at Odonopa (Kukọyi, Agẹmọ priest, #s 82.95 and 82.97). Today a tombstone marks the site. The more conventional burial sites for deceased parents, however, are under the floor of the house (chapter 3). Not only do women ordinarily control markets, but Agẹmọ titles tend to be passed through the female line to a son.[22]

As early as circa 1508, the Portuguese explorer Duarte Pacheco Pereira wrote of "a great city, called Geebu. [. . .] The trade which can be done here is in slaves, who are sold for brass bracelets (manillas) at 12 or 13 bracelets each, and some elephants' teeth" (Pacheco Pereira, quoted by Law 1986:246). From their position on the coast, the Ijẹbu during the eighteenth and nineteenth centuries were middlemen between the Ọyọ Empire inland and foreign trade from the sea, collecting high tariffs from those passing through their territory (Smith 1969:80–81). And as Ogunba (1985:298) has observed, the resident towns of the Agẹmọ priests are in close proximity to the ancient earthworks' ramparts that encircle the Ijẹbu kingdom, which Pacheco Pereira referred to early in the sixteenth century (see Smith 1969:79; Law 1986:246).

For centuries, then, the center of Ijẹbuland was urban; Ijẹbu-Ode was the economic and social focal point of the area. But perhaps more importantly, this center borders the site where the Agẹmọ priests repeat the performance they did in Imọsan, after praying for the Awujalẹ. Tami formerly met the Awujalẹ in neutral space, while the other Agẹmọ awaited his return at their own site, where they then performed for the second time during their pilgrimage. Indeed, there is a performance at each sacred site, including those owned by each priest individually. What distinguishes each of the performances in the three kinds of centers is the concept of the pilgrimage, the struggle, and the hardships along the way, not the least of which includes the cursing and the conflict.

Even today, Agẹmọ pilgrimage attempts to consolidate Ijẹbuland ideologi-

cally by bringing its administrative and spiritual centers together in close proximity. At the same time, it also preserves vestiges of a former sociopolitical
system, and it has done so through generations of change. It predates British
colonialism, which had a profound impact on the indigenous sociopolitical system (Laitin 1986). And it may very well hark back to the trade of the early
sixteenth century, when slaves were exchanged for brass *manillas* and ivory.
Perhaps significantly, the key regalia of unmasked Agemo priests—their staffs
and bracelets—are made of these very materials. It is not difficult to imagine a
time when it became necessary for peripheral markets to organize at the center
in order to control trade at the fringes. Such an organization would benefit
everybody equally by controlling prices and minimizing cutthroat competition
that could become chaotic.

   Whatever it may have been in the past, Agemo nevertheless stimulates conflict in the collective and the play of individual personalities. Neither the pilgrimage nor the ritual surrounding it is about existential communitas as Turner
envisioned it, nor is it about a clear-cut center and periphery (1977a:132).
Centers and peripheries are very much matters of individual orientation. In fact,
it may be more appropriate to say that Agemo priests have no peripheries;
rather, each has at least two sacred centers, and the majority have three. Just as
Egungun performers and devotees do in talking about Apidan masked performances, Agemo priests continually shift their orientations and assumptions.

   By many accounts, Agemo priests are "strangers." Their traditional titles,
such as Tami, Idebi, and Posa, some say are not Yoruba in origin. This is particularly curious given the length of time they are thought to have dwelled in the
land. In their own communities Agemo priests are accorded the initiations and
burials of kings and bear the title Olurin in Osugbo conclaves (chapter 3).
Much more recent emigrants—refugees from the nineteenth-century wars—are
not regarded as strangers. So why are the Agemo priests regarded in this way?

   As pilgrims with ever-shifting orientations, Agemo priests in a sense are
perpetual strangers. They assume multiple identities and allegiances like the
chameleon from which they get their name, and then they bring those identities
and allegiances into discourse each year at festival time. They do so not only
through the power of spectacle, but through the spectacle of power played out
dialectically and rhetorically on the ground, not merely enacted.

7.1 A pair of Egungun masks representing prosperous female twins dance prior to the beginning of the Agẹmọ festival in order to reap their own benefits. Ijẹbu area, Imosan, 5 July 1986.

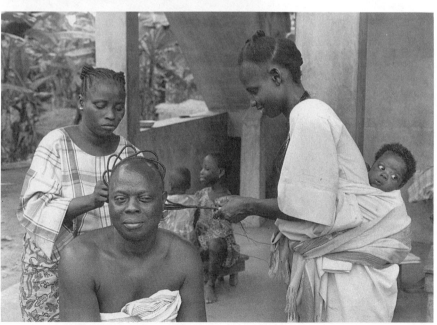

7.2 Portrait of Adie, a transvestite Agẹmọ priest, having his hair wrapped in female style by his two wives. Ijẹbu area, town of Agọ-Iwoye, 24 July 1986.

7.3 Two transvestites pause for a photograph on the road just outside the Agẹmọ grove at festival time. Ijẹbu area, Imọsan, 7 July 1986.

7.4 Outriders charge out of the grove ahead of one of the Agẹmọ masks. Ijẹbu area, Imọsan, 4 July 1982.

7.5 Tough young men lash each other with long tree branches at an Agẹmọ festival of one of the priests named Idẹbi. Ijẹbu area, town of Agọ-Iwoye, 21 September 1986.

7.6 Close-up of Agẹmọ Idẹbi at his annual festival; his headdress is surmounted by an image of the chameleon. Ijẹbu area, Agọ-Iwoye, 21 September 1986.

7.7　Agẹmọ Posa, with legs like an elephant, performing at a funeral. Ijẹbu area, village of Odoṣiwọnade, via Eguṣẹn-Ipẹja, 6 June 1982.

8. From Militarism to Dandyism: The Shaping of Performance

> It is common knowledge that the Ibadans are just merely at best tolerating the Ijebus. Their deep hatred for the Ijebus for more than a century is epitomized in the mood and manner of celebration of the Oke Ibadan. During the celebration of this Festival the Ijebus are usually made the object of ridicule, abuse and attack by their young and old. Till today, it may be tragic for an Ijebu man in Ibadan on the day of the celebration to feel himself a Nigerian and walk around the town without taking extra precaution to avoid all the trails or routes plied by the crowd that follows the masquerade, Oke Ibadan.
>
> (Anonymous n.d.:3–4)[1]

Performers not only invoke, and perhaps on occasion enact, fragments of myth in their rituals, but raconteurs represent performance in their telling of tales. The tale above was deployed to argue for "a separate State for the Ijebus" (p. 3). Indeed, in 1976 the Western Region of Nigeria was divided up into three states—Ọyọ, containing within its borders Ibadan, Ijẹṣa, and Ifẹ peoples; Ondo, with Ekiti, Ọwọ, and Ondo peoples; and Ogun, combining Ẹgba, Ẹgbado, and Ijẹbu peoples (Map 1). There is no evidence that this argument was persuasive in that decision. But why would the unnamed author assume that it might be? It is a myth about ritual, a representation of a representation with the referential power to transform consciousness, or so it was hoped.

Ritual spectacles, as do written texts, acquire referential power through what Edward Said (1978:20) terms strategic formation. In my adaptation of his concept to performance, strategic formation is an ensemble of relationships between groups of agents and the representations they employ. The ensemble acquires mass, density, and referential power within itself and in the larger society. Indeed, it is this ensemble of relationships and their referential power that in part constructs spectacle's aggrandizing ethos (MacAloon 1984; M. Drewal 1987). Through its referential power, Agẹmọ performance preserves a vestige of a former sociopolitical system, making it felt today throughout the land. The Ijẹbu celebration of 'Id al-Kabir is another spectacle of power of a different style and substance. Introduced early in the twentieth century, during a period of radical social and political change in Nigeria, it has since that time participated in an annual discourse of spectacles, set among much older, precolonial ones.

An analysis of the festival's history in this community thus provides insight into how individual interests get transformed into performance practices. To this end, I have selected two individuals for special consideration, each of whom has a different relationship to the history of the festival. The first is Balogun Bello Kuku (1845–1907), the celebrated Ijẹbu trader/warrior credited with having introduced the Yoruba version of 'Id al-Kabir that is performed today in Ijẹbu-Ode. The second is the current Ọtun Balogun of Ijẹbu-Ode, Alhaji M. O. Ṣọtẹ, alias Lovely, on whom I focused during the 1986 festival that took place from the 15th to the 17th of August.

The Ijẹbu version of 'Id al-Kabir represents an alternative identity to those constructed in the same town by other festivals such as Agẹmọ. Although its format loosely follows that of its Muslim prototype celebrated farther north in the cities of Ilọrin (Yoruba/Fulani/Hausa) and Bida (Nupe) (Lloyd 1961; Nadel 1965:143–144), it has an emergent identity all its own and is at the same time distinctively Yoruba, and more specifically Ijẹbu. Like its prototype, the festival commemorates Abraham's sacrifice to God. Yoruba also call the occasion Ileya festival, from the Hausa *layya* and the Arabic *alazha* (Abraham 1958:303)[2]

Ileya festival in Ijẹbu-Ode lasts three days. On the first day, Yoruba and other Muslims go *en masse* to the public praying ground where the king of Ijẹbuland, the Awujalẹ, presents a ram to the Imam, the chief cleric of the central mosque, for sacrifice, and all pray. In 1986, the Awujalẹ arrived in his Mercedes and was met by his palace servants with his state umbrella to escort him into the praying ground, where the chief Imam awaited. The families of the Balogun war chiefs gathered in entourages, each one parading on its own to and from the praying ground, singing and dancing to an assortment of drum ensembles that they had each hired especially for the occasion. The following day those Muslims who could afford it slaughtered their own rams to serve to their less privileged friends as well as to those of other faiths and the poor. But as Ifa diviner Ọṣitọla remarked disdainfully, "Muslims think everybody needs the same sacrifice."

On the third and final day, disparate entourages paraded simultaneously with their musicians throughout the town on various routes, sometimes criss-crossing one another at intersections, sometimes passing through each other from opposite directions, but all converging in the end on a central spot to pay public homage to the Awujalẹ. Once again, the chief Imam spoke and prayed. This last day is known as Ojude Ọba, loosely "Meeting the King Outside." In order of their rank, each entourage danced in and prostrated before the Awujalẹ. Afterward, they paraded back home making stops along their individual routes to greet important personages, be entertained, and gossip about other groups.

This last day of parading was more festive than the first. People dressed more elaborately and gathered in larger groups. Seven or more young men in each group carried their family's flags, which loomed some ten feet above the crowd and, from a long distance away, called attention to their placement within an otherwise chaotic scene (fig. 8.1). The Baloguns, or in some cases the eldest men in Balogun lineages—called Mọgaji—all dressed in large expensive garments; many wore Hausa-style robes and Fulani turbans, evoking the Muslim north (fig. 8.2). They mounted horses decked out in ornate, northern-style trappings of embroidered leather, brass, and feathers.

There were many different styles of horse-handling, too. A woman chief on horseback in one Balogun's entourage—a wealthy businesswoman—cross-dressed in a man's large embroidered garment and turban. Most women were on foot singing and dancing. Some dressed collectively in the same cloth; others wore large men's robes that in some cases belonged to their forefathers. In so doing, they could dash more actively here and there, according to one young man. Men on foot with guns fired them into the air creating terrific blasts of noise, smoke, stench, and residue that fell on everybody's heads. Between parading and visiting, the groups did not arrive back home until well after dark, around eight-thirty to nine o'clock.

HISTORICAL CONDITIONS

The historical conditions that gave rise to Ileya practice in Ijebu-Ode at the turn of the century are more accessible than those of the older Agemo festival. Data for the reconstruction of Ileya come from both Yoruba and European historians—all of whom based their analyses on primary sources from the period in question, mostly missionaries' and colonial officials' reports and correspondence.[3] Another important source is the eyewitness account of Reverend Samuel Johnson (1973), a repatriated Yoruba slave writing prior to 1897.[4] I have supplemented these writings with extant material gathered in 1986 in Ijebu-Ode, including oral accounts, local publications, the festival performance itself, and the Kuku family house.

Throughout the nineteenth century the whole of Yorubaland was plagued by wars, largely as a result of the slave trade and the decline and fall of the Oyo Empire in northern Yorubaland (Ajayi and Smith 1964; Law 1977; Atanda 1973). As war became a major preoccupation during the second half of the nineteenth century, a professional warrior class evolved from hunters' guilds (Ajayi 1965; Lloyd 1971:49). Powerful war chiefs came to dominate, with their own private armies made up of their lineage members and slaves. Contemporary expressions of this historical period are the outings of the Egungun warrior masks described in chapter 6, who storm through the streets of Abeokuta during festivals in memory of their ancestors. The Oke Ibadan mask cited at the outset of this chapter is another example.

Circa 1823–24, militant Muslim forces overthrew the Oyo Yoruba city of Ilorin, dividing it into four quarters, each headed by a war chief entitled Balogun (fig. 1.2).[5] This new military order had a direct impact on war and trade further south. The titles Balogun, Seriki, and Mogaji were introduced shortly thereafter into southern Yoruba areas.[6] In Ijebu-Ode, the titles came to prominence in the mid-nineteenth century, probably via the city of Ibadan, which had been established in the 1830s as a war camp with a military organization loosely modeled after Ilorin's (Lloyd 1971:18–19; Smith 1971:181 and 198 note 36). Bello

Odueyungbo Kuku (1845–1907) was only the second Balogun (Balogun Keji) in the city's history (Kuku 1977:1).

Today in Ijẹbu-Ode, the Balogun war chiefs are reportedly the principal liaisons between the community-at-large and the senior chiefs. How this works in practice is unclear, since there are in fact many different hierarchies operating simultaneously in Ijẹbuland whose powers have been waxing and waning in relation to each other since at least the mid-nineteenth century.[7] The Agẹmọ chiefs as a body constitute one system; the local government council, another; the hierarchies of the three precolonial administrative authorities—the Ilamurẹn, Oṣugbo, and Pampa—represent others; societies based on age grades (rẹgbẹrẹgbẹ) another; as well as the hierarchy of Muslim clerics; and so on.

In addition to its religious status as an Islamic celebration, Ileya festival gives the Baloguns of Ijẹbu-Ode—all Muslim—the privilege of displaying the nature and force of their own power through spectacle's aggrandizing ethos and mass appeal. Ostensibly, with no wars to fight, the public displays of the Baloguns, like those of the Agẹmọ priests, represent only a vestige of a former sociopolitical system, and an extremely short-lived one at that—no longer than the last quarter of the nineteenth century. Not until then did Islam become a real presence in Ijẹbu (Gbadamọsi 1978:90)[8]

T. G. O. Gbadamọsi (1978:92–94) attributes the strength of Islam in Ijẹbu to three factors: Ifa divination in which the sign Otura meji identifies "predestined" Muslims at early ages; returning long-distance traders who were converted abroad in the interest of their trade;[9] and the subsequent conversion of free-born. From Gbadamọsi's reference to Ifa (1978:92), it is clear that he means Ikọsẹ w'aye, Imori, and Itẹfa divination rituals (chapters 4 and 5). There were many "predestined Muslims" in Ijẹbu area, he notes. The processes that identify them are the same as those that directed Oṣitọla's son to acquire an Egungun mask and learn to perform it.

It is not insignificant that the first conversions of Ijẹbu citizens to Islam coincided with the development of professional militarism and a new warrior/trader class, for it is the wisdom—indeed, the pragmatism—of diviners, as Oṣitọla pointed out, to interpret Ifa texts in relation to the changing world. The direct link between internal wars and trade in slaves in particular seems obvious.[10] The northern Ijẹbu town of Oru, where the Awujalẹ stationed a Balogun and Sẹriki in the last quarter of the nineteenth century, was an important slave market. The Ijẹbu began there by selling gunpowder, guns, salt, Manchester cloth, tobacco, and spirits to the Ibadans, while they received slaves, cotton, cloth, palm oil, and palm kernels (Ayandele 1979:57). By 1888, they were demanding nothing but slaves, and by 1891 they were adding to their revenues by also collecting tolls.[11]

To protect their independence and their positions as middlemen in the slave trade between inland territories and the Atlantic coast, the Ijẹbu closed their borders to all strangers—especially the British (Ajayi and Smith 1964:121; Newbury 1971:99–100; Johnson 1973:567–568, 587, 608–609, 615; Ayandele 1966:55–66, 1983).[12] Ijẹbu isolationism provoked a British invasion in 1892.

The motive was economic.[13] This marked the culmination of a period when powerful warrior-traders became "culture heroes" with personal traits resembling deities (Lloyd 1971:6; Hopkins 1973:24, 142; Belasco 1980:152). One such individual was Balogun Kuku.

BALOGUN KUKU AND THE
REPRESENTATION OF SPECTACLE

The memory of Balogun Kuku lives in many forms of representation. It is alive in the Ijebu version of 'Id al-Kabir, which he is said to have introduced; it is encoded in his mansion on Ita-Ntebo Street, Ijebu-Ode (fig. 8.3); and it resonates from the pages of a booklet published by the Kuku family on the seventieth anniversary celebration of Balogun Kuku's death in 1907 (Kuku 1977). The latter, based on the oral accounts of family members, chronicles Kuku's life from his birth in 1845 to death. It is filled with tales of jealousy and conflict, accounts that can be evaluated based on a comparison with other primary sources. What is particularly striking is how the family history resorts to narrative accounts of spectacle to construct for the reader a sense of Kuku's power.

According to the account, Kuku's mother died when he was very young and his grandmother, a titled elder in the Oṣugbo society, raised him. She taught him trading and how to gain profits by the age of fifteen. Kuku took this job more seriously than most his age, traveling to Ibadan to sell tortoises for use in medicines. It was an inflationary time, when a system of indentured slavery known as *iwofa* was widely exploited.[14] Large debts incurred from performing family funeral rites (chapter 3) were often handled in this manner. The risk was, as Fadipe (1970:193) explained, "a boy or a girl who was in pawn as a result of the celebration of funeral customs of his father might be forgotten by his brothers and sisters whose job it was to repay the loan." Beginning services within a day of the loan, *iwofa* labored for the lender two to three days out of the Yoruba four-day week, depending on the size of the debt. Traders who accumulated great wealth could afford to loan money in exchange for *iwofa* labor and could incur quite a retinue of servants in this way. This is what is understood in references to Balogun Kuku's *iwofa*, many of whom went on to become his war boys (*omo ogun*). Initially, the account goes, Kuku's grandmother supplied him with many *iwofa* to carry his loads to Ibadan in order to help him get started in trading, and with his financial savvy, he soon became rich and famous.

From then on, Kuku's life is presented as a series of intrigues with enemies in which the performance of spectacles, re-cast in narrative form, expresses Kuku's power in the midst of conflict.[15] As the story goes, Kuku incurred the wrath of several powerful chiefs for the funeral celebration for his grandmother:[16]

> Many things happened during the Ita-Oku, the third day of the funeral. The funeral that traveled about contained different types of drumming and various cheerful plays [*ere arirya miran*]. Chief Kuku went to the celebration wearing a

combination of heavy, multicolored damask cloth and very expensive velvet. And he also carried an umbrella. People praised and respected Chief Kuku because nobody had ever done anything like that before in Ijẹbu-Ode. He spent lots of money on the various entertainments he organized on that day. Because of all the money he spent on his grandmother's funeral, which outdid what the other powerful chiefs were able to do, they prosecuted him in the presence of the Awujalẹ for using an umbrella.

In spite of his explanation that his umbrella was not the locally used one, the court fined him. And he would have been condemned to life in prison, it is said, had he not held the post of Balogun.

The Kuku family history also suggests that the Ijẹbu-Ode chiefs feared Kuku's power, advising the Awujalẹ to kill him. When this news reached Kuku, his war boys wanted to fight, but Kuku preferred to avert his enemies by moving to Ibadan. Building a beautiful "castle" there, he continued to trade, but his enemies pursued him. The history then suggests Kuku's persecutors made an about-face, now suddenly requesting him to return to Ijẹbu-Ode because of the danger of a British invasion.

The message was said to have been sent via the Baalẹ of Ibadan and his chiefs, who advised Kuku to go back home as the Awujalẹ had requested. Kuku reportedly returned to Ijẹbu-Ode with all his wives, children, and slaves in order to fight the war. As the party set out, the Baalẹ of Ibadan supplied Kuku with many musicians and instruments, including a ṣẹkẹrẹ and many *bata* drums as a demonstration of support. On their entry into Ijẹbu-Ode, his war boys rode on horseback and his family sang and danced. At first townspeople thought Kuku was coming with his army to wage war against them, but they eventually welcomed him in joy and friendship. In this way, it is reported, Kuku was the first person to bring this style of music to Ijẹbu-Ode.[17]

When Kuku's entourage arrived at his father's house, he reportedly sat down on his father's grave, where his family begged him not to fight the British. With his family's advice, Kuku decided to leave Ijẹbu-Ode and go to Ijẹbu-Ifẹ, where he settled in Ishapodo Quarter with his family and war boys, returning to Ijẹbu-Ode only after the Anglo-Ijẹbu war.[18] Various accounts agree that for one reason or another Kuku left Ibadan and stayed in Ijẹbu-Ifẹ during the war.[19]

When British troops invaded Ijẹbu-Ode, they first of all leveled the two most important sites of traditional political authority, the royal palace at Iporogun and the Oṣugbo house.[20] Three days later Kuku returned from exile. It just happened to be on the occasion of Queen Victoria's birthday celebration, which involved "imposing military ceremonies" (Johnson 1973:622).

With the colonization of Ijẹbuland, Kuku instantly became the most influential citizen in town apart from the Awujalẹ. Within a week the expedition forces departed, leaving behind a district head and a peacekeeping force of one hundred Hausas. The Kuku family history (1977:16–18), in fact, claims that the British wanted to make Kuku king, but he declined. Instead the British awarded the Awujalẹ an annual allowance of 200 pounds sterling, while Kuku received 100 for his management of "native" affairs (Johnson 1973:622).[21] No other recipients are mentioned. Already by August of that same year, Kuku had begun to plan another house in Ijebu-Ode, which was clearly not dependent on his annual stipend.[22]

Kuku called his mansion Olorunsogo, "Glory to God." If the family account is correct, its completion took approximately three years, from 1897 to 1900 (Kuku 1977:21). At the opening ceremonies in 1902, Kuku, together with a whole score of other Ijebu citizens, publicly converted to Islam (Gbadamosi 1978:97; Kuku 1977:18–21). Gbadamosi (1978:97) reports, "he turned the event into a grand occasion, inviting people from far and wide—Lagos, Ibadan, Abeokuta and Epe, and on this occasion he publicly declared for Islam, taking the name of Momodu Bello. He was joined by scores of people who were also converted. Among these were influential and highly placed Ijebu men."[23] Gbadamosi concludes that this event had considerable impact throughout Ijebuland.

The Kuku mansion was built in an Afro-Brazilian style by Balthazar Reis, a repatriated Brazilian Yoruba living in Lagos (Kuku 1977:20) (fig. 8.3). Its grandeur and detail are testaments to Kuku's enormous accumulated wealth from war and trade. The upstairs bedrooms and sitting room are maintained in the same state as Kuku reportedly left them, with all the original imported Victorian furniture, mostly of Brazilian manufacture; hand-painted wallpaper; crystal chandelier (fig. 8.4); and British ceramics, one pair modeled after the wood kola containers in the form of antelope heads that the British captured from the Benin royal palace during their punitive expedition of 1897.

An ornately carved, circular staircase, with its own entry gate, is located in the center of the house. Apart from this, the first floor is starkly furnished with only a large platform stationed at the bottom of the staircase, which is covered with linoleum that poses as ceramic tile. On the platform is a stuffed leather cushion from the Islamized north of Nigeria. The platform is located just next to the front door to the house. In the lower half of the door, shutters open to the inside. Kuku's great grandson Babatunde claimed Balogun Kuku used to recline on the cushion on one elbow. In that position he would receive his subjects. To demonstrate, Babatunde Kuku posed as his great grandfather supposedly would have done (fig. 8.5). Through the lower portion of the door, he reportedly watched to see who was approaching. If he did not wish to see a particular visitor, he could easily ascend his circular staircase and disappear.

The house is a blend of diverse cultural styles—English Victoriana, Brazilian Baroque, together with an Orientalist Islam—an exercise in style management designed to control space and what goes on in it (Rapoport 1982). As a mediator, an instrument of indirect rule, Kuku entertained the British in the second story, but dealt with "native" affairs from his sultan's platform on the lower level. Whether he served tea to the British or arbitrated a dispute among townspeople from his platform, each setting served Kuku's negotiations, constructing the power relationships between negotiators.

The reasons for Kuku's conversion are multiple and complicated. The Kuku family history (1977:23) reports that by the time Christianity had become well-established in Ijẹbu-Ode, Kuku had thirty wives, which he could not bring himself to send out of his house merely because of Christian prohibitions against polygamy.[24] He no longer wanted to worship the Yoruba deities, so he sent for Muslim teachers in Ilọrin to come and instruct his people.

Polygamy was clearly a factor; it has direct bearing on the power and prominence of the corporate family group, which is essential to the construction of the Ileya festival spectacle. Clearly, too, Kuku understood power relationships. He had successfully taken advantage of rapidly shifting conditions, parlaying his resources from trade to maximize his own personal power in the last quarter of the nineteenth century. Kuku appears to have used both Islam and colonialism to his own advantage.

Kuku's political and economic power prior to British involvement expressed a new social order. In becoming a Muslim, Kuku maintained a certain autonomy from the colonialists and the Christian clergy, many of whom were repatriated Yorubas who had taken Christian names.[25] From his position outside the dominant religious order of the colonialists, he maximized his potential to manipulate his circumstances, using the British romance with Islam and the Orient as a strategy. This is suggested by the cunning eclecticism of his mansion.

The British never had it easy in their attempts to control Ijebu and Kuku.[26] In 1903, not more than a year after Kuku's conversion to Islam, he was already "under a cloud with the Government, although he had been paid a stipend of £100 per annum from 1892 because 'he was then more loyal to the British Government than the Ijebu Native Authorities.' "[27] Then, in 1904, there were riots in Ijebu-Ode when the Awujalẹ recognized Kuku as a member of the Native Council set up by the British as a means of indirect rule, suggesting that old grievances with local chiefs were still active. In 1906, the reigning Awujalẹ Adeleke died and another king was installed (Ayandele 1970:237–238). Soon after, in 1907, the year of Kuku's death, civil and criminal courts were suspended for three months, and Kuku was fined 100 pounds on the instructions of the acting governor for "insubordination" to the new Awujalẹ (Bovell-Jones 1943:19). Kuku became sufficiently controversial that, when his son Gbadamọsi succeeded him as head of the "Kuku party," the British reduced his annual stipend to only 25 pounds, stipulating that he was to be "useful to Government." The history of Kuku's relationship with the British and with the indigenous authorities thus took a number of twists and turns from the beginning of the colonial period until his death. Whatever the state of affairs at any given time, he seems to have always made the most of it, both financially and politically.

It was sometime during the first two years after Kuku's formal conversion to Islam that he probably introduced the Yoruba version of 'Id al-Kabir. Once again, the reader of family history (Kuku 1977:24–26) is presented a narrative about the power of spectacle. Thus Kuku wanted a means of expressing his allegiance to the Awujalẹ, just as the worshipers of Yoruba deities were accustomed to doing once each year at the time of the Odela festival, when they all joined together with musicians and danced in a royal salute. During Kuku's first

Ileya festival after becoming a practicing Muslim, he sacrificed a ram in memory of Abraham. As it happened that year—the family history implies—Odela fell on the third day of Ileya festival. Wanting to express his fealty to the Awujale, he and his sons and friends dressed in expensive cloth, mounted their horses and, with guns blasting and ṣẹkẹrẹ, bata, and aro musicians playing, they paraded from the Kuku mansion to the palace singing and dancing. When the devotees of Yoruba deities and others saw Kuku's entourage coming, they dispersed thinking he was waging war. "In this way," it is asserted, "Kuku killed the Odela festival once and for all in the city of Ijẹbu-Ode, and instituted the celebration of Ita-Ọba (Ojude Ọba) which we are performing until today."[28] The following year he reportedly put on a more elaborate show. The other Baloguns of the town also joined in so that Ojude Ọba became a grand occasion when the Baloguns' families and associates parade all around the town. Ojude Ọba is thus represented as having conquered Odela, one spectacle of power displacing another.

In the Kuku family narrative, spectacle is represented as a power play in three different instances, each one articulating a point of conflict amidst implied social change. Kuku's imported war title, his economic status from trade as evidenced in his mansion, and the conflict bubbling underneath the narrative accounts of the spectacles he supposedly initiated—all are encoded in the Ileya festival. In Ijẹbu-Ode, contemporary Baloguns use the celebration of 'Id al-Kabir as a display of their personal wealth, power, and erstwhile military might, although none have been trained in militarism. Indeed, as Ọtun Balogun Ṣọtẹ performs 'Id al-Kabir today, militarism is transformed into dandyism.

ṢỌTẸ'S AESTHETIC[29]

An elephant is huge. When an elephant crosses your path, you don't need to inquire, "Oh, did something just pass by?"

Ọtun Balogun M. O. Ṣọtẹ,
alias Lovely

The elephant here, as it is in Agẹmọ (chapter 7), is a self-aggrandizing metaphor. For who can ignore a passing elephant? The allusion is to Ọtun Balogun Ṣọtẹ, whose entourage sang this song during the Ileya festival parade of 1986. Like those who tell tales of spectacle as a power play, the chiefs who parade during the Yoruba celebration of 'Id al-Kabir have a very clear sense of how performance constructs power.

A very handsome, wealthy businessman in his early fifties, Ṣọtẹ never schooled formally but at the time of my research owned a palm-oil factory, an ice-block plant, and a lace-manufacturing company that employed over five hundred people. Popularly known as "Lovely," after the name of one of his early business ventures, he is a ladies' man, a dandy who "takes wives in series," as a close friend of his was fond of putting it.

Extremely conscious of the power of corporate display, Ṣọtẹ has lots of wives and children—he could not recall the number—because as a chief he claims he has to have a big entourage. Actually, Ṣọtẹ took the title of Ọtun Balogun only in 1985 on the occasion of the Awujalẹ's twenty-fifth anniversary celebration on the throne. The Awujalẹ used Ileya festival that year to celebrate his anniversary and to bestow honorary titles. By then, Ṣọtẹ already had many wives in series and also grown children. Islamic law, he tells me, allows him only four; Nigerian law, modeled on the British system, permits only one. Ṣọtẹ handles this by periodically divorcing older ones to take new ones and boasts that the divorcees always return to participate in his festivals. They do so, he is confident, for the pleasure and enjoyment he provides.

In Yoruba society women are economically independent and, as soon as they reach menopause or become grandmothers, achieve domestic independence from their husbands if they so desire. If Ṣọtẹ's wives return, it is because divorce is only a formality to enable him to marry more wives legally. His personal relationships with ex-wives need not have changed substantially. In daily life, as in ritual, the "rules" may influence behavior, but they seldom determine it.

When I first met Ṣọtẹ's newest wife, some thirty years his junior, she had come to bring us snacks. He took her arm and pulled her down to a kneeling position, telling me that he always made his wives obey. She went along with this without any visible reaction. Later on, as they were standing in front of the VCR selecting tapes, I watched them playfully nudging and elbowing each other as he tried to persuade her to find a particular tape for him—he does not read and thus could not identify the one he was searching for. She continued to ignore his request, and soon this developed into outright horseplay. Every time he tapped her to reinforce his request, she nudged him back with her hip; both were giggling.

Scene two deconstructed the first. Later on he asked me if my husband and I had married for love, or because it was convenient insofar as we are in the same work. I attempted to explain that I could not really separate the two things out. He then pointed out how well his junior wife had danced in his parade: "she danced the whole time, and when it was over and everybody else was saying they were tired, she was saying that she wished it could go on all night. It is because I married her from the Osi Balogun's family, so she grew up understanding this performing role and so she enjoys it.[30] Such alliances perpetuate strong performance traditions, a fact that is evident to performers themselves.

In the front of Ṣọtẹ's 1986 entourage were banners displaying his name, and a boy wheeling a bicycle with a police siren mounted on it. Immediately behind them was Ṣọtẹ's horseboy riding "gently" on his second horse, kept in reserve for the time his first horse would tire. Like those of bygone days, Ṣọtẹ's horseboy is Hausa; "Yorubas don't know how to ride," he asserted. Large horses are not normally suited to the rain forest areas of southern Nigeria and require special care. In the nineteenth century, Yoruba procured northerners, either free men or slaves, whom they felt knew best how to take care of the horses (Adamu 1978:124). The horses and the Hausa horseboy are direct carryovers from nineteenth-century warfare and slavery.

Behind the Hausa horseboy was a retinue of hunters with dane guns, whom Ṣọtẹ imported from the fringe areas of Ijẹbuland. Their duty was to shoot off their guns, adding to the noise and excitement of the parade. They "represent," according to him, his traditional role as a war chief, who always had foot soldiers out in front. All of the groups have guns, Ṣọtẹ acknowledged, but in his own group he confines them to the front position, thereby keeping them apart from the ladies, who find them unpleasant.

The middle section of the parade was composed of two horsemen—a junior brother and a friend respectively in order of their ages. Each had his own set of musicians. The women followed—Ṣọtẹ's wives, daughters, and female friends in their age grades (fig. 8.6). They too had their own musicians in the lead. At the back, claiming the most senior position was Ṣọtẹ himself on horseback with another cadre of musicians, flanked by his sons and veterans of World War II in uniform acting as crowd controllers. Young men behind Ṣọtẹ carried large round fans on poles that, when extended into the air, created a visual backdrop setting him off against the landscape (fig. 8.7). Finally at the very back was a line of men, members of his age grade. According to Ṣọtẹ, "they are very powerful and very rich and, in fact, they are all millionaires"—among them, reportedly, managers of companies and general managers of banks. While they walked shoulder to shoulder, they also danced, but, as Ṣọtẹ explained, "they should be more stately and solemn."

Each segment of the entourage had its own musicians. Ṣọtẹ intended this explicitly to keep the group members "alive." He felt that if people did not have music, when they got tired they would focus on their tiredness and deaden the effect of the whole. He commented further that he also kept lively and playful, explaining, "you know, if you look up and see me on my horse and I look tired, then you will start to feel tired as well." As the day wore on he made a conscious effort to do more dancing and playing with his horse to set a positive example for the other members of the group, who by that time he was sure were tiring.

The overall organization of the group was based on a progression from the least senior in front to the most senior in back, polished off with millionaires. The order was in keeping with that of the various groups that paraded into the festival grounds. Thus the entourages holding the more junior titles as well as those lineages who do not currently have a member in office are supposed to go in front of him. Ṣọtẹ joked that sometimes the other entourages were very stubborn and attempted to delay him deliberately. In such instances, he claimed, he would parade on through them, even though they would insist he could not pass. Responding that they wasted his time, he would always push forward, forcing them to scramble to get back up in front. As he asserted, his show was so good that after he went past all the spectators would leave. In effect, that would leave no one to watch the stragglers.

The corporate display is critical for Ṣọtẹ, as it is in the Kuku tales, and he is very articulate in describing how he organized his entourage. He asked me if I had seen the siren in the front. When I said yes, he broke into joyous laughter and went on to say, "I wanted my own siren. It is for fun. You know, it fits. I am

accustomed to riding with a siren because whenever the Awujaḷe goes out any-
place there is always a police car in the front with a siren to clear the road. I am
always behind the police car with the siren because I must always precede the
Awujaḷe anywhere he goes. I am always with a siren." His use of the siren
reminded me of Kuku's use of the umbrella.

In Ṣọtẹ's case, it was clearly intended as a ruse. I observed its effectiveness
on the main road where all the groups came together before parading into the
festival grounds. The Awujaḷe had passed through moments before in a rather
large, speedy motorcade led by police, sirens screeching. Suddenly, another siren
came from behind. The entourages in front cleared the road; people stopped and
turned around; the entire crowd on the street suddenly seemed to halt and come
to attention. I turned and there behind me was the boy with the siren strolling
leisurely up the road beside his bicycle, a parody of the Awujaḷe's motorcade, a
reproduction, but with critical distance, which at the same time had the power
to move people and get their attention, if only for an instant.

Not content to proceed slowly forward, Ṣọtẹ's wives, daughters, and their
friends together with their musicians danced back and forth within the parade
itself, creating a second movement in counterpoint to the primary one. They
paraded continually between the horseman in their front, and then turning and
moving toward Ṣọtẹ in the back. Upon reaching Ṣọtẹ, their two sets of musicians came together, and they danced in front of Ṣọtẹ's horse before turning
back in the opposite direction. Ṣọtẹ controls the group from the back, commenting that there is always communication between the individual segments.

Ṣọtẹ selected all the cloth for the members of his entourage and even designed some of the costumes, in particular those of the hunters and the Hausa
horseboy. They could have come in their hunter's clothes, except from Ṣọtẹ's
point of view they were not fine enough. Ṣọtẹ and the two other horsemen all
dressed in the same traditional strip-weave cloth—red and black stripes. All
these costumes Ṣọtẹ handed out just before the parade and collected them back
at the end. Over their red gowns, the horsemen wore capes made of cloth from
Ṣọtẹ's lace factory (fig. 8.7). It was the cloth Ṣọtẹ personally handpicked for his
entourage. Everybody purchased it from him. His wives, children, and their
friends together with the millionaires all wore this cloth, white with blue, red,
and yellow dots embroidered on it (figs. 8.6–8.8). Ṣọtẹ chose cloth in what he
considered to be in his lower price range—$25 per yard, which he offered at a
bargain price of $18. Other groups he observed bought cheap cotton, no more
than $5 to $6 a yard. If he did not set a high enough price, he feared he would
attract too many people to his entourage because of his enormous popularity.
The cloth functioned as a control device to select out the more prosperous
participants and eliminate the poorer ones, an inversion of the value of the ram
sacrifice. Those who bought Ṣọtẹ's cloth designed it themselves so that women
were in everything from traditional blouses and wrappers to long gowns and
pants suits. In an added playful touch, Ṣọtẹ's wives and daughters also appliquéd their first name initials on their fannies in pale blue ribbon—R for Ronke,
K for Kẹmi, and so on (fig. 8.8).

Ṣọtẹ also went into a long unsolicited explanation of his choice of colors:

> You notice I always use red. I like red very much. And I mix it with
> other colors, but red will always be there. Red is dangerous. It is too hot.
> Yorubas run away from red; they fear it. But that is why I like to use it,
> because when you look at my group coming down the street, if it comes
> near any other group who is wearing yellow—and yellow may look good by
> itself—or they may use green—and green may look pretty—another group
> may use yellow and green together, but when it comes next to the red, red
> will swallow it. [. . .] Black is another beautiful color that people fear, or
> run from. Those two colors have power and they are able to swallow up
> other colors.

A survey of color combinations in his entourage quickly validated his claim. The
costumes of the hunters and horseboy were bright red and blue. Tall, red Hausa-
style caps, rounded at the top, were similar to the traditional Yoruba hunters'
caps designed in the past to hold medicines. Both the hunters and the elderly
women in the family wore them. Ṣọtẹ's own garment was red and black strip-
woven cloth (aṣọ oke); the same for the two other horseback riders. All of the
musicians—five groups to be exact—wore bright red Oṣugbo-style hats that
were probably modeled originally on Portuguese hats, with their wide brims and
long dangling tassels (fig. 8.6). Ṣọtẹ's wives and their friends all had on red hats
as well, designed slightly differently—carnival-style conical ones with shiny
streamers attached. The horse trappings were also red. Ditto for the gourd rattle
(ṣẹrẹ) Ṣọtẹ carried: "that one is to greet people; it is a response, but it is prepared with medicine. It is not an ordinary rattle." Everything and everybody in
Ṣọtẹ's procession was adorned with large splashes of red.

One of the most unique things about Ṣọtẹ's Ileya festival parade is that his
horses "dance." He trains them himself. In contrast to other horseback riders I
witnessed, he made his horses prance around in circles lifting their hooves,
bounce in one place on their forelegs, and rear up—all in time to the music.
One of his daughters was particularly good in synchronizing her own movements
with the horse's, matching him step for step, beat for beat, going down when the
horse's head dropped, jumping up when the horse reared. What Ṣọtẹ tried to do
in these dance patterns, he said, was to balance turns to the left with ones to the
right. As he explained it, his concern was not only to keep the horse in balance,
but also to turn his own face to the entire crowd of spectators on both sides of
the street so they could keep him in full view. His horse-handling skill gave the
members of his entourage confidence: "you see how people can come and dance
right up next to my horse. They don't have to worry, because I control my
horse. They don't run away; they are not afraid." And it was true. I often went
up very close to the horse to photograph, and at no time did I ever fear the
consequences.

Other horses were not so well trained, other riders not as much in control.
Some required assistance from comrades moving alongside to hold them, partic-

ularly when the horses reared up on their hind legs. The better horsemen and horsewomen danced in their saddles unattended. Each had developed his or her own way of going about it, but I saw no other dancing horses besides Ṣọtẹ's.[31]

Although Muslim himself, indeed an Alhaji, Ṣọtẹ associates his skill in handling horses with his personal Ifa sign, Ọbara meji, divined for him in youth during his Itẹfa ritual (chapter 5). Calling Ọbara meji his "star," he proudly displayed it next to a horse's head on his parade banner, on his horse regalia, and on decals for the festival (fig. 8.9). Ṣọtẹ also claimed to have a personal diviner residing in the Rẹmọ town of Ilisan, whom he telephones for consultations. The significance of Ọbara meji to Ṣọtẹ is that its texts deal with horsemanship, which is a central theme in Ileya festival parades as well as in nineteenth-century Yoruba history.

Apart from this, there is also another factor operating for Ṣọtẹ, that is, the legitimacy of his position. Ṣọtẹ received his chieftaincy title from his mother's side of the family, even though he also had the right to the Osi Balogun position on his father's side. This apparently caused some mild conflict in the family. It was expressed most clearly in the songs of abuse sung by the various groups during the parades. Ṣọtẹ's acceptance of the title reportedly did not make his father's house happy. But had he waited for the position to open up in his father's house, there would have been no guarantee that he would have been offered it, since there were many other potential candidates. As it was, the Osi Balogun position is one rank down from Ọtun Balogun. Since the current Balogun was reportedly eighty-five years old in 1986, it is likely that Ṣọtẹ will move into the top spot within the decade. What this means performatively is that he has the right to the last and most important position in the procession to salute the Awujalẹ at the end of Ileya festival.

Ṣọtẹ's dandyism reflects his relationship with his mother more so than with his father and the militarism implicit in the tradition of his war title. As Ṣọtẹ explained, he was much closer to his mother than to his father. A weaver and cloth trader of great foresight, Ṣọtẹ's mother, like Kuku's grandmother, taught him and his brothers and sisters the ways of business. With her foresight, she anticipated conditions some twenty years in the future, Ṣọtẹ observed, a trait he values highly and applies both to business and to his festival performances, priding himself on thinking ahead and preparing in advance.

One aspect of this is his systematic videotaping of his annual festivals. He then reviews these videotapes in preparation for the next festival. "I don't get tired," he said, "because I am well prepared." "How do you prepare?" I asked. "I am all the time looking for new ideas. And whenever I travel abroad, if I see something, I buy it and include it." This interest showed up in his parade. From the Lagos vicinity, he commissioned the red carnival-style hats with tassels, and he brought his hunters from Ikija and other fringe areas of Ijẹbu. He also imported musical ensembles from Ọyọ, Oke Iho, and Ikire, all northern Yoruba towns. When I asked how he knew where to go for the drummers, he said, "well, I've done research. It is the people from those areas who know how to play talking drums very well. In other areas, they don't know it so well." Making a specific reference to a wedding he had attended the previous week, he commented, "I was noticing the way the bridesmaids were dressed. That gave me an idea." Not wanting any "copycats" to adopt it before he had a chance to show it off, he kept the secret to himself. "I am not a copycat," he asserted. "I take ideas from other places, but I always change them." Last year he carried a peacock feather whisk, but he decided not to use it this year because too many people appropriated it. Instead, he gave it to one of his daughters to carry.

Ṣọtẹ travels widely on business, having visited West Germany, Austria, Switzerland, Italy, England, Holland, and the United States. Whenever he travels he is especially interested in attending festivals and "tries to learn about them." When Ṣọtẹ sees things he likes, he buys in large quantities and ships them back for use in his parade. On his various trips, he has purchased British bobby helmets and horrific rubber masks. Once he bought twenty-two mayors' hats from England. From constant use, such items are eventually depleted, so that by 1986 I saw only two mayors' hats, four bobbies' helmets, and one Halloween horror mask (figs. 8.10, 8.11). Over the years dominant motifs in this way dwindle, taking less prominent positions, and are replaced by new ones. They speak of Ṣọtẹ's hipness, his worldly experience gained through traveling to distant places. Worn by mere teenagers—female and male alike, the latter in Bermuda shorts—the mayors' hats and bobbies' helmets are symbols of British authority dethroned. Ṣọtẹ laughed on mentioning that he had acquired them. Other symbols used in his entourage have special meaning. To honor his mother, he commissioned replicas of the heddle sword she used in weaving cloth. One of his sons, a Brown University graduate now in banking in Lagos, carried one of these.

The various entourages sing abusive songs directed against each other. Ṣọtẹ learned to compose songs growing up in his father's house, even though he never really liked what they sang, claiming the songs were "too hard," songs such as, "we are the powerful ones;/ we are the warriors;/ we've come to fight;/ we have courage;/ we have come to fight." The style of the song as Ṣọtẹ sang it in Ijẹbu was very forceful. When people sing that kind of song, Ṣọtẹ observed, they have to be aggressive and then they attract ruffians and hooligans. "You know, if you are traveling with my group," he insisted, "you won't have your pockets picked. There are no pickpockets in my group." He sends people away that he does not know because ruffians can get inside the group and disrupt it. When the group entered the festival grounds to greet the Awujalẹ in 1986, things suddenly turned chaotic with crowding, stampeding, pushing, and shoving. Ṣọtẹ's son told me later that "ruffians" tried to insert themselves into the group to disperse and diffuse it so that it could not maintain its visual power.

A keen sense of competition with other performing entourages is evident. Ṣọtẹ told me that his brother had now come back with the word from town that his group had put on the best show. Ṣọtẹ acknowledged that he could not know the accuracy of his brother's report because, from his vantage point in the parade, he could not see the other groups. He then commented, "maybe we flatter ourselves in thinking that we are the best." The competitive mode of performance comes out most strongly in the songs the groups direct against each other. "It is not that they want to fight each other," Ṣọtẹ explained, but rather "they are playing."

Ṣọtẹ recollected two songs that were sung about him. One went, "a very rich man can pay to get his title;/ that is not the way it used to be done." Even though such songs never mention names, Ṣọtẹ claimed everybody always knows of whom they speak. A second song criticized the fact that he had taken his title in his mother's house, rather than his father's. It went, "the father fathers the child,/ or does the child father the father?/ It is the mother who will know."

Personally, Ṣọtẹ asserted, he chose not to sing abusive songs, because people would want to fight him. Instead he composes songs to flatter himself, observing that the purpose of abusive songs is to bring down the powerful but, if a person is already the most powerful, abusive songs only belittle the abuser. To bring that point home, he cited a song of self-flattery that he composed in response to the abusive songs leveled at him by his father's house: "When a dog barks, it has seen something!"

With "many songs" in his "brain," Ṣọtẹ sometimes composes on the spot, and the members of his entourage pick them up spontaneously to sing. At other times he writes them down beforehand. On Ileya festival day, he distributed a typed list of nine songs, but said they represented only a very small percentage of those he would sing on that day. The *dundun* drummers pick up the phraseology and tonal patterns and then echo them in their own music. The words are usually constructed around an adage or a proverb that reflects how Ṣọtẹ wishes to be seen. When Ṣọtẹ's entourage made house calls along his route, he would ask his hosts to sing songs they had heard from others, since he could not hear them while parading due to the logistics of the independently moving groups.

Comparing the harsher styles of the other Balogun lineages with his own, Ṣọtẹ boasted, "in my group, you know lots of young women follow me. They can join my group." Stressing gentleness and beauty, he reiterated, "you saw how neat we were; we were neat, clean, orderly, and beautiful." Instead of the physical force and songs of abuse used by other groups, Ṣọtẹ chose instead the aggressivity of colors like red to "swallow" other groups. Emphasizing color rather than physical force, he expressed his own personal power in his elegance of dress, the size and originality of his ensemble, his demonstrated ability to control his dancing horse, and the solidarity of his millionaire friends.

Baloguns do not have to be Muslim, according to Ṣọtẹ; a Christian can be a Balogun as well. At the same time, he believes that being a Muslim he would always put on the better show. "A Christian could do it, but they would just be going through the motions."

Once back home, Ṣọtẹ rested inside, watching his video of the festival with close friends. Outside in his courtyard was a party that continued unabated all night long.

OTHER DIMENSIONS, OTHER PERSPECTIVES

As a Balogun and leader of the people, Ṣọtẹ commented, "whenever there is a festival—whether Christian, Muslim, or pagan, I will always be there." During the Agẹmọ festival, however, he sent his junior brother to represent him and made a point to say that the brother stands with the palace servants who are the representatives of the Awujalẹ. When I asked specifically why he did not attend personally, Ṣọtẹ responded that he did not go because the Awujalẹ did not go. As an outrider for the Awujalẹ, he went on to explain, he must always go in front. Therefore if the Awujalẹ does not attend, neither does he.

Over the years since the current Awujalẹ's installation in 1960, he has dropped visibly out of traditional festivals and has made 'Id al-Kabir, especially the day of Ojude Ọba, the principal occasion for his annual public appearance. Even so the official program of the Awujalẹ's twenty-fifth anniversary celebration held during Ileya festival of 1985 makes no mention of his adopted role in 'Id al-Kabir, Ileya, or Ojude Ọba and continues to assert instead that the Awujalẹ appears publicly only thrice each year, at the traditional festivals of Bẹrẹ in October, Ebi in February, and Agẹmọ in June/July (Anonymous 1985a & b). What actually happens is thus not what is written down. But in a sense the Awujalẹ has it both ways. The official program is in part a reflection that it is not tradition that the Awujalẹ is practicing, although for many Ijẹbu citizens—like Ṣọtẹ and his junior wife—Ileya festival is by now a tradition. Too, the site of Ojude Ọba is not the same as that of older festivals like Agẹmọ. Rather, it takes place on the grounds of the former colonial administrative office building.

On the eve of Nigerian independence from Britain in 1960, P. C. Lloyd (1961:267–278) also documented 'Id al-Kabir in the northern Yoruba city of Ilọrin. The Baloguns rode independently with their own followers to and from the prayer ground. On the return, the Emir at a certain point took the lead. The Baloguns followed in order of seniority, led by the Mọgaji Arẹ, the linear descendant of Afọnja, the pre-Fulani ruler of Ilọrin. Reaching the palace, the Emir received the horsemen following him. Lloyd noted further that the festival had been adapted to the colonial situation.

> Before the return of the Emir from the prayer ground, the Resident of the Province, together with the senior officers of the administration and their wives—all in their best clothes—gather on the tower of the palace gateway to watch the ceremonies. The police band marches and counter marches, playing everything from highlifes to Scottish laments. As the Baloguns and their followers disperse, the Resident greets the Emir and introduces his subordinates. On the following day the Emir and his chiefs ride in procession to the Residency, where they are entertained, as the Emir had earlier entertained his Baloguns.

Lloyd concludes that the festival symbolizes the political structure of the town. And indeed the British clearly encoded themselves at the apex of that structure. The very fact that the word *durbar*—taken from British colonial experience in

India—is in common usage among Africans for festivals such as 'Id al-Kabir in former British colonies like Ghana and Nigeria hints at the colonists' effective use of such festivals to encode their own positions in that hierarchy.

During World War II, 14 December 1942, Abdul Aziz b. Sa'id spoke in Mecca expressing his gratitude to the British government for their generous support of Nigeria. Circulating a copy of this speech to the Resident of the Western Province of Nigeria, the secretary to the government of these provinces commented: "In it (the speech) his majesty (Abdul Aziz b. Sa'id) expresses strong pro-British sentiments and it is thought that if the address was brought to the notice of leading Muslims they might like to quote part of it on the occasion of Id al-Kabir."[32]

What all this suggests is that a spectacle like 'Id al-Kabir can accommodate the expression of many diverse and competing interests simultaneously. While the colonialists were busy encoding themselves in this hieratic structure of unified appearances, I have little doubt that Yorubas, masters of the art of spectacle, "circumcised" them without their knowledge in, for example, abusive songs in Yoruba.

On the occasion of the 1941 'Id al-Kabir in Bida among the Nupe, S. F. Nadel (1965:144) wrote of the "binding forces" present that refer

> to a largely abstract and timeless collective identity which no longer needs the sustaining symbol of kingship. These 'binding forces' implant in the minds of the people of the state the realization that, over and above tribal sections, cultural and class divisions, they form a single human material, living an identical life. They teach a new meaning of the word Nupe, which is the meaning of *nation*.

Clearly, the Ijẹbu version of 'Id al-Kabir is just the opposite of Nadel's model. It is about the time-centered identities of individuals and their self-interests, sectionalism, class, and differentiated lives, which set the pickpockets into nonverbal discourse with the millionaires.

Nadel (1965:143–144) reported that on the first day of 'Id al-Kabir in Bida, also known as *Sallah*,

> after the service the procession returns to the royal residence. Here a great display of horsemanship takes place, at which the bodyguard of the king, his police, and officers of state parade before him and his guests of honour—the foremost among whom are the District Officer and all the Europeans living in Bida Emirate. [. . .] For two days tens of thousands of people crowd the streets of Bida and assemble in front of the royal residence. [. . .] There they watch their rulers ride past in all their splendour, equipped with their paraphernalia of rank; they listen to music, drum signals, and songs of praise etc. [. . .] Here, then, it falls to the elements of worship and secular display, inextricably fused, and supported by the stimulus of mass experience, to mobilize periodically sentiments of loyalty and the consciousness of unity.

Like Lloyd, Nadel focused on the structure of the event rather than on its internal dynamics from the vantage point of individual participants. Equally prominent in both Lloyd's and Nadel's descriptions is British colonial involvement.[33]

In 1942, one year after Nadel's Nupe experience, the Chief Imam in Ijẹbu-Ode refused to go to the praying ground to accept the ram because of grievances the quarter heads had with the Awujalẹ (Bovell-Jones 1943:44). Although Muslims who supported the Awujalẹ attended, those on the side of the quarter heads and the Imam stayed away. How is this to be reconciled with the British perception of such festivals as binding forces that are about a timeless collective identity, mobilization, loyalty, and consciousness of unity?

In Nadel's description, the Europeans are placed side by side with the Emir; in Lloyd's, the hierarchical arrangement is more clear-cut. Thus, as the chiefs paraded to greet the Emir, the Emir paraded to meet the colonials on the following day. In Ijẹbu-Ode, the Awujalẹ stations himself in the position of the former colonial officials—on a grandstand in front of the colonial administration building.

How is it that the same occasion, with essentially the same structure, mode of performance, and symbols clustering around horsemanship and warfare, appears so radically diverse in the three places? Clearly there is a difference between an external view of seamless, surface appearances—the outer structure—and a view from within of the internal dynamics of individual interests all competitively playing that structure to their own advantage. But it is not really an either/or issue. More critical is that the style and flavor of 'Id al-Kabir as it is performed today in Ijẹbu-Ode is understandable only in relation to the historical conditions that gave rise to the practice and the subsequent transformation of militarism into dandyism by a time-centered individual shaping spectacle to suit the way he wishes to be socially regarded.

8.1 Flags and fans project above the crowd on the third day of
     'Id al-Kabir, when the entourages of the war chiefs parade
     into the festival grounds to salute the Awujalẹ. Ijẹbu area,
     Ijẹbu-Ode, 17 August 1986.

8.2 A Yoruba war chief on horseback parades dressed in Fulani
     garb reminiscent of the Muslim north. Ijẹbu area, Ijẹbu-Ode,
     17 August 1986.

8.3 The mansion of Balogun Kuku was built in an Afro-Brazilian style circa 1902 by Balthazar Reis, a repatriated slave from Brazil. Ijẹbu area, I j ẹ b u - O d e , 1 9 8 6 . Photograph by Henry J. Drewal.

8.4 Interior of the Kuku mansion is shown with Victorian decor and a portrait of Kuku beneath the table. Ijẹbu area, I j ẹ b u - O d e , 1 9 8 6 . Photograph by Henry J. Drewal.

8.5 The grandson of Kuku poses on a platform as his grandfather supposedly would have done in the lower level of the Kuku mansion, where he received his people. Ijẹbu area, Ijẹbu-Ode, 1986. Photograph by Henry J. Drewal.

8.6 Ṣọtẹ's wives and daughters wear outfits made of lace from his factory and carnival-style hats. Their musicians precede them. Ijẹbu area, Ijẹbu-Ode, 17 August 1986.

8.7 Ọtun Balogun Ṣọtẹ on horseback is foregrounded by huge fans at his back and flanked by men in military dress. Ijẹbu area, Ijẹbu-Ode, 17 August 1986.

8.8 Ṣọtẹ's wives and daughters assemble for the parade, one with her first-name initial playfully appliquéd on her buttocks. Ijẹbu area, Ijẹbu-Ode, 17 August 1986.

8.9 Detail of Ṣọtẹ's decal showing a horse's head and the sign of his personal set of divination texts. Ijẹbu area, Ijẹbu-Ode, 1986.

8.10 A teenage boy in Bermuda shorts wears a British bobby's helmet. Ijẹbu area, Ijẹbu-Ode, 17 August 1986.

8.11 A young boy in the festival parade wears a ghoulish mask brought from Europe by Ṣọtẹ. Ijẹbu area, Ijẹbu-Ode, 17 August 1986.

9. Reinventing Ritual: The Imewuro Annual Rally

In the last chapter, I examined how individual interests gave rise to and shaped performance practices among Muslim Yoruba, and I contrasted the internal dynamics of the spectacle with its surface appearance as a unified whole. In this chapter, I explore that line further by examining the structured appearance of the Annual Rally in the community of Imewuro in relation to its internal dynamics and the values of the organizers.

In Imewuro, a Western-educated, predominantly Christian "elite" have reformulated "traditional" ritual as a strategy to collectivize and mobilize the townspeople to accomplish a common goal. The idea is implicit in the name Rally given to a week-long celebration, which I attended in 1986 from August 24th to 31st. The Rally possessed all the characteristics of a sacred festival, including sacrifice and play. As Eric Hobsbawm (1985:5) observes, novelty is no less novel for being able to dress up easily as antiquity.

Planned at the convenience of the town's "elite" and publicized in the news media of the area, the week's festivities began with an all-night vigil that included a torchlight parade, the sacrifice of a dog to the ancestral hunters at the Ijasi shrine, and the Yọyọ dance performed by a raffia fiber mask. On the following morning were sacrifices at four shrines—two for the trickster deity Eṣu, one for the local river deity Oluwẹri, and one for the water spirits known collectively as Ekine. Jigbo maskers paraded and performed around the town throughout the entire day (fig. 1.2). The third day was devoted entirely to performances of the Agbo maskers, while the fourth day was for the Egungun maskers (fig. 9.1). Day five was another of sacrifice, first to the deities that the original settlers brought with them when founding the town and then to the founding forefathers themselves to whom the ruling houses trace descent. The sixth day of festivities fell on Friday. The day's official events included praying in the Mosque and a football match between the local Youth Club and the Welfare Association. On Saturday, after the environmental sanitation exercises, a national clean-up campaign scheduled for three hours on a morning near the end of each month, there was a massive town party to launch a $100,000 project to bring electricity to the town.[1] The final day was a thanksgiving service at each of the town's two churches—St. Peter's Catholic

9.1   Egungun masks dance at the Imewuro Annual Rally. Ijẹbu area, village of Imewuro, 27 August 1986.

Church and The Anglican Church of Our Saviour. The complete week's events were printed in a program (fig. 9.2).

Imewuro is a small settlement some twenty-five miles northeast of Ijẹbu-Ode with a voter registration in 1983 of some five thousand people (see Map 1).[2] Not all of its citizens actually reside in the town; however, all were born there and maintain residences and family. Many are professionals who live most of the year in Ijẹbu-Ode, Abẹokuta, Ibadan, or Lagos. Through communal effort and the political contacts of the educated elite, the town has built over the last ten years a maternity clinic and a secondary school compound with about twenty-two classrooms.

Although small in comparison to other Yoruba towns, Imewuro, with its two Christian churches, one Mosque, and many shrines to the Yoruba deities, is characterized by religious pluralism. Lloyd (1959:53) reported such Ijẹbu villages to be 56 percent Christian and 41 percent Muslim, in comparison to Ijẹbu-Ode, which he calculated to be 69 percent Muslim and 31 percent Christian.

Imewuro residents divide their town further into two parts based on ancestral city identities. The lower part of the town houses those who, according to oral tradition, are the descendants of the original settlers, said to have migrated from Idowa, a town southwest of Ijẹbu-Ode. In 1974, when the headman of Imewuro, the Olumewuro, wrote to the Ministry of Local Government and Chieftancy Affairs to request that his position be turned into a kingship, he argued that his forefather was the fourteenth Awujalẹ of Ijẹbu-Ode, who once upon a time left town to take his ill son to Idowa for treatment.[3] On his return, he found that another Awujalẹ had been installed in his place, and his palace servants begged him to go back to Idowa and take up the kingship there. He did, but with this his son set out on a journey to found his own town. Following the advice of his diviner, the son settled at the place where there were many bitter leaf trees, named Imewuro, "Sweet after Labor." The letter concluded by reminding the Ministry that the Awujalẹ was a direct descendant of Oduduwa, the first king of Ifẹ, where all Yoruba peoples originated. By implication, then, so too is the current Olumewuro a direct descendant of Oduduwa. The truth value of the claim is not what is important here; what matters is the way the claim constructs ancestral city identities in relation to the towns of Idowa, Ijẹbu-Ode, and Ile-Ifẹ. By contrast, the people in the upper part of the town identify their ancestral home as Ijẹbu-Igbo, just a few kilometers to the north, and support the view that the lower part of the town is senior.

Equally important, each of the two parts of town has its own distinct ritual traditions that express its separate identity. Each part has its own Ẹṣu shrine dedicated to the divine trickster. The shrines for Oluwaye, deity of contagious diseases; Ọṣun, a river goddess; and Oṣi, the ancestors, belong to the lower part of the town, as does the Ekine water spirit masking tradition. The upper town owns the Ijasi shrine dedicated to hunter-warrior ancestors and the Egungun masking tradition.

David Laitin (1986:146) questions, "why ancestral city identity is subjectively felt to be primordial while religious identity is not." For him, this discrepancy hints at cultural hegemony and the instrumental management of Yoruba identity by the elite, a strategy initiated and set in action by British colonial rule. But Laitin gives the British too much credit. What needs underscoring is that the British had no viable alternative means of colonizing the Yoruba other than using an already extant symbolic repertoire (Laitin 1986:168). In the process, they created a privileged elite. I would argue, however, that the assumptions the elite operate on with regard to ancestral city identity are not significantly different from precolonial ones.

The reason that religious identity is not felt to be primordial is that the traditional religious system engenders extreme diversity through its processes of divination and ritual performance. If the changeability of the ancestral city would seem on the surface to undermine arguments of primordial ties, then the fluidity and the multiplicity of religious practices carried out side by side within the same community or the same family, or even performed by a single individual, would appear to destroy them altogether. In my experience, Yoruba neither construct, nor live, either religious or ancestral city homogeneity.[4] Laitin's observation (1986:118, 145) that identities are not always "given," but "taken"—

PROGRAMME OF EVENTS

SUNDAY 24TH AUG. 1986
1. Torch light Parade
2. Bibo Ijasi
3. Yoyo Dance

MONDAY 25TH AUG. 1986
1. Bibo Esu
2. Jigbo Dance
3. Bibo Oluweri
4. Bibo Ekine

TUESDAY 26TH AUG. 1986
Agbo Dance

WEDNESDAY 27TH AUG. 1986
Egungun Dance

THURSDAY 28TH AUG. 1986
1. Bibo Oluwaiye
2. Bibo Osun
3. bibo Osi

FRIDAY 29TH AUG. 1986
1. Praying in the Mosque
2. Football Match
   IMEWURO YOUTH CLUB
   VERSUS
   IMEWURO WELFARE
   ASSOCIATION

SATURDAY 30TH AUG. 1986
1. Itoju Ayika Ile Eni
   (ENVIRONMENTAL
   SANITATION)
2. Launching of ₦100,000.00
   Electricity Project
3. Dance! Dance!! Dance !!!

SUNDAY 31ST AUG. 1986
Thanks Giving Service at
1. St. Peter's Catholic Church
2. The Anglican Church of Our Saviour
   Imewuro

COME ONE   COME ALL

9.2 Programme of Events, Imewuro Annual Rally. Ijẹbu area, village of Imewuro, 1986.

that they are fluid and changeable—in no way lessens their significance *as* identities, or constructions of self.

What the organization of the Imewuro Annual Rally revealed is the heterogeneity of its citizens' origins and religious practices, all juxtaposed side by side in serial fashion within the span of a week. Indeed, the Rally drew upon the town's heterogeneity and its richly diverse traditions in its organization as a strategy for unification. Its organizers pulled together segments of the town's annual festivals and reconstituted them as a "Rally" for its own purposes.

The very fact that the organizers felt a need to reinvent ritual in this way in order to collectivize the community is a rather glaring testament that the rituals on which the Rally was based were not considered adequate for accomplishing this purpose. It calls into question the assumption that ritual by its very nature is communal. The critical question, it seems to me, is *how* a group of organizers and performers of a particular ritual is made up and for what purposes?

As a reconstituted ritual based on disparate other ritual festivals, the Annual Rally has been contextualized alongside its various models in the yearly calendar since 1959. As one of its organizers, the late Chief Philip B. Rennaiye explained, "the reason why we are performing this Annual Rally is to bring all our people abroad home to see each other once a year. The majority of them like to spend three days, four days, and see all our culture, all our performances, like Jigbo, Egungun, any deities" (Rennaiye #86.59). There was a concerted effort to represent all the religious factions of the town. The organizers of the event used ritual very consciously to construct what Turner (1974a:169) has called ideological communitas, that is, a blueprint formulated by the organizers to supply optimal conditions for existential communitas. The Annual Rally incorporated all the community's festival traditions into its structure and also added to them praying at the Mosque and Sunday services at each of the two Christian churches. In this way, the elite members of the community directed "the flow of symbols" (Laitin 1986:176). In a town where old ways are alive, why was ritual reinvented and juxtaposed with preexisting ones? The answer was implicit in the organization of the Rally itself and was also expressed verbally by the organizers.

The Rally has its roots in the progressive or improvement union movement that developed in Yorubaland during the colonial period in response to the changes in local government that were instituted by the British (Lloyd 1959:55).[5] The home branches of these unions are usually in small rural communities. Made up of those who have had Western-style educations—clerks, teachers, and so forth—they serve as pressure groups on the headman and the chiefs to introduce amenities into the community. Their strategy is to help the chiefs understand, rather than to oppose, the latest technological developments. Progressive unions also tend to function as age grades. Branches of the unions abroad stimulate the one at home, keeping it active. In Imewuro, it was the progressive unions that organized the Rally.

The first Annual Rally was organized under the auspices of the Imewuro Liberty Congress, a small group of citizens with Western-style educations. The Congress was founded in 1957, probably in anticipation of Nigeria's independence from Britain in 1960. Eades (1980:62–63) suggests that it was the colonial government's unequal development and allocation of amenities that directly shaped the activities of such organizations. The prospect of Nigerian independence would have stimulated further a desire on the part of Western-educated citizens to get a jump on any late-breaking developments under the new government. The purpose of the Imewuro Liberty Congress was reportedly to unite sons and daughters living outside the town into an effective cooperative body that could benefit the home community. The Annual Rally was seen as one effective means of accomplishing this goal.

In 1970, as more and more citizens of Imewuro received formal educations, the leaders decided their numbers had become unmanageable, and they reorganized the Congress and regrouped into smaller associations based on traditional three-year age sets. This reorganization marked the resurgence of a precolonial social formation (Lloyd 1959:51–52). In the most senior association of men between forty-five and forty-eight, who call themselves the Imewuro Charity Club, wives were also considered members.[6] In the remaining associations, age sets were divided further by sex and location. For example, there is an Imewuro Unity Club stationed in Lagos and another in Ijẹbu-Ode. The Jolly Sisters are a group of professional women in their mid-thirties—all born in Imewuro. The groups proliferate as more young people receive secondary-school educations and take up professional jobs as civil servants, clerks, shopkeepers, and so on. The "elite" in this sense refers to local people at the upper echelons of political and economic power within their own communities, in contrast to what Lloyd (1974:67) calls the cosmopolitan elite, focusing more on national capitals and external opportunities. In 1984, the various groups re-formed themselves once again into a larger cooperative body known as the Imewuro Development Council.

The names that the groups have chosen for themselves imply their values and aspirations. Named predominantly in English, rather than Yoruba, the groups in 1986 included—in addition to those mentioned above—the Friendship Association, the Committee of Gentlemen, the Co-operative Association, the Progressive Association, the Welfare Association, the Elites Club, and so forth. Nineteen such groups contributed money for the 1986 Annual Rally, although there were more than that in the town as a whole. Only those associations that were financially solvent participated on the Council. This was pragmatic. Thus,

we are only just beginning the electricity project this year. We only collected 10,000 dollars. They didn't collect enough, being that things are so expensive. So we have to launch another fund-raising on December 26. [. . .] We were expecting about 80,000, so we still have a long way to go.

There was a levy of 200 dollars for each group for the Rally, because we are spending a huge amount every year buying sheep and everything [for sacrifice]. And we are giving the participants something. The Development Council bought all the sacrificial animals. A hen for Ajẹye [water spirit], a hen for Ọṣun [deity of the Ọṣun river], a dog for Ijasi—just like iron god—

a he-goat for Oluwaye [deity of contagious diseases], and a ram for Osi
[the ancestors]. We gave all the musicians something. Every year we give
them beer and food plus some money. And the printed program and
announcements for the radio cost a lot of money. There was also an
announcement in the newspaper. We printed up 500 copies of the program.
(Rennaiye #86.59)

Students who had no money, for example, did not participate on the Council
even though they had also organized themselves into associations based on age
and sex. The Development Council cut across both religious and ancestral city
identities.

ORGANIZING PLURALITY

Likewise, the Annual Rally's week-long series of performances incorporated
the entire community, cutting across religious, class, and ancestral city identities
by appealing to its citizens' attachment to their own birthplace (*ibile*). By bringing diverse traditions together in one festival, including Christianity and Islam,
the organizers of the Rally reconstructed the *ibile*, the birthplace, as pluralistic
and highly stratified. Equally important, it provided each faction its own separate time and place within that plurality. This concern was expressed by Rennaiye in explaining how the festival was organized:

In the year 1959, we decided we were going to spend a week because it
is a week program. So we said we would perform them in a day—let's say
Jigbo, we perform that one in a day because Jigbo and Egungun cannot see
each other. They cannot perform them on one day because they cannot see
each other. So that's why we separate it. That is why we give them one day,
one day, Jigbo—one day, Agbo—one day, Bibo Oluwaye—one day,
Egungun—one day. So we give them one, one day. That one will cover all a
week program. (Rennaiye #86.59)

The organizers faithfully followed the order of the traditional calendar in pro-
gramming the performances. They started with a program of masked performances in the category of "Children of the Owner of the Sea" (Omolokun).
First in the program were the Yoyo masks, who performed overnight on Sunday,
followed on Monday by the Jigbo masks (see fig. 1.2). These two types of masks
ordinarily perform during the Erena festival. Falling in December, this period is
conceived as a period of "walking through the gate," or crossing the threshold
into another year (Ositola #86.65). Wearing matured palm fronds, the Yoyo
and Jigbo masks are associated with the dry season. Also at this time were
sacrifices to Olueri, a river deity, and the water spirits known as Ekine.
    In the annual calendar, after Erena is Ebibi, considered a New Year festival,
which goes from the end of December through February. During this period, a
whole repertoire of masked forms called Agbo, representing various water spirits,

perform over the weeks in sets of three (see H. Drewal 1986). The order is determined by divination. In Imewuro, because of a death in one of the families only a day or two earlier, the Agbo performance was sedate. Three sets of masks performed on August 26th. The common practice during Ebibi festival, however, is for only one set to perform per day.

On Wednesday, August 27th, the Egungun masks performed (fig. 9.1). They normally perform during the last quarter of the year when yams are harvested and offered to the ancestors. At the Rally, there were two broad categories of Egungun, each with a wide range of costuming forms, as well as two distinct types of drum ensembles. They danced under a large shade tree, one group before the other. A dispute erupted, however, one group accusing the other of not giving them an equal chance to perform. The complaining group asserted that, when they arrived on the scene, the first group should have relinquished the performance space. Everything came to a halt while members of the Development Council negotiated with the musicians and masked performers. They decided each group should go its separate way around the town until they met up at a particular junction of four roads. There they would perform jointly.

The day after the Egungun performance was a procession to each of three shrines. The procession was led by the Olumewuro, the head of the town, with drummers, chiefs, and members of the Development Council and other townspeople. At each shrine, the headman prayed for the well-being of the town and its citizens. The members of the Council stood by in support, holding the tethered animals that the headman then sacrificed at the shrine sites. Rennaiye, who is Christian, explained:

> We perform these rituals just to see that the deities never go from our town. That's why we must perform them during the Rally. It has been many years since we began this Annual Rally. Many people don't want to perform the rituals because of the missionaries. They were telling them you must not perform the rituals. If you are a Christian, no need to go and worship any god. So it made them leave everything. When we brought this rally it renewed everything.[7]

Me: But why did you decide to renew the ceremonies for the deities and the ancestors and so on?

Rennaiye: Suppose we have left all of them now, my son won't know what is called Egungun or Jigbo. He will only see them in the streets. He won't know that Egungun belonged to his family. But when he begins to perform it, then everybody knows that this Egungun comes from my area. This Jigbo is from my area. This Etiyeri is from my area. Everybody knows their fate. (Rennaiye #86.59)

To know one's "fate," or destiny, is by implication to know one's origins. The idea is implicit in the divination rituals performed for children (chapters 4 and 5).

DIALOGUING WITH CHRISTIANITY

The same concern for preserving tradition was expressed by another member of the Development Council, the Reverend Father Valentine Awoyẹmi, a rather hip-looking Catholic priest who often dresses in jeans, T-shirt, and sunglasses. "Having lived with christianity for 200 years," Father Valentine wrote (Awoyẹmi 1985:64), "we now endeavour to dialogue with Christianity which as it were was imposed in 1892;[8] compare notes with it with respect to reconciliation, thereby rectifying a part of the anomaly of the unintegrated African christian." Unintegrated African Christianity is a phrase Valentine prefers to religious syncretism. Valentine is interested in melding traditional religion with Catholicism because he is convinced that that is the only way Christian religion can make sense among the Yoruba. But his phrasing is interesting: Christianity is the object being operated upon, not traditional religion.

As an example of his dialogue with Christianity, Father Valentine explained the Ebibi festival, celebrated throughout Ijẹbuland at the beginning of the new year. Ebibi festival begins, Valentine observed, about the same time as does the Lenten season. He described how each person in the community gathers firebrands and runs into his or her own room of the house yelling "witches, begone, wizards, begone," *ajẹ yo, ọṣo yo*. In this way, they send evil spirits out of the house.

> After going into their own room, they go into the sitting room and then take the firebrands outside. They put them at a particular crossroads in the center of the town, pushing the evil spirits outside.
>
> Finally they run to the river to put the firebrands into the water to quench them, and gather *woro* leaves that grow in cool places [that is, in the shade down by the river]. They pick handfuls, as many as possible— each person—and they put a group of them at four different shrines in the town—Oluwaye, Ọṣun, Eṣu, Oṣi. They are a sign of peace from a cool place.
>
> They also put *woro* leaves over the threshold into the house so that any evil spirit would see that the house had been purified or cleansed and evil had been driven out. (Awoyẹmi 1986)

Valentine compared these acts with the Old Testament story of the Passover, "where they put the sign on their doors and death passed over them. The *woro* leaves are a sign of peace in the house, and evil spirits will not come there." He also drew a correlation between Christ's death on the cross and the extinguishing of firebrands. For Valentine, Ebibi festival expresses reconciliation in the same sense that Pauline philosophy does. Both present ways for man to remove negative forces and ensure peace and prosperity. Valentine participates wholeheartedly in Ebibi festival, but resisted when young men in an Egungun family asked him when he would perform Egungun. Valentine joked that the only Egungun he would perform would be Egungun Jesus Christ.

Valentine's concern relates to that of the retired Bishop of the Anglican Church in Ijẹbu-Ode, Theodore Kalẹ, whose son is the head priest of the deity Ọbalufọn in Mọbalufọn quarter, Ijẹbu-Ode. By virtue of having been installed as quarter head, Kalẹ's son is responsible for performing the rituals associated with the deity. Kalẹ was adamant that his son had accepted the position, agreeing to perform all the rituals as the deity's chief priest, including the sacrifices, in order to imbue them with Christian values. Kalẹ sees his son as transforming "pagan" ritual practice. By contrast, Valentine wants to change the way Yoruba Catholics worship in order to tap and bring out the values he believes Catholicism shares with traditional Yoruba religion.

RECONSTITUTING CONVENTION

From all outward appearances the ritual performances during the Imewuro Annual Rally were the same as those of any other religious festival in their combination of prayer, sacrifice, and play and in their faithfulness to given styles of dance, music, and costumes. On closer inspection, there was a double standard operating in at least one aspect of Egungun performance, as Rennaiye indicated:

> During the annual Egungun festival, you won't see any of our boys go and visit it. But at the Rally, the day festival, you will see many of them— graduates and secondary school families—who are working and getting money. They will try to perform Egungun on that day just for the Rally only. After that you won't see them at the Egungun festival. They will leave it to those concerned.
>
> During the annual festival many of them will try to perform, like Agbogegẹ and others. But, take for example Oloko, you won't hear him say he is going to come and perform Egungun during their own Egungun festival, because by that time they will begin to claim seniority. So they will begin to use *juju* [magical medicines] and start saying things nobody wants to hear. So we leave them to do their own.
>
> At Oloko's house that day [during the Rally], you saw one Egungun enter into their room. Immediately he entered you saw that we were worried. An elder came in and said that Egungun was a strange Egungun. He did not belong to Egungun Imewuro. We don't want to see him until he takes off his dress. We want to know that he belongs to Imewuro, because during the rally you won't see any people using any *juju*, or carrying any knife in their pocket. That is a rule. You must not bring any *juju* in your pocket or anything that can charm anybody. We don't allow it. And that is why during the Annual Rally you won't see them. You only see them in their cloth dancing around to make fun everywhere.

Since the Liberty Congress, they have made this rule. Now the Imewuro Development Council reinforces it. You saw the headmaster and that police officer. They just perform for the interest of the Annual Rally. It will be next year's Annual Rally before you will see them again. Oloko is going to do Egungun again at next year's Annual Rally. You won't see him at the Egungun festival proper. But the Egungun Ẹlẹru, you will see them. This Alagogo, you will see them. But all those small, small Egungun you saw on that day, you won't see them]in the annual Egungun festival[because if there is trouble it won't be very easy for their parents. That Egungun Rally is for funning. If anything happened, the parent would take the child and go home.

If I am in town, I won't go to see the Egungun during the festival. If I go to see them, I will stand far, far from them because of their *juju*. Many people are running away from them. (Rennaiye #86.59)

One of the other things the Rally does is to give those citizens living and working in other towns a venue for performing family traditions that they otherwise would not have done because of their physical absence and lack of commitment to traditional worship. But the Development Council takes the teeth out of Egungun when it bans harmful medicines and "word fights," verbal duels in the form of improvised poetry called *ijala*. Rennaiye distinguished the "funning" of the Rally's Egungun with what is considered harmful wordplay, when Egungun curse each other somewhat as Agẹmọ priests do. Apart from this, the Council members performed other elements of traditional festivals, including all the sacrifices and the spectacle.

There was some overlap between those who performed in the Rally and those involved in the annual Egungun festival. At one level, the so-called elite of the town have in some sense appropriated Egungun for their own use. At the same time, all the Rally's Egungun have inherited the authority to perform within their lineages. In this sense, then, they have not appropriated it, but have merely incorporated what they see as theirs by birthright. Meanwhile, the two kinds of Egungun coexist in the same segment of one small community. Going beyond their ancestral city identity with Ijẹbu-Igbo, where their Egungun reportedly originated, they have now differentiated themselves still further in their performance practices.

Ọṣitọla, who is a close friend of Rennaiye, attended the Annual Rally. His own view of what was going on is instructive. He believes that rituals should be performed in accordance with the traditional calendar, which is calibrated on the phases of the moon. But when I asked him specifically about how he viewed the Annual Rally, he classified the sacrifices as *etutu* (ritual) and the football match as *ayẹyẹ* (celebration). The sacrifices were ritual, he argued, because "if they are ignorant]of the traditional calendar[, it is pardonable" (Ọṣitọla #86.66). At the same time, he did not agree that the performances in celebration of a king's twenty-fifth anniversary were rituals, *even if* the parties concerned made sacrifices. The reason: anniversary celebrations were introduced by the British.

In rapidly changing circumstances such as those that set the improvement union movement into action, and which in turn led to the invention of the Imewuro Annual Rally, people had to determine for themselves how to apply old rules under new conditions. For example, it is a rule that Jigbo and Egungun must never meet face to face, so the organizers of the Rally scheduled them on separate days during the Rally. Normally Jigbo and Egungun are performed at completely different times of year. The organizers of the Rally upheld the rule, allocating to each a separate day, but changed the practice by placing them back to back within the same period. Deprived of their magical medicines, organized outside the ritual calendar along with disparate other traditions, and confined to only one day, the Egungun performances at the Rally differed from those performed during the annual Egungun festival. New versions of "the practice" thus emerged as participants seized the moment to alter their current situations. And indeed they invented new rules to attempt to control those situations. The Development Council's "rule" banning harmful medicine and verbal duels is one clear example.

Throughout the previous chapters, I tried to indicate the various ways performers "play" ritual, constructing identities, transforming consciousness—their own and others—through spontaneous interruptions and interventions in ritual, competitively pulling and tugging it to shape performance to suit their immediate interests and needs. In this chapter, I showed how a sector of a typically heterogenous Yoruba community transformed ritual altogether, recombining elements from diverse other rituals into new syntheses, reshuffling segments, reinventing it. The organizers of the Imewuro Annual Rally did all of this. In the last chapter I turn to focus specifically on gender play in ritual performance, something that has been integral to all the rituals I have discussed thus far.

10. Gender Play

The issues of sex and gender are deeply embedded in all of the rituals I have considered thus far. In funerals, in Ifa divination rituals, and in the various types of spectacles, including masking, men have formally dominated. It is they who have taken the key roles in organizing and directing the ritual performances treated here. Indeed, men are the organizers of most large public displays. Furthermore, in funerals when men manifest the deceased's spirit voice, or when diviners initiate novices inside Odu's sacred bush (*igbodu*) during Itẹfa, or when Agẹmọ priests pilgrimage on public roads or encamp in Agẹmọ groves—in all these cases women are excluded, and at times even confined. Women organize spectacles too, but they tend to be more localized within individual compounds and do not attract men like men's spectacles seem to attract women. By the same token, there are more restrictions placed on women in performances organized by men than there seem to be on men in women's performances. Why?

I have pursued this question with male ritual specialists in Ẹgbado, Ọhọri, and Ijẹbu Yoruba areas. They invariably have told me that women are much more secretive and exclusive than men are. Women, however, do not seem to be as preoccupied with the idea of secrecy as are men, and in a curious way this makes women appear all the more secretive. I have sensed this attitude strongly on occasion when I would deny that women are secretive. And yet to agree that women are secretive is, ironically, to demystify and trivialize the idea. Men believe women's animating spirits (*ẹmi*) leave their bodies and transform into birds or animals. When priestesses are possessed by their deities and go into trance, for example, their spirits are temporarily displaced. Men say these displaced spirits transform into birds and use this opportunity to gather and hold secret meetings in the treetops.

These beliefs and practices have important implications for understanding the power relationships of men and women in Yoruba society. As Gayle Rubin has argued (1975:178), divisions of roles by sex are in effect taboos that divide sex into two mutually exclusive categories that exacerbate biological differences and thereby create gender, which is a socially imposed construction. Sex role divisions are as highly formalized and exclusive in the Yoruba practice of everyday life as they are in ritual. The media artists work in, for example, are divided by sex. Thus women work in clay, while men specialize in wood, metal, and beads. Gender-specific rules dictate the use of media, but there are no comparable rules dictating representations, so that, theoretically, women can choose to represent any role they wish. Even so, women as artists tend to focus on images of mothers and priestesses; men, on the other hand, represent a much greater range of subject matter.

The reason most often given for such divisions of labor involve perceived differences in the natures of men and women. It is considered more fitting for men to work in hard materials and for women to use soft ones. By extension, men work with iron tools that require direct, forceful action—striking, slashing, hammering, or even "beating," as in the process of palm-nut divination. Women, on the other hand, work directly on their material—clay—firmly molding and shaping it with more indirect gestures.

Then again, there are always exceptions. Adefowora Ọnabanjọ, an elderly woman artist living in the Ijẹbu town of Imodi, carves twin figures. The granddaughter of a carver, she made figures for Ọṣitọla's parents in the early 1940s. Only one among the many, she nevertheless contravened normal practice; she had the power to "act otherwise" (Giddens 1986:14). Yoruba women on horseback cross-dressed as men during the Islamic 'Id al-Kabir festival, as I understand they do elsewhere in Africa. A female chief riding in Ijẹbu-Ode, 1986, settled way back in her saddle, moving her rib cage side to side like a mother hen nestling her eggs, swaying her shoulders and waving a fly whisk over her head with large sweeps of the arm. Such examples may be rare in the whole scheme of things, but what seems most important is that the rules are susceptible to negotiation. I am reminded of the Yoruba adage "concede to each person her or his own character."

The formalization of sex roles lends itself easily to deconstruction, not only by ethnographers, but by the performers themselves. In this way, performers use the structure of ritual to reflect on gender and sex role divisions. This is what Iya Ṣango in effect accomplished in aggressively commandeering an Apidan performance ordinarily dominated by men, inserting herself into the action, turning their show into her own, transforming caricatures of undesirables into ironic objects of her own desire (chapter 6).

The rules, such as they are, relate directly to Yoruba concepts of power in the construction of gender. In the Imori ritual performed to determine the nature of a child's inner head (chapter 4), the husband brought a bush rat to represent the energetic, agile action of males, according to Ọṣitọla, while the wife brought a mudfish, alluding to the coolness and easiness ordinarily associated with females. These items then come to stand for each side of the family broadly, composed of both men and women. Culling relevant material on gender from earlier chapters, I have analyzed the relative positions of men and women in both male and female dominated performance and examine the ways in which each constructs gender in those contexts, adding a further dimension to issues of identity, individuality, play and power, and the multiple discourses of spectacles.

Actors as agents not only shape roles that become models for future performances, but they shape, and reinforce, analogous roles in everyday life. This is particularly true in societies where trained specialists perform rituals that are intimately interwoven into the ongoing fabric of everyday life. Ritual is quite literally and explicitly "actor-mediated." But like the metaphorical actor in the social drama of life, whose perceptions are "shaped by" the structure of the practice, actors in formal performances are equally engaged in shaping perceptions of the world in their practice of the structure (Sahlins 1976). I have argued, "practice" from a Yoruba perspective is by definition play. It is improvisational. Rituals operate not merely as models *of* and *for* society that somehow stand timelessly alongside "real" life. Rather, they construct what reality is and how it is experienced and understood.

As a body of data, Yoruba representations of gender can be analyzed in terms of what Said (1978:20) calls "strategic location" and "strategic formation." Strategic location is the artist's own position in her/his creation in relation to the image of gender he/she is creating. Said gets at this essentially through an analysis of style, images, themes, and motifs. The relationship between various representations, and the way in which groups of representations "acquire mass, density, and referential power among themselves" and in the larger society, constitute a strategic formation.

What attracts me to Said's methodology is that, unlike the Orientalists, Yoruba re-presenters of gender differentiate themselves by the very constructs they are representing. Or, stated simply, Yoruba artists and performers are representing primarily their own culture and sometimes foreigners, although gender is an aspect of identity and is fundamentally about selves and others—man/woman, male/female—inclusivity and exclusivity, depending on one's orientation. Artists and performers alike represent their own gender as well as the opposite.

Most of the binary oppositions invoked in literature on gender, like Said's orient/occident, are Western asymmetrical constructs that have a strong political grounding.[1] They say perhaps more about how the West thinks than they do about any non-Western reality. To assume that power always resides in the male side of the equation by applying an asymmetrical model to the analysis not only biases the results, but creates the impression that women universally are in a rather hopeless position of eternal subordination. In order to get beyond what Karen Sacks (1982) labeled a social Darwinist perspective on gender,[2] it is necessary to address the following questions: 1) Is the construction of gender in Yoruba art and performance always in fact asymmetrical? 2) And, if it turns out that it is, does the "power" always reside in the male half of that structure?[3] 3) How are these relationships represented in art and performance as models for future roles and action?[4]

STRATEGIC LOCATIONS/STRATEGIC FORMATIONS

For the most part, Yoruba art depicts ritual roles of men and women so that there is a thematic consistency between the two forms of representation. Each derives meaning in relation to the other in time and space. The dominant themes of maleness depicted in sculpture are hunter/warrior, herbalist/diviner, drummer, king, bush animal, and woman's partner. In contrast, females are typically shown as mother, priestess, bird, and man's partner. The depiction of motherhood, I will argue, has ritual significance even though it is not often a ritual role *per se*.

Allusions to motherhood in ritual construct women as nurturers of the deities and the community broadly. In their roles as mothers, women are usually depicted in sculpture either breast-feeding or carrying a child on their backs, the traditional method of portage (fig. 10.1). Ọṣitọla invoked this image explicitly through incantations during Itẹfa ritual as a woman danced with a calabash containing the male initiate's divination palm nuts (chapter 5). In this way, diviners appealed to women for their support on behalf of male initiates.

In sculpture, the role of priestess is often combined with motherhood, a reality of everyday life. Thus, a woman in priest's regalia is often—though not always—shown breast-feeding or carrying a baby on her back. An extension of this idea is the image of a woman offering her breasts, that is, giving of herself to nurture another. This image speaks of the mother/child bond, the pact between them that is invoked during Itẹfa rituals. The physical bond implies spiritual support. The image of woman as gift giver—usually kneeling or sitting holding a bowl—is a further development of the idea of sacrifice, giving freely of oneself to nurture another. The analogous male act of nurturing is the blood sacrifice, which involves a death. Additionally, the images of man as bush animal, as Gorilla or Patas Monkey, and woman as Bird among other things hint at another dimension of performance—the power of transformation.

In paired brass objects known as "the-owners-of-the-house" (*onile*) and smaller ones known as *ẹdan*—both emblems of the Oṣugbo society (chapter 3)—males and females are presented as equals (fig. 10.2). A chain at the top often links the castings together and evokes the importance of the bond between males and females, both within the judiciary and in the larger society. As the custodian of a pair of these figures, Ọṣitọla commented, "they have joined them together to make one couple. It's for oneness. It's for [the] oneness of Oṣugbo [the judiciary]." Both types of objects are prepared with "medicine." The smaller ones are portable; the larger figures reportedly are cast at the founding of a town and are enshrined permanently. Except for certain priests, nobody should see them once they have been installed inside the inner sanctum in the enclosed meeting house (*iledii*).[5]

Myth relates how the paired images were originally human beings, progenitors who established communities and governments. Whenever communities are founded, the elders either migrate with the paired figures to their new site or, in some cases, they commission a brasscaster to create them anew. All those concerned gather before the figures to swear an oath (*ibura*) of truthfulness and secrecy. As Ọṣitọla explained, "it has the most aṣẹ [generative power] because it is the thing that combines all of them together. [. . .] It is a symbol of unity."

The male and female figures reflect the makeup of the traditional judiciary, which includes both men and women, although males are in the majority. The head female title, Iya Abiye, senior among the Erelus, is in many cases a relative of the king. The paired brass figures signify the union of men and women, the founding of a community, which represents their progeny, and the oaths of truth and secrecy sworn by the members of the town's judiciary in the witnessing presence of earth, the abode of spirits and the ancestors.

The smaller brass staffs modeled on the larger figures have a variety of other important functions. Being portable, they are carried publicly as insignia of membership and as messages. S. O. Biobaku (1956:259–260) has noted that an appointed male messenger holds the staves in his two hands and strikes them on his forehead and chest before a summoned individual. The recipient in turn holds the staves, strikes them on his or her own forehead and chest to acknowledge the society's authority. Reportedly, to receive the male of the pair signifies "wrath," while receiving the female conveys "friendly greetings."[6] A titled elder, or his surrogate, may also place the staffs across the path or at the entrance of disputed farm land to prevent either party from entering while the case is under discussion. Violation of this sanction may bring a stiff fine or supernatural retribution (Lloyd 1962:20). In other civil or criminal matters, the traditional judiciary can impose a form of house arrest, or injunction, by placing the staves across the compound entrance of the accused; the person cannot leave, nor supporters enter, without permission from the judiciary.

The paired representations of males and females—cast in brass by men—portray a symmetrical power relationship. One figure mirrors the other except in the depiction of breasts and genitalia, in which they are sexually differentiated. In a few instances the two are hermaphroditic. In both cases, the figures command equal visual attention, offsetting and balancing each other. Neither dominates visually. In performance, equality is expressed in the sequentially ordered solo dances of women and men.

The representation of symmetrical power relationships in Eṣu staffs for the trickster deity, also carved by men, frequently draw visual analogies between the male's medicine gourds and the female's breasts, both in their shape and in their positioning in relation to the body (fig. 10.3). Such symmetry is particularly revealing when compared with Yoruba parodies of European couples, such as in the Egungun skit described in chapter 1 in which the European female laid her head on the shoulder of her male counterpart as he chucked her under the chin and clutched the sides of her neck with his hands, pulling her forward to kiss her on the lips (see fig. 1.1). For Yoruba, the public display of affection was the essence of the joke. The dominant/submissive relationship was encoded. The frozen wooden face mask each wore made kissing itself an absurdity, calling attention to the parodic intent.

In ritual, men portray spirits in masks, such as Egungun, Agẹmọ, and Jigbo, that represent both males and females. In contrast, women as priests and mediums of the deities portray female as well as male deities, often carrying carved weapons, or staffs, as insignia of office while dancing in states of possession trance (M. Drewal 1989). Sometimes women possessed by the divine mediator

Eşu become tricksters wearing a carved wooden penis and testicles (fig. 10.4); at a Gelede festival in Ketu, 1971, one with a deadpan face went up to other women seductively pulling her wrapper back to reveal her equipment. Their renditions turn the male organ into a toy, a plaything for comic display.

In addition to these roles, there is also some cross-dressing by both men and women during public festivals (figs. 7.3, 10.5). The Agemo priest Adie is supposed to wear his hair plaited in female style throughout his life (fig. 7.2). Not only that, each time I saw him on various festival occasions, he always had a different hairdo that had been wrapped or plaited by his wives. During the annual festival, only Adie and Ewujagbori reportedly entered the inner shrine of Agemo, and they did so dressed as women. Unlike the transvestites with padded breasts and buttocks who stormed into the Agemo grove as the women cheered, these Agemo priests were not engaged in comic parody.

Similarly, I have seen women dance what are technically classified as men's dances (ijo ako). During Egungun's day at the Imewuro Annual Rally (chapter 9), a woman suddenly started dancing with large, forceful gestures that included high kicking and rapid spinning. As soon as she began, a man rushed forth and gave her his own outer garment to wear. As another male observer explained to me later, he gave her his garment "to make the dance look fine." The large, strong gestures characteristic of male dancing were thought to look best aesthetically in a large, loose-fitting, male-style garment. In the same vein, women at the Ileya festival parades dressed in their fathers' garments, supposedly to be more physically active in dashing about.

As a medium of the tough, hot, male warrior deity, Iya Şango literally becomes male on certain ritual occasions through possession trance. She can also turn Şango himself into a comic lecher by enacting fucking with other men. Is she a woman constructing men as her objects as if she were male, or is she a man playing to other men as if they were women? Iya Şango "came to the world" through Şango, rather than from her mother's or father's side of the family, according to her "Knowing the Head" ritual. Not insignificantly, her father was a Şango drummer; her mother a dancer. She thus grew up performing the songs and dances in the Şango tradition, although she was not formally initiated as a priest until the mid-1960s (Iya Şango #75.6b). Her identification with Şango guides and licenses her behavior. Most people would call this her destiny.[7] Although interpretations of divination parables are intended to provide people models for further reflection and behavior, ultimately what they do is out of the diviner's hands, a matter left to the parents and child.

According to Yoruba belief, the concentration of vital force in women, their aşe, their power to bring things into existence, to make things happen, creates extraordinary potential that can manifest itself in both positive and negative ways. Phrases such as "one with two faces" (oloju meji), "one with two bodies" (abara meji), and "one of two colors" (alawo meji) aptly express this duality and allude to their alleged powers of transformation. The Yoruba word for these special powers and a woman possessing them is aje, which has been translated in the literature as "witchcraft" or "witch." All elderly women are aje, as are priest-

esses of the deities, wealthy marketwomen, and female title-holders in prestigious organizations. Collectively, such women are affectionately called "our
mothers" (awọn iya wa). The positions they have attained, it is felt, are evidence
of their power. One day in the traditional Yoruba week is devoted to them.[8] It
was on this day that I first met Ọṣitọla; he took that to be significant. From then
on, he always reserved Our Mothers' day for our discussions, never budging from
that schedule the entire time we worked together, except when my time grew
short.

Ọṣitọla told me Ifa speaks of three categories of powerful women—referred
to euphemistically as ẹlẹyẹ, "owners of birds," to allude to their powers of transformation—white, red, and black (ẹlẹyẹ funfun, pupa, ati dudu) (Ọṣitọla
#82.46). White ẹlẹyẹ are beneficial; they bring prosperity and the good things in
life. Red ẹlẹyẹ, on the other hand, bring suffering (ipọnju), while black ẹlẹyẹ
cause death. It is the nature of human action, rather than the person, that is
color-classified in this way. Therefore a powerful woman may bring prosperity on
one occasion, but suffering or death on another.

Unlike the predominantly negative connotations of the English word
"witch," elderly women and female priests are not necessarily either antisocial or
the personification of evil. Rather, they form an important segment of the population in any town and are given respect, affection, and deference. Because of
their special power, they are thought to have greater access to Yoruba deities.
They occupy a position subordinate to the supreme deity, Olodumare, who is
genderless, and to Ọrunmila, the deity of divination, but equal, or even superior,
to the deities. In their roles as mediums, they are thought to exert a certain
amount of control over the deities.

When angered, the mothers operate surreptitiously in seeking and destroying
their victims. Their attacks are believed to result in stillbirth and conditions
such as elephantiasis, impotency, infertility, and false pregnancies that "turn to
water," or in debilitating diseases that destroy slowly and silently with no visible
signs. In contrast to destructive images of males that express overt aggression in
representations of radical male sexuality and themes of war and hunting, female
images of the transformed bird stress secrecy, elusiveness, and covertness.

Genitalia become metaphors for the two kinds of power. As the invocations
below suggest, males and females are both portrayed as sexual beings and both
can be intensely creative or destructive.

> Honor, honor, honor today, honor to the deities
> Honor to Ogun, my husband
> Ogun the brave one in firing, in firing
> Ogun killed his wife in the bathroom
> Ogun killed the swordsmen
> He destroyed them with one blow
> Ogun, I asked you to chase them, not to lick their bones
> Honor to the one whose penis stood up to father a child in the room
> He made his penis lengthen to father a child in the house of Ijana

We heard how the penis struck those in the market
Ogun, the one who saw the king's mother and did not cover his penis.
[. . .]
Honor, ooooo, honor today, ooooo
I honor you today
Old bird did not warm herself in the fire
Sick bird did not warm herself in the sun
Something secret was buried in the mother's house
A secret pact with a wizard
Honor, honor today, ooooo
Honor to my mother
Mother whose vagina causes fear to all
Mother whose pubic hair bundles up in knots
Mother who set a trap, set a trap
Mother who has meat at home in lumps
(recorded in Emado Quarter, Ayetoro, 1971).

Yoruba concepts of female and male power to a large extent derive from shared cultural values in the interpretion of biological factors, expressed as binary opposites.

As indicated in the invocations above, anatomical features are metaphors for spiritual power. The male is portrayed as overtly aggressive; he destroys with one blow. His penis is at once destructive and creative, a weapon and a procreative tool. Because male power is overt and expressed physically, men are at the peak of their power in their forties. In contrast, women are thought to become even more powerful after menopause, when menstrual blood ceases to flow.[9]

According to Ọṣitọla (#82.107),

you see, men and women, they all came to the world at the same time.
There has never been a time when we have men and we don't have women.
And there has never been a time when we have women and we don't have
men. So everybody comes to play his role successfully. If you leave men,
then the role of the women cannot be played successfully. If you leave
women, then the role of the men cannot be played successfully. That's how
they have been mixing every issue, and everyone has his own secrets, too.
Men have the secret and women have the secret, just to trouble each other,
just to add more spice to the world.

By oral tradition, it was the wife of the deity of divination who taught her husband how to perform Itẹfa ritual (chapter 5). Through her he fathered sixteen children, that is, the sixteen major sets of divination texts. Thus "she is the most significant among Ọrunmila's wives. Ọrunmila has no power besides her. She is the backbone for Ọrunmila in all his endeavors."[10]

The female deity Odu is represented in Itẹfa rituals by a closed calabash placed inside a larger container (fig. 5.3). Always carried by a woman, I am told—this container is a primary symbol of female power; in Itẹfa ritual this was represented both literally and metaphorically. As I have said, both the male and his mother, or wife, performed most of the ritual acts together up until the time the initiate entered the restricted sacred grove to learn the divination texts that brought him into the world. Couples also participated in a similar fashion after leaving the grove on the third, seventh, and fourteenth days, often exchanging positions in relation to each other as dancer/spectator or diviner/client.

Women are prohibited from entering Odu's grove, and there is a well-known story that Odu made Ọrunmila promise to keep Odu away from other women, for she is thought to be harsh and vindictive. Not only that, but women cannot be initiated through Itẹfa rituals. Nor can they participate in the rituals of rebirth that take place on the inside, even though they can interpret Ifa and, in other contexts, they can divine. When I asked diviners how it was possible for men to give birth to children without women, they quickly pointed out to me that Odu is a woman, and it is her power they were using inside the grove.

Whenever women were physically excluded from ritual, men tended to appropriate female gender to construct representations of them. In Agẹmọ, for example, it was only two male transvestite priests who were allowed to enter the main shrine in the Imọsan grove. Curiously, the majority of the Agẹmọ priests were also excluded from this shrine. Women were present symbolically in this way, if not physically. That is, female gender was present even when women were not. And indeed men believe that powerful women always gain access to men's secrets in spite of it all. Women's spirits (ẹmi) are believed capable of going where their bodies fear to tread at risk of being discovered and punished.

One of the underlying purposes of Itẹfa was to prepare the male initiate's personal set of divination palm nuts, which would be used initially to divine the texts that "brought him to the world" and then throughout his life whenever he should consult a diviner. This personal set of divination palm nuts represents the male client's rebirth, his personal destiny, and, by extension, the deity of divination.

During the *iyi ifa* ritual segment when a woman danced holding the palm nuts in a calabash, the diviners invoked the spiritual support of women through a series of songs and incantations. To demonstrate respect for women broadly, one of the diviners prostrated himself before the dancer. Throughout the processes of Itẹfa, either the mother or the wife, as the case may be, provided all the various containers to hold the palm nuts. There was a contiguity between the palm nuts in the calabash and the unborn child in his mother's womb. The ritual privileged the association of the palm nuts with men and their destinies.

THE CONTAINER AND THE CONTAINED

The symbolic relationship of the male initiate's palm nuts to their containers sets up a structural relationship of woman as container, man as contained. This construction precludes any identification of women with the palm nuts other than as container. Generally speaking, ritual containers in Yorubaland are a primary symbol for female power. The notion of woman as container is based on cultural interpretations of biological factors, for women possess the secret knowledge of life itself.

In contrast to the types of containers that hold a man's or boy's personal set of palm nuts, those containers used by diviners on behalf of their clients report- edly must live in a carved wooden container known as *agẹrẹ* in order to be proper. According to a legend told to me by Ọṣitọla, Agẹrẹ was once upon a time another one of the divination deity's wives, who hid her husband inside her stomach to save him. She was so industrious that he always worked with her. Thus, the *agẹrẹ* (a carved wooden caryatid container that holds the palm nuts) is female wood and serves two purposes: it works very hard (i.e., it is prepared with medicines), and it contains the divination deity (i.e., the sacred palm nuts), just as the deity's wife of the same name had done according to the story. For this reason, images carved on *agẹrẹ*, according to Ọṣitọla, should be female, although sculptors have flexibility in what they choose to carve, often depicting men on horseback, or other animals, so that there is a discontinuity of meaning. When an *agẹrẹ* begins to deteriorate, it should be buried in the sacred grove like the other containers, and like the birth caul, because "it is a delicate thing which should not be burned, [be] used as a toy, or otherwise."

Both males and females perform "Stepping into the World" and "Knowing the Head" rituals (chapter 4). After that, males and females go their separate ways, ritually speaking. According to Ọṣitọla, in the past girls performed a ritual called "Tying the Bracelet" (Isodẹ) in which they were "married" to a diviner's palm nuts. This ritual supposedly put the girl under the protection of the diviner until her actual marriage, when the diviner performed "Breaking the Bracelet," or bond (Itudẹ). A woman is then "married" to her new husband's palm nuts, but not until Ifa has agreed that their destinies, or their inner heads, are compat- ible. Ever after, whatever the palm nuts say as a result of the divination process applies equally to both of them.[11]

What is particularly interesting to me is that, today, Isodẹ and Itudẹ are performed rarely, if ever. I have yet to witness or even hear of one. Itẹfa rituals, on the other hand, are quite common both for youngsters and adults. Men who have performed Itẹfa rituals often display on their walls photographs of them- selves all in white after just leaving Odu's grove. Perhaps women are somehow not as susceptible to shattered, scattered lives as men are. Woman's role as mother is rather clear-cut, although it does not prohibit her from other activities such as trading. Or, perhaps it is that there are other institutionalized ways for women to deal with shattered lives, for example, by becoming priests of deities. I met a priest of Are in Ilaro in 1975 who explained that she was initiated after the birth of her first child, when she was drawn inexplicably to Are's shrine in another town. Before then, she had been sitting for days on end in silence, and she had no interest in feeding or caring for her baby. From her description, it sounded as though she might have been experiencing postpartum depression. Her initiation would have reoriented her, providing a model for action in some ways similar to Itẹfa.

The spiritual powers attributed to women make them the primary candidates for priesthoods in Yoruba society. The only categories of women eligible to carry the concealed shrine of Odu on their heads are diviners' wives and priestesses. The fundamental role of a Yoruba priest is that of a medium between the world and the spirit realm. As a medium, the priest becomes possessed by her deity. She thus becomes that deity's physical representation in the world. To acquire such a spiritual role, women go through elaborate initiations during which the deity is installed on their heads. During this period, devotees are prepared for spirit mediumship. Like the Itẹfa initiates, they metaphorically die and are re-born. Their clothes are taken away, their heads are shaved, and they are se-cluded in a dark shrine where they must remain quiet and still for some weeks. During this time, the head is bathed and painted regularly in an amalgam of leaves, animal blood, and pulverized minerals, which signify the vital force of the deity (fig. 10.6) (Verger 1954:324 and 1969:65 note 2). It is also rubbed into incisions made in the shaven head. This is thought to fix the power of the deity in the head of the devotee and to stimulate possession trance. Like their roles as nurturers, women then become the caretakers and nurturers of the gods. Indeed, in these initiations, in contrast to Itẹfa, women retain control of the rebirth.

The initiate is now known as *adoṣu*, one who has received, in her head, the ball of medicine, or *oṣu*, that signifies the deity. Later, special hairdos are often worn by the newly initiated to identify them with their particular god and to show that this is a head endowed with power (fig. 10.7). Iya Ṣango's hair was shaven clean to the crown and then braided from that point back. Her receding hairline had the visual effect of expanding her forehead, thereby creating the illusion of swelling, a reference to the state of possession trance in which the head is said to swell or expand (*wu*). Finally, the initiated receives a special new name, which suggests the deity's hold or claim on the initiate, such as Ọdakusin, "The-one-who-fainted-while-worshiping," implying that the devotee bearing this name fell into trance, signaling the deity's strong influence.

With the deity's power inserted into the head of the priest during rites of initiation, she becomes the deity's medium, his or her conduit into the world. Even in cases where Yoruba men become possession priests, they are referred to as the "wives" of the deity and often dress in female garb and hairstyles. The male Ṣango priests from the town of Ẹdẹ plaited their hair in two different female styles (fig. 10.8)—the three priests on the left wore the *ṣuku* style, which refers to the round basket in which marketwomen carry their wares on their heads, and the two on the right had the traditional Yoruba bridal hairstyle known as *agogo*.[12]

Just as women receive the spirit of the gods in possession trance, they at the same time master that spirit through training and turn its power to their own advantage. This is analogous to the power relationship between mother and child. The mother sustains the child, who in turn gives the mother power and support throughout the rest of her life. Mothers have influence with their chil-dren in a way that is not possible for fathers in the polygamous household. By the same token, possession priests are perceived to have influence on their deities. They are providers, and they are receptive. They are indeed receptacles, or containers for the deity. This is conveyed in ritual sculpture depicting kneeling females supporting bowls on their heads, which serve to contain a representation of the deity's power. During the 1971 Ṣango festival in Ila Ọrangun, an Igbomina Yoruba town, Ṣango priests sacrificed a cock, pouring its blood over a neolithic thundercelt placed inside the bowl depicted on top of the kneeling female's head (fig. 10.9). On one level, head loading reflects actual behavior. But in this case it also alluded to the idea of receptivity, that priests' heads contain the power of the deity. I believe it is not by chance that these caryatids almost without exception depict women.

Through dance, spiritual forces materialize in the phenomenal world. The god is said to mount the devotee and, for a time, that devotee becomes the god. Temporarily, then, the animating spirit of the deity (ẹmi oriṣa) displaces the ẹmi of the individual being mounted. Whatever the priest does from the moment she enters the trance state is thought to represent the deity's own actions. Possession trance states are most often expressed through the medium of dance.

Spirit mediumship is the most significant role of a priest. The uniting of devotee and deity into one image often causes some confusion for researchers who try to establish the identity of figures represented in Yoruba sculpture. Sculpture represents the union of the priest and deity by depicting the former with accoutrements associated with the latter. It is through dance, however, that the priest brings the active deity into the phenomenal world for other devotees. To become possessed by one's deity is the primary role of the medium.

Chanting and drumming performed prior to the onset of possession trance invoke the deity, bringing him or her into contact with the priests. In a festival for the deity of smallpox and contagious diseases known as Omolu, which took place in the Ẹgbado town of Igbogila in 1978, a medium of Ogun, the god of war and iron, gazed downward; her dance movements diminished (see M. Drewal 1989). There was a transformation of her attitude: from outgoing and playful to concentrated, serious, and inwardly focused. As if bound to the spot, she stopped moving her feet; her upper torso veered to the side; her head dropped; and her left knee quivered, causing the entire body to tremble. A priest in this state is called the "horse of the god" (ẹṣin oriṣa). Attendants rushed to straighten the clothes of those becoming possessed, binding their waists and breasts tightly in much the same way a rider saddles a horse, pulling the straps tightly to secure the saddle in place, for the deity "mounts" (gun) and rides the medium. The Ogun medium became fully transformed into the deity, repeatedly licking her lips in an agitated fashion. Her upper torso dropped forward, her head fell back, and her eyes rolled upward into the sockets. Attendants quickly closed the eyelids and brought the head forward.

Finally Ogun signaled his presence when the medium emitted a deep guttural yell. Leading with the whole left side of her body, the possessed medium took giant steps to make her way to the gathered crowd. Now the deity, he placed his hands on his hips and lifted his knees and feet, extending each one in turn forward as he walked in a stylized fashion. After greeting the entire assemblage with "Ẹ ku o!," Ogun sang, danced, and prayed, all the while directing the drummers.

In these kinds of performances, spectators give money to the deity and the drummers. The amount in 1978 ranged from several cents to one dollar with an average of about twenty cents. By "spending money" (*nina'wo*) for the deity, spectators receive his special recognition and blessing. In a sense they invest in his dynamic power and in return receive its benefit. In dance, possessed mediums express particular deities' powers in the dynamic qualities of movement (M. Drewal 1989). *What* a medium does in the dance is not as crucial as *how* she does it. Meanwhile the head remains calm in contrast to an active body.

When Iya Ṣango went into trance in 1975, she performed large, angular, asymmetrical, forceful gestures that evoked Ṣango's stormy manner (fig. 10.10). A small dance staff (*oṣe*) carried in her hand depicting paired thundercelts added its own statement to the intensity of her actions. She also danced with knees flexed and torso pitched forward from the hips. Iya Ṣango commented that hers was "a dance performed *kikan kikan* with forcefulness" (*ijo kikan kikan to l'agbara*) (Taiwo #75.6b). The word *kikan* is idiophonic and simulates orally the effort quality of Ṣango's dance, that is, one in which a dominant motif is raising (*ki*) and then percussively dropping (*kan*) the shoulders, or the torso, repetitively, i.e., *kikan kikan*. *Ki* is quick, sharp, and high (or up) in tone; *kan* is forceful, full, and heavy, dropping in tone in a manner analogous to the way Iya Ṣango plunged her body forward in her dance, thrusting her dance staff of paired thundercelts, fan, and medicine horn toward the earth.

According to Rowland Abiọdun, *kikan* connotes a forceful release of energy as if under pressure (personal communication, 1981). When Iya Ṣango danced, she evoked this in her speed and thrust, playing on the dynamics of lightning and thunder—in that order—that is associated with Ṣango. Indeed, the force of lightning and thunder is felt in its actual dynamic qualities, qualities which in turn reflect the nature of his own power as Iya Ṣango expressed it in dance. When Ṣango left Iya Ṣango's head, he withdrew suddenly. Her body tensed up, and an attendant ran to grab her, holding her to prevent her falling.

Once a deity leaves the head, attendants take measures to clear the medium's head and return her to normalcy either by pouring gin over the head and rubbing it in, or by blowing into the ears and onto the top of the head. Attendants also press their hands on the base of the medium's neck or press their foreheads to the medium's forehead and tap the back of her head. Sometimes they stretch her arms up and place them on her knees and then pull her legs out straight and forward by the big toes—all the while calling the medium's name. The medium finally comes to, as if having just awakened from a deep sleep, and sits silently gazing into space.

Whereas it is primarily women who nurture the gods, men in Yoruba society mask. Yoruba construct performance roles like they construct gender, that is, based on the anatomical and biological features involved specifically in procreation. This is consistent with the stress in Yoruba society on progeny and the perpetuation of the lineage through the reincarnation of the souls of forebears.

In masking, men cover and conceal their exteriors. But when women are "mounted" by a deity in possession trance, the spirit of that deity enters her "inner head," her interior.

Men, in becoming possession priests, are therefore like women in their relationship to the deity; they are receptacles. Crossing gender boundaries, male priests cross-dress as women, and priestesses possessed by male deities select out forceful, direct dynamic movement qualities ordinarily associated with men.

Here again the sexual metaphor comes into play. The male is contained during intercourse, just as he is by the spirit's cloth in masking and just as his palm nuts are by the calabash or bowl. In contrast, the female contains during intercourse and pregnancy, just as she does the spirit of the deity at the onset of possession trance and just as the container holds the male initiate's palm nuts. What is represented in both cases is the union of spirit and devotee, in each instance by the corresponding metaphor that plays on the binary oppositions of inside/outside.

The metaphoric contiguity between the conditions of pregnancy and possession trance was revealed most clearly in the personal history of a little girl named Tinusin, literally "From the Inside Worshiping." According to the child's grandmother, the mother went into labor and gave birth to her child while in a state of possession trance. The child thus came to the world "worshiping," and so at a very early age was initiated as a priestess of her mother's deity. Only three years old in 1978 when I met her, she was already a confident dancer, and I observed her imitating her mother's gestures as if she were entering a trance state.

In a sense, the child in the mother's womb is the ultimate masker. Men play on this idea in Apidan performance, masking as pregnant females, a kind of mask times two (fig. 6.12). The play on the idea of mask as womb and womb as mask is the primary theme in performances of miracle worker masks (figs. 6.7–6.11), whose form and performance allude simultaneously to a pregnant womb that "gives birth" and to the dress of Muslim women in Purdah.

The pregnant woman in a sense becomes a mask, and indeed when a child is born in the birth caul, it is often taken by Yoruba as a sign that he should perform in a mask, if male, or become a member of a masking society, if female. Phenomenologically speaking, to mask is to conceal something. At the basis of the taboo against women wearing masks may be a tacit understanding of what Christopher Crocker (1977:59) calls the contagious power of metonymic conjunction. That is, there is an analogical relationship between a pregnant woman and a full body mask. This metonymic conjunction may explain the prevalence of African myths that attribute the very origins of masking to women (Cole 1985:15). Metaphorically speaking, woman was the original mask.

The same kind of idea may be the basis for excluding women from certain portions of ritual. I have never known a Yoruba women to mask, nor have I ever seen one make a blood sacrifice. And although women menstruate, the phenomenon is associated with conception. The threat of metonymic conjunction would have been even more problematic during the historical period before 1892 when the Agẹmọ, Oro, and Oṣugbo societies reportedly executed criminals and made human sacrifices. It is significant that women were excluded precisely from those portions of ritual that in the past reportedly contained such sacrifices. Not only were they prohibited access, but they protected the illusion that they did not know what was going on. The seriousness of these practices in Yoruba thought, it seems to me, is directly related to the precariousness of human spirits as expressed in rituals of birth (Ikọsẹ w'aye and Imori) and death (Isinku).

Even with the sexual divisions between masking and possession trance, both men and women have institutionalized opportunities to take on the attributes of the opposite gender temporarily, either glorifying it or satirizing it, in either case engaging in a ongoing dialectic on gender. In figure 10.11, a priestess possessed by the hot male warrior deity Ogun, wearing a man's hunting outfit, rears back with hands on her hips as devotees prostrate themselves before her. In contrast, a male priest of the river goddess Ọya displays in his house a photograph of himself dressed as a woman with plaited hair, flanked on either side by his two wives (fig. 10.12).

That Yoruba shift back and forth between gender roles in ritual situations, and are not necessarily construed as either comical or horrendous, is in and of itself significant. It suggests that Yoruba are conscious that gender is a construction dividing sex into two mutually exclusive categories to underscore biological difference. What this does in effect is to channel human behavior that is not biologically determined. Why? By constructing gender to underscore sexual difference, Yoruba place primary value on procreation.

Implicit in funerals and the divination rituals for children was the participants' concern with the continuity of the human spirit from birth and death to reincarnation. This is at the basis of Yoruba ontology and being. Continuity can be accomplished only through progeny, what Yoruba perhaps value most in life. It is from the reference point of the fixed role of woman as childbearer and nurturer that Yoruba construct female gender. This role becomes the dominant representation of women in the visual arts. It suggests the strategic location of male and female artists in relation to the role they are representing, which evokes the mother/child bond even when the child is physically absent, as when women are portrayed holding their breasts or offering containers.

The ontology of the human spirit's journey between the otherworld and earth and the value Yoruba place on progeny also explain why homosexuality as a way of life is absent in Yorubaland. Although homosexual relations are known to exist, it would be inconceivable for Yoruba not to perpetuate the spirits of their forebears. Both men's and women's significance in life is judged by the number of children they bring into the world. To have no children is regarded as a great human tragedy.

SEX AND POWER RELATIONSHIPS

Because of the emphasis placed on progeny, women possess—from a male perspective—the quintessential power, childbearing. For men, the patrilocal residence of women during their childbearing years is a means of establishing and verifying their own paternity. This is reinforced legally by giving the father rights to the children. Even then, women often return to their own family compounds to give birth. Because of the importance of establishing paternity, women during their childbearing years are usually subordinated domestically in the patrilocal compound. The strong bond between mother and child that is sustained throughout life poses an additional threat to husband/wife relations as well as to father/children relations. This bond also gives mothers a significant amount of power with their children that extends more broadly to younger generations. Both Balogun Kuku and Otun Balogun Sotẹ considered their mothers the greatest influences in their lives (chapter 8).

The literature often stresses that the Yoruba family is patrilineal and patrilocal, although reality does not always bear out this assertion. In fact, Yoruba sociologist N. A. Fadipẹ (1970:134), who was trained in the British system, began his discussion of Yoruba descent by stating: "Although the patrilineal form of organization prevails, the Yoruba reckon descent bilaterally." Women inherit property from their parents.[13] When a man dies his property is distributed among his wives and their children; when a woman dies her property is distributed only to her children. It cannot go to the husband or his family. If she has no children, her property goes to the children of her brothers and sisters. Although women own property, they do not often farm. This task would be left to their male children or to hired labor.[14]

In the traditional Yoruba system, children were betrothed by their families at a young age (Lloyd 1963). There was no concept of romantic love. During the betrothal, a young man had certain obligations to his future wife's family. The family of the husband paid a "bride price" to the family of the wife. Part of the money went to the mother to buy her daughter goods and supplies to help her set up her new household. The remainder was distributed equally among the rest of the family members, including females, as a symbolic compensation for their loss. The wife, however, remained a full member of her own lineage.

The bride price in theory also gave the husband rights to the children born to the wife, and sole sexual access. In practice, women have sole rights to a child until it is weaned, and strong allegiances between mother and child often mean that, when children are old enough to choose, they opt to be with the mother. This is the major cause of lineage segmentation (Lloyd 1963:36). As Lloyd notes (1962:281), "the Yoruba always state that their emotional ties with the mother are much stronger than those with the father." This sentiment is expressed in the Yoruba adage "Mother is gold, father is glass" (Iya ni wura, baba ni digi). By middle age, women's domestic roles shift from mother to grandmother. And, if a woman is residing in her husband's compound up until the time her own child bears a child, she may return to the compound of her own parents or, if she is financially able, may build her own house. She is under no obligation to remain in the husband's compound.

Seniority is also a factor, since men normally marry younger women. Even so, I did not get the feeling that Sotẹ's young wife was all that subordinate to him as

I watched them engaged in horseplay in front of the VCR. Each wife in the patrilocal compound has her own room. Wives cook for themselves and for their children, and often take turns cooking for the husband. More senior wives also delegate domestic duties to junior ones. A wife's rank in relation to other wives depends upon how long she has been married. Yoruba women who value the polygamous system argue that it gives them freedom and more time for independent activities because they share domestic responsibilities. The system is also highly competitive, although a husband is ideally supposed to treat each of his wives and her children equally. Whereas a woman shares what she has with her children alone, a man who has multiple wives must share what he has among all his wives and their children equally. This appears to be one of the dominant sources of disputes within households. This theme was expressed in Egungun by the "miracles" representing the husband and his three well-dressed wives who got into a fight.

During a long nursing period—up to three years—a woman's menstruation is suppressed and women practice sexual abstinence (Jelliffe 1953; Caldwell and Caldwell 1977; Adeokun 1983). At such times she is considered ritually pure, perhaps one reason that nursing priestesses are often depicted in Yoruba art. Ọṣitọla's junior brother once told me:

> It is our belief that if you give birth to a child, and you don't breast-feed him or her, in the long run he may not like you, because he doesn't get served from your own breast. In our area here, if you give birth to a child and within the next year you give birth to another, we call you "prostitute" because you never allowed the first child to be well fed. (I. Ọṣitọla #82.28)

The close physical and emotional bond that develops between mother and child during the first three years of a child's life creates an image of woman as soothing, indulgent, and enduring (Abiọdun 1976; in press).

Concepts of female power to a large extent seem to derive from these cultural practices. Thus women are said to possess patience (*suuru*), gentleness (*erọ*), coolness (*itutu*), and endurance (*iroju*). Breast-feeding sets up an unequal power relationship between mother and child. It then becomes a metaphor for spiritual power. Thus during the *iyi ifa* segment of Itẹfa, Ọṣitọla prayed: "You see mother, you are my mother, and we have the belief that through your power you can make all these sacrifices, all these ceremonies we have been doing efficacious. We are begging you because remember the day that you delivered us, and the breast-feeding. Come and help this ceremony be efficacious. Put all your powers into it so that it will come true, by the grace of the songs." The idea is that the mother has an unspoken pact with her child. The metaphor applies equally to adult males.

From a Western perspective, it would be tempting to view Yoruba women as restricted; quite the contrary, they have a great deal of flexibility and independence. Once a woman ceases to give birth, usually around age forty, whether she returns to her own family compound or builds her own house, she becomes even more independent and indeed has significant influence over the men in her household. Furthermore, Yoruba have a very high divorce rate, but there is little or no stigma attached to being divorced. Divorce appears to be a traditional practice, for verses from the oral divination literature speak of man's fear of desertion by his wife or of her seduction by another man (Lloyd 1963:37).

Perhaps most significant of all is that women in Yoruba society are economically independent from their husbands. Trading is their most common profession. Women control the central market; its administrative head holds a position on the king's council of chiefs. In this sphere, there is clear asymmetry, the power residing solely in the female domain, which is public rather than private or domestic.[15] Since a woman is economically independent from her husband, she often provides greater economic support for their children than he does. Farmers wholesale their perishable produce to middlewomen, who turn around and resell it to other marketwoman. In this system, farmers are totally at the mercy of marketwomen, who can manipulate and control commodities and prices either by hoarding or flooding the market with goods.[16]

Husbands are expected to help their wives establish trades by giving them money but, beyond this, husbands and wives borrow money from each other with the expectation of paying it back. If a wife is a food seller, for example, and the husband wants to partake of her wares, he must purchase them from her as he would from anyone else. And if the husband is a farmer, the wife does not necessarily specialize in selling the crop her husband raises. A husband, on the other hand, may enlist his wife's assistance in selling, because it is generally felt that men can be more easily cheated in the bargaining process than women (Sudarkasa 1973:120).

A woman's status therefore derives largely from her own reputation as a trader, or a craftsperson, and from her wealth rather than from her husband's social importance. Trading gives women economic as well as spatial mobility. In 1826, British explorer Hugh Clapperton (1829:21) observed wives of the king of Ọyọ "in every place trading" and "like other women of the common class, carrying large loads on their heads from town to town." Through trading women can acquire greater wealth and higher social statuses than their husbands (Lloyd 1963:39). It is thus possible for him to be a nonentity in the town by comparison.

If a woman is a successful trader, which gives her autonomy, her status within her husband's compound grows stronger in relation. A woman also acquires status in the patrilocal compound by the number of children she brings into the world. If Yoruba women are subordinated within the context of the patrilocal compound during their childbearing years, in the public sphere they are economically independent, dominate the marketing system, and hold important chieftaincy titles, such as Erelu in Oṣugbo, Iya Agan in Egungun, Iyalaṣẹ in Gẹlẹdẹ. This public sphere is reflected in the balanced presentation of male/female relationships in the sculptures that embody the power of Oṣugbo, the traditional Yoruba judiciary. It is also reflected in ancestral Egungun masks that honor women, even though they are performed by men. While women dominate

Yoruba markets, their roles as businesswomen are seldom represented except in the context of Gẹlẹdẹ spectacle, which explicitly celebrates female power (H. Drewal and M. Drewal 1983).

Women also dominate the sphere of the deities, a fact that is evident in Yoruba art. Thus women and men each dominate different spheres at different times in their lives. There is, however, an egalitarian ideal built into the system, and this—accompanied by a great deal of economic independence and mobility and a need on the part of men to establish paternity—results in intense competition for power. But, to a large extent that power is negotiable, depending on the personalities involved. This is what Ọṣitọla really meant when he said, "men have the secret, and women have the secret—just to trouble each other, just to add more spice to the world."

Equally significant is that in ritual there is some amount of cross-dressing by both men and women, and in possession trance there are more literally gender transformations. So even with rigidly structured gender roles, both men and women in Yoruba society have institutionalized opportunities within ritual contexts to cross gender boundaries and to express the traits assigned to the opposite gender. Just as Yoruba construct gender, they also deconstruct it. Iya Ṣango becomes Ṣango himself in possession trance realigning sex and gender. Her representation is not a structural reversal that merely reinforces an asymmetrical system; rather, she achieves a new synthesis. Iya Ṣango partakes of her deity's masculine character even in her daily life. She is never merely not not herself, not not Ṣango. Rather, she is a third term, a trickster shifting positions. It is the nature of her "inner head." Unlike cross-dressing and female or male impersonations in the West, her results are true reversals—temporary gender transformations, opposite and symmetrical.

10.1 Detail of a pot depicting a nursing child holding the mother's breast. 37 cm. Institute of African Studies, University of Ibadan, #69.8.

10.2 Pair of brass Onile figures—male left, female right. Ijębu area, Imodi, 22 April 1982.

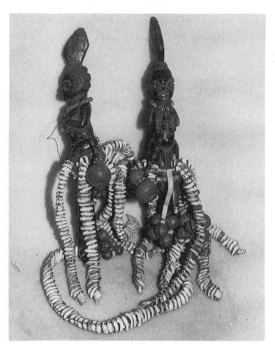

10.3 Pair of Eṣu staffs. The female on the left holds her breasts, while the male on the right holds medicine gourds. Musée de l'Homme, Paris, #31.21.11.

10.4 Woman possessed by the trickster deity Eṣu, wearing a carved penis and testicles under her wrapper. Ketu area, village of Idayin, 8 June 1971.

10.5 Women crossdress as men during an Ebibi festival. Ijẹbu area, Ikija, 28 February 1982.

10.6 A female initiate, with head shaved and painted, is being prepared for Ṣango. Ijẹbu area, village of Iparinla, via Imọpe, 6 August 1986.

10.7 Iya Ṣango dances in possession trance. The crown of her head has been shaved, giving an illusion of a swollen head to evoke the state of possession. Ẹgbado area, Ilaro, 14 November 1975.

10.8 Male Ṣango priests perform with their hair plaited in female styles. Ọyọ area, town of Ẹdẹ, 13 October 1970. Photograph by Henry J. Drewal.

10.9 A caryatid bowl contains a neolithic thundercelt representing Ṣango's power. Over it, a priest pours the sacrificial blood of a cock. Igbomina area, town of Ila-Ọrangun, 11 February 1971. Photograph by Henry J. Drewal.

10.10 Iya Ṣango performs a strong, angular style dance associated with thunder and lightning. Ẹgbado area, Ilaro, 14 November 1975.

10.11 A female priestess possessed by Ogun (right) wears men's hunting garments and carries a rifle. Ẹgbado area, Igbogila, 6 February 1978.

10.12 Detail of a framed photograph of a male priest of Ọya, goddess of the whirlwind and wife of Ṣango, who dresses in women's clothes and plaits his hair in female style. He is flanked by his two wives. Ijẹbu Rẹmọ area, town of Iṣara, 16 March 1982.

Envoi

The rituals I examined were neither unidimensional nor authoritarian, that is, no more so than any other kind of performance. Instead, they were multidimensional, indeed, multifocal and heterological, with participants' shifting their perspectives as well as their operating assumptions. Much Yoruba ritual involved a great amassing of participants, layers upon layers of highly charged visual sensory stimuli, an aggrandizing ethos, intense competition, and multiple and simultaneous channels of interaction so that the word dialogic cannot even begin to convey the dynamics of what went on. Graphic writing does not lend itself easily to evoking this kind of ritual, what Yoruba at the same time refer to as "spectacle."

Ritual is for experiencing and contemplating, according to Ọṣitọla. Thus even ritual specialists themselves, in his words, become "new to the world." Specialists and others "played" ritual, intervening in ordered segments called *aito* to surprise and be surprised, to disorient and be disoriented, to turn one condition into another through a series of exchanges that brought revelations, altered perceptions, or even a reorientation of the participants. Through playful improvisation, through what Afro-Americans might call "signifyin(g)," meanings slipped and slid and got transformed into others; they remained unfixed. Recall white man's bush spirit, the rite for the founder of London, playing *ayo* as a ritual act, the bobbies' helmets—symbols of British authority—carnivalized by young boys in Ṣotẹ's parade, and the bicycle with the police siren in the lead, Iya Ṣango's nonverbal discourse with the Hausa meat-seller masker and the lead drummer.

The rules, such as they were, were often averted and broken; new ones were invented. Contention over rules was part of Agẹmọ practice, but the very histories of Ijẹbu-Ode's 'Id al-Kabir festival and the Imewuro Annual Rally were ones of rule-making, breaking, and reinventing. This process is not only evident in the performances themselves, as well as in the consciousness of participants like Ṣotẹ and Rennaiye, it is also embedded in oral tradition. The Kuku tales are exemplary. Practices changed, along with the very principles on which they were based.

Individuals inserted themselves into ritual at their whims; they elaborated and embellished, deleted, and even impeded or disrupted the action; they also recontextualized, transposed, and transformed its elements. In this way, the rituals accommodated diverse and competing interests as well as different points of view. Yoruba ritual was thus a playing field of individual interests, continuously generated, never cyclical in Eliade's sense—neither timeless nor seen as participating in primordial time. That is one of the main ideas behind the metaphor of the journey.

The only point of correspondence between Yoruba rituals and Turner's liminal category (1977b) was that they had a sacred dimension—which I do not want to demystify at the risk of being accused of exposing secrets. Then again, "secrets get rotten," Ọṣitọla would tell me, "for each one that is revealed, there is another behind." Yoruba rituals combined genres such as spectacle, festival, play, sacrifice, and so on, as well as integrated diverse media—music, dance, poetry, theater, sculpture. They may have been collective in the sense that they involved more than one person, but so do most performances in the West. Characteristically, Yoruba rituals were produced and consumed by known, named individuals. This was true of divination rituals, funerals, Agẹmọ and Egungun masked performances, 'Id al-Kabir, and more.

The central political and economic processes in Yorubaland have been in flux since at least the nineteenth century, and ritual often exists outside them, or even in spite of them. There is no evidence to suppose that things were ever otherwise. Egungun piggybacked Agẹmọ to reap its own benefits. Agẹmọ in turn coexisted with 'Id al-Kabir, though some would have preferred it not to be that way. Through Ifa divination, children were directed toward Islam or perhaps Egungun, or whatever, and more. But then, too, Alhaji Ṣọtẹ found Ifa divination useful in validating his authority to hold the title of Balogun. The Egungun of Imewuro's Annual Rally was set against the annual Egungun festival in the same small sector of one small community. How wonderfully messy it all was!

Yoruba religion is structurally pluralistic, just as Yoruba communities are heterogenous. There was no ritual that I experienced that could be said to be centrally integrated into any totality. To assert such would be to say nothing more than that Yoruba performance is part of Yoruba culture—but, for that matter, American performance is part of American culture. Neither unified, nor coherent, conservative, generalized, nor normative, Yoruba rituals were instead plural, fragmentary, experimental, even idiosyncratic and quirky—the ritual burning of the foam bed pillows, the disruptive fighting, the commandeering, the ruses, the millionaires walking in solemn solidarity behind Ṣọtẹ in nonverbal discourse with the pickpockets, the Christian elite sacrificing to the deities to dialogue with Catholicism.

If there was any common intellectual and emotional meaning, it was certainly not shared by all members of the community, nor even all the participants in any of the rituals. Indeed, Yoruba rituals competed in the cultural market and appealed to specific tastes. The most obvious example was the contrast between the Egungun performed during the Imewuro Annual Rally and that performed at the annual festival. But it was also true of funerals, Ifa divinations, Agẹmọ, and 'Id al-Kabir. Furthermore, ritual specialists and others not only inverted and reversed mundane order, they also subverted it through power play and gender play. Iya Ṣango, Ṣọtẹ, and the Agẹmọ priests excelled in this. The expression "to circumcise a white man" [that is, without his realizing it] is a rather clear testament of the operating idea. And, finally, communitas of any sort need not be involved. Taussig (1987:442) has already called our attention to this. In their multifocality and simultaneity, what Yoruba rituals did most effectively was to accommodate optionality and individual choice—through reflexive, interactive play; interpretation; parody; and competition.

Oyekan Owomoyela (1987:89) has observed that the Yoruba proverbs "the white man who made the pencil also made the eraser" and "today is not necessarily a reliable preview for tomorrow, hence the diviner consults his oracle every fifth day"—both:

> point to the preference for a medium that does not fix one in positions but permits a cleansing of the slate when and as necessary. The African perception of the fixity writing represents comes across quite clearly in the words of a fictional character infatuated with the European way, and, to some extent, alienated from the African. In Chinua Achebe's *No Longer at Ease* (1960:120–21) the apostatic Isaak tells his son Obi:
>
> > Our women make black patterns on their bodies with the juice of the *uli* tree. It was beautiful but it soon faded. If it lasted two market weeks it lasted a long time. But sometimes our elders spoke about *uli* that never faded, although no one had ever seen it. We see it today in the writing of the white man.
>
> He goes on to explain that in the court records nothing ever changes or is alterable, because " 'What is written is written'. It is *uli* that never fades." If philosophers argue, therefore, that traditional proverbs indicate the authoritarianism of traditional systems, one could very well riposte that documents, *uli* that never fades, exude their own sort of authoritarian and restrictive oder [sic].

I am reminded of the time I gave John Mason a copy of a paper I had just written on the practice of Yoruba religion in New York. He is a diviner and priest of the Yoruba deity Ọbatala. I had been hanging with him and his wife, Valerie, and other friends, attending *bembe*, talking *orisa*, and just plain having a good time.

The next time I saw him after handing over the paper he told me that he had found it disturbing. He went on to explain that as he read it, Valerie, sensing a problem, had asked him what was wrong; had I misrepresented the religion? No, he reportedly said, the problem was that I had been all too accurate. He then told me that he was surprised by the detail with which I reported our conversations. The problem, he decided, after giving the issue some thought, was that in my concretization of his words in black and white on paper they took on a kind of reality and permanency of their own that he found frightening.

I have now once again committed the same frightening authoritarian act, implicating the performers, putting them on record by objectifying and freezing their words and their positions to create a permanency they would have otherwise not had without my interventions. There is only one excuse I can make: the absolute necessity of engaging the one mode of the production of knowledge that a Western mentality seems to recognize or understand. The problem is that this mode has not generally served ritual well, representing more our own authoritarianism as if it were that of ritual. This to my way of thinking is the real crisis in the humanities.

Aware that I was returning to the United States to write a manuscript on Yoruba ritual performance, Ọṣitọla informed me just before I left Nigeria that we had only reached the end of chapter 1. That was his way of telling me that no matter how many chapters I wrote they would not add up to more than that. He did not imply that I should not be writing, but rather he wanted to impress upon me that it is the nature of *awo*, esoteric knowledge, "secrets," that once revealed it merely leads us to more . . . .

As the Yoruba adage goes, "what comes after six is more than seven" (*oun to'nbe lẹyin ọfa o ju ọje lo*). Indeed, the journey continues.

Glossary

àbíkú	A child "born to die," that is, a spirit child who continually dies and is reborn.
Agẹmọ	Literally, chameleon; also refers to an Ijẹbu masking society.
àìtò, ètò	Discrete segments within ritual.
àjẹ́	Any woman with extraordinary power; sometimes translated as "witch."
àjò	A journey; a metaphor for ritual and the life cycle.
àjò l'áyé	Life's journey.
ajogún	Spirits of hardship.
alábala	Type of ancestral Egúngún mask constructed as a loose-fitting sack with a multicolored patchwork facing.
Alágẹmọ	Member of the Agẹmọ masking society.
aláṣẹ	One who possesses performative power and authority, that is, the power to accomplish things, to get things done, to make things come to pass.
aláwo	One who has acquired esoteric knowledge through training and initiation; used more specifically to refer to an initiate into Ifá divination.
Apidán	Literally, a performance of "miracles." The name of a type of performance within the Egúngún masking complex in which a miracle worker mask "gives birth" to a whole series of masks that playfully parody people, animals, and spirits.
àṣẹ	Performative power; the power of accomplishment; the power to get things done; the power to make things happen.
awo	Esoteric knowledge.
Awùjalẹ̀	Title for the King of Ijẹbuland.
àyànmọ́	Literally, "that which is affixed to one," that is, associated with one's prenatal destiny.
ayé	The visible, tangible world of the living.
babaláwo	Literally, "the father of esoteric knowledge"; also used to refer to Ifá divination priests, or diviners.
baba parikoko	Type of ancestral Egúngún mask constructed as a long, loose-fitting sack that trails on the ground. Such masks represent the spirits of "the original" Egúngún lineages.
Balógun	A warrior's title.
bàtá	A double-membraned drum used for performances for the thundergod Ṣàngó and for Egúngún ancestral masks.
dùndún	A double-membraned tension drum; called "the talking drum," because it can imitate the tonal patterns in Yorùbá language.
égún	Ancestor, as well as masks representing the ancestors.
Egúngún	Ancestral spirits who are manifested in the form of masked performers.
èpé	A curse.
eré	Play; improvisation.
eré isinkú	Play segment in funerals.
Èṣù	The mediator deity, guardian of the crossroads.
ètùtù	Literally, an act of cooling or soothing; also any ritual or segment of a ritual.

ẹbọ	A sacrifice, or offering, to the Yorùbá deities, ancestors, spirits, and extraordinarily powerful women.
Èfè	Literally, "joking"; the night of singing during Gèlèdé masked performance.
egọ	Complex, irregular drumming; also used to designate the dance that goes with the drumming.
Ẹlégba	A name referring to the mediator deity, Èṣù, the guardian of the crossroads.
Ẹléni	Dancing mat mask of the Agẹmọ masking complex.
ẹmí	Literally, "breath." Also refers to the soul or animating spirit of a living being.
ẹmi òrìṣà	The spirit of a deity that on occasion possesses mediums to send them into trance states.
èrò	Gentle, soothing; a quality generally associated with women.
ẹrú	Slave.
ẹrúbọ	A sacrificial burden offered willingly; more specifically, any ritual sacrifice.
ẹsẹ Ifá	The verses contained within the sets of Ifá divination texts known as Odù Ifá.
èyọ Ifá	The explanation of Ifá divination verses in narrative form provided by the diviner or by a priest of a deity.
Gèlèdé	Masked performances found predominantly in western Yorùbáland that honor the extraordinary powers of women; also refers to the masked performers themselves.
ibéji	Twin(s), regarded by Yorùbá as special or sacred children; also refers to the deity of twins.
ibó	Instruments of divination symbolizing good and/or bad destiny.
idán	Literally, a "miracle," but also refers to certain types of masks in Apidán performance that parody people, animals, and spirits in the Egúnún ancestral masking complex.
Ifá	The name for the system of divination.
igbó	Bush, or forest.
igbódù	Sacred ritual space constructed by a diviner as a forest grove to contain the shrine for the deity Odù, the wife of Ọrúnmìlà, the deity associated with the Ifá divination system. It is in this sacred space that diviners are initiated into Ifá practice.
Ìgunnuko	A type of tall, cylindrical, cloth mask introduced into Yorùbá country by Nupe immigrants.
Ìkọsẹ w'áyé	Literally, "a step into the world"; the name of a divination ritual performed for babies from three to seven days old in order for the parents to know the quality of the child's entry into the world.
ilé	House; by extension, one's family.
ilédì	Literally, "house with an inner sanctum"; the meeting place of the Òṣùgbó society.
ilè	Earth, ground.
Ilé-Ifè	The ancient city where, according to oral tradition, Yorùbá peoples originated.
Iléyá	The Yorùbá name for the Muslim 'Id al-Kabir festival; derives from 'Id al-Adha, "the Feast of Immolation," an alternative Arabic name for 'Id al-Kabir; the folk etymology is *ilé yá*, "let us go home."
imò	Knowledge.
Imorí	Literally, "know the head." A divination ritual performed for a child between three and seven months old in order to know which ancestor's or deity's spirit the child has reincarnated.

inú	Inside; more specifically, refers to the spiritual aspect of a being.
ìran	Spectacle, based on the verb radical *ran*, which has the sense of at once repetition and transformation.
ìrìn	A walk.
ìrìn àjò	A journey on foot.
ìrójú	Endurance; a quality generally associated with women.
Ìṣasà	The section of Ijẹbu-Ode where the Agẹmọ priests perform during the Agẹmọ festival.
isìnkú	A generic term for a funeral ritual.
Ìtẹfá	A fourteen-day ritual initiation into Ifá during which the initiate learns the nature of his inner head and receives his personal set of specially prepared palm nuts that will be used throughout his life in divination to consult Ifá.
ìwà	Character; inherent nature of a person or thing; in the broadest sense, existence.
iwòfà	Indentured servant.
Jìgbò	Masks found predominantly in the Ijẹbu area and associated with the forest and Ekine water spirits. They wear cloth from local markets and freshly cut palm fronds; also refers to masked performances by the above-mentioned masks.
kádàrá	Hausa loan word meaning destiny.
létòlétò	Based on *ètò*, a ritual segment. Literally, in a series, one after the other, conveyed by the repetition of the word *ètò*.
obìnrin	Woman.
òdodo	Justice.
Odù	The two hundred fifty-six sets of Ifá divination texts; also the name of the wife of Ọrúnmìlà, the deity of divination, herself a deity.
Odù Ifá	The two hundred fifty-six sets of Ifá divination texts.
Ògbóni	Literally, a "wise elder"; also refers to members of Òṣùgbó, the precolonial judiciary in Yorùbáland, who were the most senior members of the families in Yorùbá communities.
Ògún	Deity of iron and war, whose devotees are hunters, warriors, and other professionals who use iron, like truck drivers and taxi drivers.
Ojúde Ọba	Literally "a meeting with the king outside," or in public; public outing to honor the king.
ojú òrèrè	The shrine for a diviner's ancestors, marked by an iron staff called *òpá òrèrè* or *òpá osun*.
òkú	A corpse.
ológbẹrì	A person who possesses a naive perspective, who is untrained and unknowing.
ologbón	A person who possesses wisdom and knowledge.
Olókùn	The deity of the ocean and, by extension, all waters.
Olúrin	Literally, "owner of the metal objects"; the title given to the king in the context of Òṣùgbó societies and/or his representative at Òṣùgbó meetings.
onídán	Literally, "owner of miracles," or "miracle worker." The Egúngún ancestral mask with a large, circular, womb-like garment who performs, "gives birth to" miracles in Apidán.
orí	The head.
orí inú	The inner head, or spiritual head, often represented by a cone-shape.
oríkì	Praise epithets chanted during celebrations.
òrìṣà	A deity, or deities collectively.
Òrìṣànlá	Male deity who creates human beings.

oríta	Literally, "where three roads come together"; an intersection; symbol of the point where the world and the otherworld intersect.
oṣi	Ijẹbu Yorùbá term for ancestor.
Òṣùgbó	Society of elders who formed the judiciary in precolonial Yorùbáland.
òtító	Truth.
Ọbàlùfọ̀n	The deity of artists, particularly brass casters.
Ọbàtálá	The deity of creation.
odún	Literally, a "year"; also refers to annual ritual festivals.
ògbẹ̀rì	The naive and uninitiated, the untrained and unskilled.
ogbón	Wisdom.
ojà	Market.
Ọjọ́fà	Section of Ijẹbu-Ode where the Agẹmọ priests exchange blessings with the King of Ijẹbuland.
Ọlọ́ja	Literally, "owner of the market"; also the title given to all Agẹmọ priests.
ọmọ arayé	Literally, "children of the beings in the world"; usually used to speak of troublemakers who cause harm and hardship to people because of jealousy.
ọmọ awo	Literally, "children of ancient, esoteric wisdom"; those who have been initiated into Ifá.
òrò̀ ijinlẹ̀	Literally, "deep words."
òrun	The spirit realm; the otherworld; sometimes translated as "heaven."
Ọrúnmìlà	Deity of Ifá divination.
òsẹ	A Yorùbá week, calculated as four days; also refers to any ritual performed weekly.
Ọ̀tun Balógun	A warrior's title.
rìnrìn	A walk; a trip.
Ṣàngó	Male deity of thunder and lightning.
ṣe	To perform; to do; to make; to create; to become.
ṣ'ẹ̀pẹ̀	Literally, "to perform a curse"; to curse.
ṣeré	Literally, "to create or make play"; to play.
tẹ	To establish.
titun	Newness.
tù	To cool.
yẹ̀yẹ́	Foolishness; nonsensical, gratuitous play, in contrast to *eré*, serious, transformational play.

Notes

1. THEORY AND METHOD

1. Gates himself is engaged in signifyin(g) on Derridean ideas by superimposing Yoruba references. One example—"Esu's representations as the multiplicity of meaning, as the logos, and as what I shall call the Ogboni Supplement encapsulate his role for the critic" (36). "Ogboni Supplement," here, signifies simultaneously on Derrida and on the often published, esoteric Ogboni adage *Ogboni meji, o di eta,* "two Ogboni elders, it becomes three." The supplemental third Gates interprets as the transcendence of binary oppositions and contradiction.

2. Some wear ornate headdresses with wire frameworks adorned with colorful yarn tassels and plastic toys.

3. See Robert Farris Thompson's pioneering work on African dance and its relation to drumming (1966; 1974).

4. As Chernoff (1979:125) points out, "in a context of multiple rhythms, people distinguish themselves from each other while they remain dynamically related." Or, as Thompson (1966:91) suggests, "multiple meter is, in brief, a communal examination of percussive individuality."

5. It is significant that the point beyond which she decided she could not ride was the crossroads. In Yoruba thought, the crossroads represents the juncture of the spiritual realm and the phenomenal world. It is a liminal space where sacrifices are often placed and where the trickster deity, Eṣu, is said to reside. As an ambivalent spot, it is also a perfect place to make a ritual adjustment.

6. See Fabian (1983) on the problem of co-evalness and the use of ethnographic tropes to create temporal and spatial distance between researchers and their Others.

7. In the past, Yoruba kings were sacred ("second to the gods") and did not travel outside their domains. Indeed they never appeared publicly except on certain ritual occasions. On his expedition to the Qyọ Yoruba capital in the 1820s, Clapperton (1829) visited with the king, who sat behind a screen so that no one could view him. Even during rare ritual appearances, the king's face was covered so no one could gaze into his eyes. Although kings travel today, there is still a lingering sense of uneasiness involved in contravening old rules, for not only is a king treading on someone else's territory, but in leaving his own domain he makes himself vulnerable to his enemies at home. Among the Yoruba, it is understood that any powerful individual, particularly an enormously popular one, has enemies.

2. YORUBA PLAY AND THE TRANSFORMATION OF RITUAL

1. All Yoruba festivals are spectacles, but not all rituals. Divination rituals, for example, are not usually called spectacle, because they are private, small, and

sedate. However, when rituals are public and the intention of the organizers is to amass people, attempting to attract the entire community as well as strangers from other places, they can also be referred to as spectacles. A well-known saying about the rituals of the Gẹlẹdẹ masking society, performed to "cool" or appease spiritually powerful women, declares: "the eyes that have seen Gẹlẹdẹ have seen the ultimate spectacle" (H. Drewal and M. Drewal 1983). The number of spectators such spectacles draw is considered indicative of their success as rituals.

2. In Czikszentmihalyi's words (1975:181), "a matching of personal skills against a range of physical or symbolic opportunities for action that represent meaningful challenges to the individual."

3. *Ere* is also pronounced *ire* and *are*, depending on the geographical area (Abraham 1958:314).

4. Thus when Yoruba say *o nṣe yẹyẹ*, the phrase is often translated into English as "he is making nonsense," as opposed to *o nṣ'ere [nṣe ere]*, "he is playing."

5. *Ọdun* literally means "year" but, when used in conjunction with performances of Ifa or Oṣugbo *(ọdun Ifa, ọdun Oṣugbo)*, refers more specifically to the annual festivals of Ifa and Oṣugbo. Similarly, *ọsẹ* literally means "week," but is also used to speak of rituals performed weekly—*ọsẹ Ifa* and *ọsẹ Oṣugbo*, for example. Apart from the temporal spacing between each ritual repetition, the main difference between weekly rites and annual festivals is one of scale and expense.

6. As Omari (1984:25) notes, "public festivals *(xire,* Yoruba for play, gala, party) provide an opportunity for aesthetic and theatrical display. Initiates are able to be 'onstage' and the focus of attention for a time. When viewing these attempts to please the Orixa [Yoruba deities] through a rich and colorful exhibition of beautiful and unusual costume elements, an etic interpreter will discern a competitive aspect to Afro-Bahian ritual art—attempts by initiates to outdo 'sisters' or fellow initiates with their display."

7. Ọlabiyi Yai (personal communication, 1990) tells me that the uses of *iran* as both generation and spectacle can be traced to the verbal radical *ran*, which at once entails repetition and transformation.

8. See below, chapter 8, on Balogun Kuku and the representation of spectacle.

9. Turner (1977b:40; 1982:32, 55; 1986:123–138) has acknowledged these capacities of play, but tends to associate them more with so-called "liminoid" phenomena, like Mardi Gras. Thus, *"liminal* phenomena, may, on occasion, portray the inversion or reversal of secular, mundane reality and social structure. But *liminoid* phenomena are not merely reversive, they are often subversive, representing radical critiques of the central structures and proposing utopian alternative models" (1977b:45).

10. Urbanism has been a subject of much debate in the literature on Yoruba since the late 1950s. See Bascom (1959, 1973); Mabogunje (1968); Krapf-Askari (1969); Wheatley (1970); Lloyd (1973). Eades (1980:43) argues that the impressive scale of urban development among the Yoruba does not predate

1800. And even though he acknowledges the preexistence of certain urban centers like Ifẹ, Ọyọ-Ile, and Ijẹbu-Ode—the latter having been mentioned in early sixteenth-century Portuguese travelers' accounts—he maintains that these are exceptions. But exactly how many ancient cities does it take in order to classify a society as urban?

11. Yoruba are socially heterogenous in that, in Wirth's words (1969:156), "no single group has the undivided allegiance of the individual. [. . .] By virtue of his different interests arising out of different aspects of social life, the individual acquires membership in widely divergent groups, each of which functions only with reference to a certain segment of his personality." In addition, Yoruba cities have historically been gathering places for diverse cultural groups, including Hausa, Fulani, Fon, and Nupe peoples, among others. Yoruba towns fit Wirth's definition of a city, but not his theory of urbanism, a point that has been argued convincingly by Krapf-Askari (1969:155).

12. Law (1977:75–76) calculates that Islam was introduced into northern Yorubaland during the seventeenth century, but it did not have much impact on southern Yorubaland until the late nineteenth century. See below, chapter 8.

13. The former domain is sometimes translated as "heaven" in the literature, although the term does not have the same sense as it does in the Judeo-Christian tradition, for Yoruba themselves conceptualize ọrun in different ways. Sometimes it is the cool watery environment beneath the sea, so that going to the home of the God of the Sea (Olokun) is the same as going to ọrun. Sometimes ọrun is conceived metaphorically in the Christian sense as the space in the sky, but it is difficult to say to what extent this notion derives historically from missionary education.

14. In the latter category are the *ajogun,* the spirits of hardship, among them Death, Illness, Infirmity, Loss, Litigation, Debt, Disaster, and Conflict.

15. The power of utterances has been widely documented in Africa (see Ray 1973; Peek 1981) and in Yorubaland (Prince 1960; Beier 1970:49; H. Drewal 1974, H. Drewal and M. Drewal 1983, M. Drewal and H. Drewal 1987; Verger 1976–77; and Ayoade 1979:51).

16. The diverse practices that make up Yoruba ritual have their roots in what Laitin (1986:146) terms "ancestral city identities." This is true in the New World as well, particularly in Brazil, where adepts of Candomblé classify themselves according to the "nations" from which they originated, such as Ketu, Jesha (Ijẹsa), Nago, or Gege (Ewe) (Bastide 1978:160, 193–195). Ketu was a Yoruba city-state in the Republic of Benin; Ijẹsa is a central Yoruba town located in Nigeria; Nago is what the western Yoruba call their language; while Ewe is a distinct culture in southern Benin, Togo, and Ghana.

17. See, for example, Bloch (1974); Gell (1975:217–218); Peacock (1975:219); Goody (1977:30); Rappaport (1979:172, 175–176, 183, 208); and Tambiah (1985:131–166).

3. THE ONTOLOGICAL JOURNEY

1. Biblical phrasing is contextualized here.

2. *Kijikiji* is an ideophonic word meaning "rowdiness."

3. The printed literature on Ifa texts and the divination process is enormous, some of it in Yoruba. The most extensive works are by Abimbọla (1968; 1969; 1975; 1976; 1977); Bascom (1969); Beyioku (1971); McClelland (1982); and Epega (1987). They tend to focus on the content of the texts, literary devices, the instruments of divination, and the casting process rather than on the situated context of meaning or the social use of metaphor. For a piece specifically on the training of diviners, see Abimbọla (1983).

4. Interestingly, the journey as metaphor in African ritual may be quite widespread. In addition to Ọṣitọla (1988), see Ottenberg, Nevadomsky and Rosen, and H. Drewal on the journey's manifestation in other African ritual practices in *The Drama Review: A Journal of Performance Studies* (1988) on Ritual Performance in Africa Today.

5. This society is also known as Ogboni. On the role of Oṣugbo/Ogboni in Yoruba society, see, among others, Dennett (1916); Bovell-Jones (1943); Bascom (1944); Biobaku (1956); Morton-Williams (1960a); Agiri (1972); Atanda (1973); and H. Drewal (1989).

6. Literally, "we are going to the beneficent king's palace."

7. *Kadara* is the Hausa word for destiny; *ayanmọ* is Yoruba for the same idea.

8. "The spreading world" is a reference to the way people put on weight in middle age.

9. The relationship between esoteric verses and improvised narratives comes up again in chapters 4 and 5 on divination rituals. By juxtaposing the verse with the narrative here, I have tried to give the reader a sense of their relationship and the extent to which the narrative elaborates and deviates from the verse. In the following chapters I have provided only the performer's re-tellings of the narrative. For discussions of the social use of metaphor and a distinction between narrative performances and reports of narrative performances and their relative value, see Kirshenblatt-Gimblett (1976).

10. Cyclical time in this sense is "a reactualization of the cosmogony," implying "starting time over again at its beginning, that is, restoration of the primordial time, the 'pure' time, that existed at the moment of Creation." The phrase as used by Eliade should not be confused with ritual cycle—the periodic recurrence of ritual.

11. With the increase in Christianity and Islam, fewer people have such funerals than they would have in the past, although certain elements carry over. For comparison, see Peter R. McKenzie's study of Christian burials and his composite account of "traditional" funerals based on secondary sources (1982:12–13).

12. This seven-day period corresponds to two Yoruba four-day weeks in which the last day of the first week is also counted as the first day of the second week.

13. Ọṣitọla's account is an edited transcription of taped discussions #s 86.94, 86.144, and 86.145, Ibẹju-Ode, 1 December 1986.

14. The voice in this sense represents the living spirit itself.

15. This practice follows literally what parents do to a newborn baby as an abbreviated initiation into the world.

16. The "white cloth" from heaven refers to the birth caul. Like the birth caul, the cloth of ritual novices is white, while the cloth of elders is multicolored and often highly patterned.

17. The patterns on the cloth do not express this in any literal way. Rather, the complexity of the designs as they float over sometimes strong horizontal stripes suggests the complexities of life itself and the elder's mastery of them.

18. This ceremony begins the process of interring the body, from which the entire process derives its name. The corpse is usually buried under the floor of the house.

19. Although "he" is used throughout, the description applies equally to men and women. Pronouns in the Yoruba language do not specify sex. Thus Yoruba speakers of English often use English pronouns interchangeably without reference to gender. Ọṣitọla also often uses he/she interchangeably.

20. Or, to put it another way, the amount by extension constructs the quality of the donor's relationship to the deceased.

21. The children often dress in clothes of the deceased, and it has recently become the style to hold up a framed photograph of the deceased as a kind of centerpiece of the group.

22. Oro is a society whose membership overlaps that of Oṣugbo. It is concerned specifically with spirits of ancestors and with death. In this capacity, its members were the executioners of those criminals condemned to death by Oṣugbo. However, people say Oro, not a human being, takes the lives of criminals.

23. This is done with bullroarers—rhombs that are swung around in the air, producing a shrill, eerie sound to represent the ancestor's voice. The source of Oro's voice is regarded as a secret even though people have an idea what it is, and there are many Oro rhombs in museums around the world.

24. The ancestor's endorsement had been in evidence the previous day through the sound of Oro's voice.

25. That is, through the sound of the Oro rhombs accompanied by drums.

26. An honored ancestor is thought to develop and expand in the otherworld and then return in generations of grandchildren.

27. These are extremely secret and involve the removal of active medicines from the deceased's head that were placed there during initiation. This practice persists in the United States among priests of Yoruba deities.

28. A more detailed treatment of Yoruba concepts of identity and personality is in chapters 4 and 5.

29. For a fairly recent attempt to grapple with this issue, see J. D. Y. Peel (1984), who concludes that both concepts coexist among the Yoruba.

4. NEW BEGINNINGS

1. The process has been described by Bascom (1969:26–75) and Epega (1987:4–5).

2. My understanding of Ikọsẹ w'aye is based on conversations with Ọṣitọla (#s 82.116 and 86.102).

3. For a description of reading kola nuts, see Epega (1987:58–66).

4. *Iyẹrosun* is the white wood dust (*iye*) created by borer insects in the Baphia Nitida tree (Papilonaceae) known as *irosun* (Abraham 1958:316, 334), which is then medicinally treated for use on the divination tray.

5. The order of the sets of texts and their corresponding graphic signs are given by Epega (1987:7–38). The order varies somewhat from place to place. If the diviner accidentally drops a palm nut, he quickly apologizes and reciprocally knocks his own knuckle on the divination tray. That particular cast does not count, and he continues.

6. That is, it posited a life situation and a projected resolution (Kirshenblatt-Gimblett 1976:123).

7. This section is based on my attendance at three Imori and on taped discussions with Ọṣitọla—#s 82.103 and 82.104 (20 July 1982), 82.116 (28 July 1982), 86.117 (9 November 1986), Ijẹbu-Ode.

8. For a study on the Yoruba ontology of personality and motivation, see Morakinyo and Akiwowo (1981).

9. Returning souls always skip one generation, so the child may be either the grandfather or grandmother, or from previous generations.

10. The truth is that Ọṣitọla had always served me *ẹba*, and I on occasion gave *him* spaghetti and the backs of beans (string beans), which were available in local shops but were not the dishes he was accustomed to or preferred.

11. These symbols have to do with Yoruba constructions of gender and power, a topic I will cover specifically in a later chapter.

12. The male stick (*iṣẹmọkurin*) was from the Newboldia Laevis (Bignoniaceae) tree (*akoko*); the female stick (*iṣẹmobirin*) from the White Star Apple tree (Chrysophyllum Albidum, Sapotaceae) (in Yoruba *ọlọsan* or *agbalumọ*, noted for its fruit with many seeds).

13. This is at times a problem, and Ọṣitọla has to stop and make his own sacrifices. The assumption is that either the deity of divination, Ọrunmila, is annoyed for some unknown reason or that the head of the child is very stubborn, or hard, inhibiting the identification of the soul.

14. If the girl had been from a deity, then he would evaluate all of the sets of texts that had appeared in order to establish which deity spoke through them most frequently.

15. Known as *iwoye*, this is also the generic name for any title-taking ceremony.

16. The *akoko* leaves he used are symbols of title-taking in Yorubaland; three is the symbolic number of *awo*, or esoteric knowledge, but also the number of directions from which the child's spirit can come. Perhaps not insignificantly it is also the number of scientific probability.

17. *Ọmọ w'aye e ni, abi ko w'aye e ni o?*

18. When Imori is performed for twins, according to Ọṣitọla, the divinations occur consecutively. The same diviner divines for both in the order that the

twins were born. The feeling is that twins cannot be divided between two diviners, because their spirits chose to come to the world in the same womb. This is so even though the two will likely have different spiritual origins and will also have different destinies.

19. *Dede Igunugun abọwale o, Dede Igun abọwale.*

5. ESTABLISHING THE SELF

1. *Mọ iwa fun oniwa. Iwa,* "character," refers to an aspect of the individual's inner head, or personality.

2. Taped discussion #86.143, Ijẹbu-Ode, 30 November 1986.

3. Itẹfa means literally to establish Ifa (*tẹ* Ifa), but this refers to the Ifa texts that will guide the person for the rest of his life. Thus it is the establishment of self.

4. I have attended three Itẹfa—one in 1982 and two in 1986. These three performances led by Ọsitọla generated approximately thirty-nine hours of discussions with him in 1982 and twenty-three hours in 1986. Our 1982 discussions naturally influenced the way I viewed and understood the 1986 performances. More importantly, in these three performances I was able to see similarities and differences. I have cited only those taped discussions I have quoted.

5. It is impossible within the limits of this chapter to unpack Itẹfa semiotically or even to convey all of what goes on. I have tried to present just enough to give some indication of its richness and complexity without at the same time oversimplifying it.

6. This discussion is based on three Itẹfa that I attended in 1982 and 1986 and a series of twenty-four hour and a half discussions with Ọsitọla in 1982 [tape #s 82.28 (7 May), 82.31 (11 May), 82.35 (18 May), 82.37 (21 May), 82.38(I) (21 May), 82.38(II) (25 May), 82.39 (25 May), 82.42 (27 May), 82.44 (31 May), 82.45 (31 May), 82.46 (31 May), 82.47 (31 May), 82.48 (1 June), 82.49 (1 June), 82.57 (8 June), 82.58 (8 & 16 June), 82.66 (16 June), 82.67 (16 June), 82.68 (16 & 20 June), 82.70 (20 June), 82.71 (20 & 24 June)]; and in 1986 [#86.138 (30 November), 86.142 (30 November 1986), 86.144 (30 November)].

7. Markets in Yorubaland are ordinarily controlled by women.

8. Ọsitọla (1988:36) suggests other explanations.

9. Confinement to the *itẹn,* and a ritual segment known as *ilẹtẹn,* are also performed during the installation rites of kings and other chiefs.

10. *Ijenla* means literally "big seven." Or, in other words, it is seven times two.

11. According to an Ifa text, Ọrunmila himself was instructed to paint his head with star chalk for protection when going to meet with "our mothers," the spiritually powerful women in the world. The relationship between one's personality, a shining star, and protection from the mothers was not a topic Ọsitọla was willing to discuss, although I speculate it is one dimension of the discourse on autonomy and dependence, which is implicit in Itẹfa performance.

12. By "playing the tropes," I mean—following Fernandez (1986:viii, x)—bringing differing domains together (utterances, images, acts) into metaphoric comparison through the logic of implication.

13. As one diviner explained, Christian preachers pray to go to Paradise when they die, diviners pray to go to Olokun.

14. See Sapir (1977:22) for a discussion of the container/contained structure of metonyms. The actions put into effect, in Fernandez's words (1986:42), "metaphoric predications upon the pronouns participating in the ritual."

15. The women's divination system, called "sixteen cowries," practiced by priests of Yoruba deities, draws from the same corpus of verses as the Ifa system. Ọṣitọla claims his grandmother, a priestess of the deity Orisanla, knew more texts than the men in the family. Thus, she chanted verses and interpreted them, but had to do so from outside the sacred grove.

16. The following parables are edited versions of those told by Ọṣitọla (#s 86.138 and 86.142). They are retellings of those told inside the restricted grove.

17. *Ọta maa fẹ pa na ọla Ojo.*

18. *Eṣuwata* implies devotees of Eṣu.

19. *O fi'gbalẹ gba a loju.*

20. That is, just as the sun blinds those who look directly into it and just as the eyelashes protect the eyes.

21. A second narrative from Ọyẹku meji presented a similar kind of conflict, warning a mother that her son had been born in a dangerous place, full of so much evil that they had to prepare them both so that Death did not take them away. The diviners hung a live chick on the front door of Ọṣitọla's house as a decoy, which after some time Death took.

22. The remaining parables in this chapter are edited versions of Ọṣitọla's retellings, taped interviews #86.143 and #86.144.

23. *Omi igbin*, "snail water," its "blood," is clear and cool in contrast to the warm red blood of the sheep and pig. And indeed the name Amututu means "One who brings coolness."

24. *O fi ọgbọn ọlọgbọn ṣ'ọgbọn.*

25. Or, in other words, nothing can take its place.

26. *Ma ri ibilẹ aye.*

27. The fourth child was constructed as an aggressive conqueror and identified with the deity of lightning, Ṣango, whom all the deities face to fight, but who throws a stone and everybody scatters. The diviners predicted a hot-tempered, flamboyant personality, like Ṣango, who is destined to conquer or to win people over by force.

28. See also Abiọdun (1983) on Yoruba concepts of character and beauty.

29. Known collectively as the "people of the world," *ọmọ araye.*

6. RITUAL PLAY ABOUT PLAY

1. Sometimes Egungun masks represent the spirit of the deceased in funeral contexts. Several scholars have briefly described such cases (for example, Talbot

1926:iii, 476; Bascom 1944:54; Morton-Williams 1960b;36). Babayẹmi (1980:51–53) has provided the most detailed account to date. He reports that, to separate the deceased from his or her family, an Egungun of the same stature as the corpse appears dressed in the deceased clothes to imitate his or her mannerisms, walk, and general comportment. If the deceased is male, then the Egungun often verbally reassures the deceased's family, clearing up doubts about the circumstances of his death and encouraging unity and solidarity within the compound. Such masks differ radically from other Egungun. They appear privately, rather than in public, and only once, never to return as other Egungun do who have been created to perform publicly.

2. The name Kulodo means literally "The-Dead-One-in-the-River" and derives from a narrative that connects the origin of this particular lineage mask to a forefather's death by drowning.

3. Sometimes myth exists separately from the performance it validates, known only to a few specialists; at other times, recitations of myth form part of the performance itself to substantiate the action within its ritual processes (Ọṣitọla 1988). In this latter case, ritual's authoritative sources are cited within its framework.

4. This parallels the practice of giving cloth to the deceased in Ọṣitọla's account of funeral performance. In the latter case, however, the deceased is buried in the cloth. The process of making an Egungun loosely follows that of site sacralization as outlined by Dean MacCannell (1976:44–45), that is, naming, framing and elevation, enshrinement, mechanical reproduction—on T-shirts, for example—and social reproduction.

5. For a more detailed discussion of *alabala*-type costumes and movement style, see M. Drewal and H. Drewal (1978:29–31).

6. Actually there are many Egungun origin myths that feature the monkey.

7. I have seen more Apidan than any other kind of Yoruba performance, sixteen to be exact, between 1973 and 1982 in the towns of Pobe, Ilaro, Ibese, Ijado, Imaṣai, Iboro, Iṣaga Orile, Abẹokuta, and Ilogbo—all western Yoruba towns. I have also seen variants of the Apidan form among Ijẹbu Yoruba in the south, where characters appear independently, rather than serially in a single performance. Given this broad experience with a particular form, I have adopted a comparative approach to Apidan performance for this chapter, in the end treating a specific performance in greater detail.

8. Most Yoruba performers would be unfamiliar with the English word "parody"; however, the parodic intent is evident in their conscious choice and use of alien images and ideas to signal both similarity and difference, thereby foregrounding the play of the signifier.

9. The name Ajofunoyinbo harks back to the colonial period when dancing for the British would have been considered an honor since they held the positions of power (Taiwo, #75.27b). For examples of these invocations, see Adedeji (1973) and M. Drewal and H. Drewal (1987).

10. As Taiwo (#75.6b) put it, "Iyawo represents the time that you will become old, that all your children will come to say 'Ah Mama!' "

11. Gotrick (1984:108) apparently did not understand tbe relationship between the miracle worker and Bride; however, it was this double-edged intentionality of Bride's dance that led her to observe that the mask "can be the young, newly wedded bride, full of life and expectations. She can also be an old woman, leisurely, dignified, and graceful."

12. See, for example, Gotrick (1984:129).

13. This tradition appears to have been revitalized by repatriated Yoruba slaves in Freetown, Sierra Leone, as documented by Nunley (1988).

14. I discussed a similar phenomenon in chapter 3 in the context of a hunter's burial known as *aṣipadẹ*.

15. For another example of the Yoruba use of performance for political opposition, see Peel (1984:126).

16. The dancing mats too represent foreigners in that the mask originated among, and is identified with, the Ijẹbu Yoruba subgroup located to the southeast of the Ẹgbado area where this performance took place (see chapter 8).

17. See also Barber (1984) on the same kind of paratactical form in Yoruba praise poetry performance.

7. THE COLLECTIVE IN CONFLICT

1. *R'eṣu rẹ wa pẹlurẹ Agẹmọ.*

2. Invariably, people said Ṣerefusi is "very jolly"; the idea is built into his title. Ṣerefusi boasted that his title implied, if six people were around and he came out dancing, five would follow him (Ọnafowokan, Agẹmọ priest, #86.14).

3. I have benefited from many hours of stimulating discussion on Agẹmọ with Henry John Drewal and John Pemberton III, both during the 1982 and 1986 annual festivals and subsequently. They attended portions of the goings-on to which I had no access as a woman. As with many Yoruba institutions, there is a growing literature on Agẹmọ. See, for example, Ogunba (1965, 1967, 1985) and Pemberton (1984, 1988).

4. Ọnafowokan, #86.14; Odunsi, Agẹmọ priest, #86.20 and #86.21.

5. Osilaja, Agẹmọ priest, #s 86.22 and 86.23; Agbadagbodo, Agẹmọ chief, #s 86.23 and 86.24.

6. Ogunba (1965:177–178; 1985:286–287) gives two other variations on these stories, both of which are about the tensions between the king and the priests.

7. Chanted by Sanni, Agẹmọ priest, #86.20. Ogunba (1985:282) gives another variation.

8. J. A. Okunuga, Pastor-in-Charge, to His Worship, The Regent of Ijẹbu-Ode, 30 June 1939, IJE Prof 1/779, pp. 57–60, University of Ibadan Library, Ibadan.

9. Even when an Agẹmọ priest dies and his office has not yet been filled, his loads are still expected to be carried on the pilgrimage.

10. Reported to me by H. Drewal and Pemberton. They were permitted to enter the encampment.

11. By some accounts, this title refers to the Oloko of Idoko, a king residing on the eastern fringe of Agẹmọ country, whose ancestor supposedly arrived in the land before the Awujalẹ invaded (cf. Smith 1969:78; Ogunba 1985:286–287). There is a further tradition that the Agẹmọ performed for Oloko's wife, who is synonymous with the Bethsheba of biblical fame (Ogunba 1985:287). Others argue that Oloko simply refers to the original ancestor, who brought a sacred stone and installed it within the grove as a symbol of the establishment of Agẹmọ. The title, Oloko of Idoko, they contend is quite separate.

12. The most detailed account of this process is in Ogunba's dissertation (1967). For an explanation of the relationship between invocations and the activation of medicines, see Verger (1976–77).

13. Neither of these two accounts explains why these two priests dress in female style, yet Adie is pictured this way on every annual Agẹmọ calendar that I have seen, at least six or seven.

14. Thus, when a priest dies, those more junior move up one in rank and the next priest installed takes the last position.

15. It is a role similar to that of Ojubọna, "One-who-faces-the-road," in Ifa practice and the Apena in Oṣugbo.

16. That is not the case in fact, since the Agẹmọ priests met periodically with the Awujalẹ during my stay in 1986.

17. Funeral performances drew mainly family and friends of the deceased, but since they occurred in the open air they also attracted passersby.

18. This was reported to me by a participant in those decisions, whose name will remain anonymous because of the sensitivity of the matter.

19. Odunsi #s 86.20 and 86.21.

20. Now it is the Local Government Council that assumes the expense of the sacrifices, a condition the Awujalẹ set before he agreed to be reinstated to office.

21. Even though there seems to be some vestige of a former sociopolitical system, there are a few Agẹmọ priests who do not make a connection between their titles and specific markets.

22. Whenever priests claim descent from their father's side, it often happens that they were also eligible for the title on their mother's side as well. The choice to take a title from the father's line when it is forthcoming from the mother's line is one of expediency since it means the candidate must await another titleholder's death and the rotation of the title among several lineages.

8. FROM MILITARISM TO DANDYISM

1. Olisa's Palace, Ijẹbu-Ode, Nigeria, Untitled Manuscript, n.d. (typewritten).

2. Ryan (1978:280, and 300 note 87) suggests that Ileya derives from Id al-Adha, the "Feast of the Immolation," an alternate Arabic name for 'Id al-Kabir, and that the folk etymology of Ileya is *ile ya*, "let us go home," a reference to the practice of returning home to celebrate the festival.

3. For example, Ayandele (1966, 1970, 1979); Gbadamọsi (1978); Ajayi (1965); Ajayi and Smith (1964); Smith (1971); and Law (1977).

4. Johnson's original manuscript was lost mysteriously by the publishers and was reconstructed posthumously by Johnson's brother, Dr. O. Johnson, from "copious notes and rough copies left behind by the author" (Johnson 1973:ix).

5. The Balogun Fulani and the Balogun Gambari—Yoruba name for Hausas—had jurisdiction over the Fulani and Hausa segments of the town, while the Balogun Ajikobi and the Balogun Alanamu controlled the Yoruba ones (Lloyd 1961:267–268, 1971:40–46; Law 1977:259; Eades 1980:101).

6. Seriki, the second in command to the Balogun, is a Hausa loan word in Yoruba signifying "king" (Johnson 1973:132–133, 135). It is the Hausa equivalent of the Fulani title Emir. In Ilorin, although prestigious, it conferred little political power and no rights to territory (Lloyd 1971:40, 46).

7. See Ayandele (1969, 1970) and Lloyd (1971, 1977).

8. Islam had been introduced into the Oyo Empire as early as the seventeenth century (Law 1977:75–76). The first Muslims in Ijebu were Hausa slaves. See Gbadamosi (1978:90–91), Abdul cited in Clark (1982:168), and Anonymous (1967:5). Christian missionaries like Bishop Oluwole of the Church Missionary Society—finally allowed into Ijebu-Ode officially after British occupation—began to lament by 1896 that Islam had become "the religion favoured by the chiefs" (quoted in Gbadamosi 1978:96).

9. The locally published *History of Ijebu-Ode Central Mosque, Oyingbo, Ijebu-Ode* states quite frankly that some of the early converts were "Ijebu traders who became muslims in the cause of their trading activities abroad" (Anonymous 1967:5).

10. For insight into the inland slave trade, see Adamu (1979). Bovell-Jones (1943:76–77) was told that the Pampa society—to which the Balogun and Seriki belong—was originally established for war, but during peacetime it supervised the markets. Ayandele (1970:235), on the other hand, claims that trade became an issue only in the second half of the nineteenth century. That is more likely because of the new resources that the nineteenth-century wars generated and from which war chiefs profited (Lloyd 1971:6).

11. According to oral tradition, Oru derived its name from *eru*, slave. Alhaji S. A. Onafuye (#86.69) claimed that Ijebu encouraged the slave trade through their territory in order to collect tolls. How the supervision of markets shifted from the Agemo priests (chapter 7) to the Baloguns is uncertain.

12. An expression well-known even today about the insular nature of Ijebu society is "Ijebu-Ode, a town forbidden to strangers; if a stranger enters it in the morning, he is sure to be made a sacrifice in the evening." *Ijebu-Ode ajeji ko wo; bi ajeji ba wo laro, won a fi sebo lale* (cited in Smith 1971:195 note 3). The slave trade thrived throughout the nineteenth century even though the British, with limited success, had been trying to abolish it since 1807 (Crowder 1968:26–28; Curtin 1969:222, 231; Law (1977:274, 281); it is known to have continued in Yorubaland until 1891 (Ayandele 1966:6). Indeed, the British did not discourage slavery in Ijebu-Ode after their Ijebu Expedition because they feared the land would go uncultivated. See letter from Denton to Ripon, 7 March 1893, quoted in Aderibigbe (1962:195).

13. Smith (1971:174–175) contends that, in order for the Lagos Colony to

be self-sustaining financially, the British depended on trade revenues, which they could not control as long as Ijẹbu trade routes inland were closed to all foreigners. Smith's assessment seems accurate. The colonial commissioner, Alvan Millson, in a letter to the colonial secretary dated 14 February 1890, estimated that with open trade to the interior the Lagos Colony could increase its revenues by at least 300,000 pounds sterling annually without developing land resources (reprinted in Newbury 1971:445–447).

14. Yoruba translate *iwọfa*, as they do *ẹru*, slave. It is the latter term that is used in the widely known nineteenth-century Ijẹbu expression "except for whites and Ijebus, all the rest in the world are slaves. There is no market where whites are sold, there is no market where Ijebus are sold." *Afi Oyinbo afi Ijẹbu, dede aiye dede ẹru ni wọn. Ko si ọja ti a ita Oyinbo, ko si ọja ti a ita Ijẹbu* (Johnson 1973:610). In contrast to *ẹru*, an *iwọfa* provides services to a moneylender, in lieu of interest, on behalf of the borrower, often a senior relative (Fadipẹ, 1970:190–193).

15. The pamphlet reports that among Kuku's enemies were the Oluwo of Oṣugbo, the Olisa of the Ilamurẹn, and the Agbon of the Pampa—not insignificantly the three most powerful chiefs in the precolonial administrative authority of Ijẹbuland (Bovell-Jones 1943; Ayandele 1970:235). Being at odds with them suggests a rather radical power struggle, a situation that characterized much of nineteenth-century Yorubaland (Lloyd 1971).

16. Translated from Yoruba.

17. Meanwhile, according to Johnson, Kuku's Ibadan house was demolished by his enemies.

18. Again Johnson's version, which sympathizes with Kuku, is slightly different; however, it confirms Kuku's movements. According to him (616), the Ijẹbu chiefs picked another quarrel with Ibadan, threatening to stop all arms and ammunition if Kuku was not expelled. They succeeded, and he returned to Ijẹbu territory, this time to Ijẹbu-Ifẹ, which had been known throughout Ijẹbu area as a refuge center. Such towns were known in the 1810s (Lloyd 1967:285–286).

19. Another version of the story given by Gbadamọsi (1978:97) also has Kuku returning initially to Ijẹbu-Ode, but getting "involved in partisan politics supporting the Awujale against the 'party of young men,' which was against trade with Ibadan and the Colonial government." Smith reports (1971:189–190) that, having suffered severe losses during their final battle in the Anglo-Ijẹbu war, the Ijẹbu soldiers turned and fled toward Ijẹbu-Ode. "As they went, they learnt that Kuku had placed himself with his war boys from Ijebu Ife between them and the capital, and fear spread that the Seriki would bar their retreat. But Kuku, who had taken his stand where the track from Ilese joined the Epe-Ijebu-Ode road about a mile to the north-west of Imagbon, was content to laugh at his unhappy compatriots and made no attempt to impede them as they passed by." The source of Smith's information is unclear.

20. See Johnson (1973:622); Carter to Knutsford, 20 June 1892, cited in Ayandele (1966:267); and, for a detailed historical treatment of the British invasion of Ijẹbu-Ode, see Smith (1971).

21. This is corroborated in Kuku (1977:18).

22. Correspondence from the colonial governor, cited in Gbadamọsi (1978:117 note 101).

23. To the Shaikh ul-Islam of the British Isles, one prominent Muslim wrote in 1902: "Kuku one of the leading men of Ijẹbu-Ode: and over 600 of his people declared their belief in the one and only eternal God and His Glorious Prophet (eternal peace and rest be upon Him) and have been received into the holy Islamic faith" (quoted in Gbadamọsi 1978:97).

24. Johnson (1973:612), who knew Kuku personally, claimed Kuku seized Ọyọ women in lieu of debts owed him and "once in his harem" never agreed to release them thereafter. What Johnson describes sounds like a corruption of the *iwọfa* system. Yoruba Christians often attribute the popularity of Islam to polygamy (Kalẹ, personal communication, 1986).

25. According to Crowder (1968:358–361), the colonial government gave Islam more active support than Christianity, indeed punishing administrators in the "Holy" north by posting them to the "pagan" south. Moreover, British officials overwhelmingly preferred the conversion of "pagans" to Islam rather than to Christianity, viewing Christian converts from Sierra Leone, Liberia, the Gold Coast, and southern Nigeria—in the words of one colonialist—as "extravagant caricatures" of themselves in their "preposterous, tall chimney-pot hats, their gaudy Manchester prints, or suits of heavy black coats and trousers and double-breasted waistcoats" (quoted in Crowder 1968:359). As a world religion, Islam appealed to the British as more dignified than "paganism," and Muslim justice was easier to administer than all the varieties of traditional law.

26. See, for example, Bovell-Jones (1943); Ayandele (1969, 1970); and Lloyd (1977).

27. Bovell-Jones (1943:18) extracted this information from a Confidential Minute dated 17 December 1903.

28. *Eyi ni gege bi Oloye Kuku ti ṣe pa ọdun Odela rẹ patapata ni ilu Ijẹbu-Ode, ati ibẹrẹ ariya Ita-Ọba (Ojude Ọba) ti a nṣe titi di ode oni* (Kuku 1977:25).

29. The following discussion is based on conversations with Alhaji M. O. Ṣotẹ, Ọtun Balogun of Ijẹbu-Ode, on the 15th and 20th of August, 1986, as well as on my participation in his Ileya festival parades.

30. Osi Balogun is third in rank after the Balogun and Ọtun Balogun. When one of the top two dies, the third moves up one position.

31. One rather wild rider, dressed American cowboy style—ten-gallon hat, chaps, and all—rode into the festival grounds where the Awujalẹ was stationed. Rumor had it that he was a decoy to distract people while pickpockets worked the crowd.

32. Letter from the Secretary of the Western Provinces to Resident Ijebu Province, 17 December 1942, quoted in Clark (1982:195).

33. Indeed, Lord Lugard in the Foreword to Nadel's book (1965:iv) praises it as "an objective study" used "in conjunction with the researches of District Officers." Then Lugard observes, "the annual festival of the Sallah (*Id el Kebir*) [sic], attended by immense crowds, became a day of national ceremonial and national unity."

9. REINVENTING RITUAL

1. At the time of this research, the official currency exchange rate was one Nigerian naira to one American dollar. Hereafter I use the word dollar instead of naira.

2. Chief P. B. Rennaiye, personal communication, 17 September 1986. The legal voting age is eighteen.

3. Letter from Chief S. A. G. Ogunbajo, The Olumewuro of Imewuro, 10 January 1974.

4. See, for example, H. Drewal and M. Drewal 1983 (Chapters 7 and 8) and H. Drewal 1984.

5. Lloyd reports that Improvement Unions were active in Ijẹbu-Ode at the beginning of this century, while Eades (1980:62) suggests they developed in the 1920s and 1930s.

6. Since the wives of Imewuro men are often citizens of other towns, and are economically independent as well, their participation automatically increases the financial power of the body as a whole.

7. That is, for Christians. The non-Christian participants also perform in the older annual festivals, depending on their affiliations.

8. This is the date of the British invasion of Ijẹbu territory.

10. GENDER PLAY

1. See Ortner (1974) on the nature/culture dichotomy; Rosaldo (1974) on public versus domestic domains; and Strathern (1981) on "self-interest" versus the "social good." As Leacock observes (1981:246), if Ortner's men/culture, women/nature dichotomy—or for that matter Rosaldo's or Strathern's—is to hold up, it "must be reflected in symbolic clusterings associated with female and male terms in worldwide ideological materials over recorded time."

2. Herein lies the essential problem with Rubin's "traffic in women" (1975:177). Rubin's access to the rest of the world is through the lens of Darwinist anthropologists, such as Lévi-Strauss, Evans-Pritchard, and Mauss, and Darwinist psychologists, such as Freud. Thus, she argues, "if Lévi-Strauss is correct in seeing the exchange of women as a fundamental principle of kinship, the subordination of women can be seen as a product of the relationships by which sex and gender are organized and produced." She then concludes, "the 'exchange of women' is an initial step toward building an arsenal of concepts with which sexual systems can be described." But the whole argument rests on a big "If." Thus, when Rubin goes on "to explicate the logical structure" underlying Lévi-Strauss's analysis of kinship, she treats her subject as kinship, when in fact it is, more accurately, Lévi-Strauss (p. 179). Rubin herself acknowledges the problem. Thus, "the danger in my enterprise is that the sexism in the tradition of which they [Lévi-Strauss and Freud] are a part tends to be dragged in with each borrowing" (p. 200).

3. Following Giddens (1986:14), I use power to mean the individual's

capability to act otherwise, either to intervene or to refrain from intervention, in this way influencing a specific performance or state of affairs.

4. I have benefited from conversations with Constance Sutton on the problems involved in trying to determine the nature of power relationships cross-culturally. Any shortcomings are my own.

5. Since British colonialism, however, these figures have found their way into museums all around the world.

6. This seems to support data collected by Denis Williams (1964:141) about Ajagbo, that is, brass castings with aggressive phallic imagery said to be associated with execution.

7. The fourth child who performed Itẹfa (chapter 5) was likewise identified with Ṣango. Using his personal texts as paradigms for examining the child's personality, the diviners constructed him as an aggressive conqueror.

8. The other three are dedicated to Ifa, the deities as a group, and Eṣu the divine trickster.

9. The essential problem with Hoch-Smith's paper (1978) on radical female sexuality in Yoruba ritual and symbolic representations is that it totally ignores radical male sexuality, which is equally prominent, and therefore does not give us a full picture of power relationships. By her omission, she leaves the impression that only female sexuality is represented in art and performance and that it has only negative connotations. It is in fact the male of the paired brass objects used by the traditional Yoruba judiciary that carries negative connotations, however. And indeed a perfect example of radical male sexuality is the aggressive phallic imagery associated with execution in male Ajagbo figures (cf. Williams 1964:141).

10. Reflecting this metaphor, the wife receives the backbone of sacrificial animals. But, as Ṣotẹ commented when it was suggested that the backbone has no meat: "it's not the meat; it's the meaning!"

11. Ọṣitọla told me of an instance he experienced when Itẹfa was performed for a married couple, only to find out that they should never have married in the first place. Thus they were advised to divorce.

12. The ṣu in ṣuku refers to oṣu.

13. The more prevalent portrait is perhaps the result of British colonialist anthropologists (male) interviewing male heads of households. It was the British judiciary system during colonial rule that gave primacy to patrilineal descent.

14. It is common for Yoruba to hire Hausa migrant labor to clear and burn fields and sometimes to plant.

15. This is just the reverse of Rosaldo's men/public, women/private dichotomy (1974).

16. Hausa men sell beef in the market and sometimes hire Yoruba men to do it for them. Otherwise, Yoruba men sell only metal implements and prepared medicines in the market. In each case, however, they are subject to the regulations laid down by the marketwomen's association.

Sources Cited

Note: Below, interviews and discussions with Yoruba specialists are listed in order according to their audio tape number. The first two digits of these numbers indicate the year they were taped.

Abimbọla, Wande
1968   Ijinle Ohun Enu Ifa, Apa Kiini. Glasgow: Collins.
1969   Ijinle Ohun Enu Ifa, Apa Keji. Glasgow: Collins.
1975   Sixteen Great Poems of Ifa. Zaria, Nigeria: UNESCO.
1976   Ifa: An Exposition of Ifa Literary Corpus. Ibadan: Oxford University Press.
1977   Ifa Divination Poetry. New York: Nok Publishers.
1983   Ifa as a Body of Knowledge and as an Academic Discipline. Journal of Cultures and Ideas 1(1):1–11.
Abiọdun, Rowland
1976   The Concept of Women in Traditional Yoruba Religion and Art. Paper presented at the Conference on Nigerian Women and Development in Relation to Changing Family Structure, University of Ibadan, April 26–30.
1981   Personal communication.
1983   Identity and the Artistic Process in Yoruba Aesthetic Concept of Iwa. Journal of Cultures and Ideas 1(1):13–30.
1990   The Future of African Art Studies: An African Perspective. In African Art Studies: The State of the Discipline, Papers Presented at a Symposium Organized by the National Museum of African Art, Smithsonian Institution, September 16, 1987, pp. 63–89. Washington, D.C.: National Museum of African Art.
in press   Woman in Yoruba Religious Images: An Aesthetic Approach. In Visual Art as Social Commentary, ed. J. Picton. London: School of Oriental and African Studies, University of London.
Abraham, R. C.
1958   Dictionary of Modern Yoruba. London: University of London Press.
Adamu, Mahdi
1978   The Hausa Factor in West African History. Zaria, Nigeria: Ahmadu Bello University Press.
1979   The Delivery of Slaves from the Central Sudan to the Bight of Benin in the Eighteenth and Nineteenth Centuries. In The Uncommon Market: Essays in the Economic History of the Atlantic Slave Trade, eds. Henry A. Gemery and Jan S. Hogendorn, pp. 163–180. New York: Academic Press, Inc.
Adedeji, Joel A.
1967   Form and Function of Satire in Yoruba Drama. Odu 4(1):61–72.
1970   The Origin of the Yoruba Masque Theatre: The Use of Ifa Divination Corpus as Historical Evidence. African Notes 6(1):70–86.
1973   Trends in the Content and Form of the Opening Glee in Yoruba Drama. Research in African Literature 4(1):32–47.
Adeokun, Lawrence A.
1983   Marital Sexuality and Birth-Spacing among the Yoruba. In Male and Female in West Africa, ed. C. Oppong, pp. 127–137. London: George Allen & Unwin.

Aderibigbe, A. B.
  1962   Trade and British Expansion in the Lagos Area in the Second Half of the
                    Nineteenth Century. *Nigerian Journal of Economic and Social Studies*
                    4:188–195.
Agbadagbodo. Oliwo Agbadagbodo, Ijasi Quarter, Ijẹbu-Ode
  #86.23   Taped interview, 27 July 1986.
  #86.24   Taped interview, 27 July 1986.
Agbelelu, Jami. Olori Onibata, Ilaro
  #75.13b   Taped discussion, 4 November 1975.
Agiri, B. A.
  1972   The Ogboni Among the Oyo-Yoruba. *Lagos Notes and Records*
                    3(2):50–59.
Ajayi, J. F. A.
  1965   Professional Warriors in Nineteenth-Century Yoruba Politics. *Tarikh*
                    1:72–81.
Ajayi, J. F. A., and Smith, Robert
  1964   *Yoruba Warfare in the Nineteenth Century.* Cambridge: Cambridge
                    University Press.
Anonymous
  n.d.   Untitled manuscript (typewritten). Olisa's Palace, Ijebu-Ode.
  1967   *History of the Central Mosque, Oyingbo, Ijebu-Ode.* Lagos. In the
                    Collection of Alhaji S. A. Onafuye.
  1985a   *Silver Jubilee Anniversary of Oba Sikiru K. Adetona, Ogbagba II, Awujale of
                    Ijebuland.* Lagos: Pacific Printers Ltd.
  1985b   *Silver Jubilee Coronation Anniversary: Programme of Events.* Abeokuta,
                    Nigeria: Ogun State Printing Corporation.
Arens, W., and Karp, Ivan
  1989   Introduction. In *Creativity of Power: Cosmology and Action in African
                    Societies*, eds. W. Arens and Ivan Karp, pp. xi–xxix. Washington:
                    Smithsonian Institution Press.
Artaud, Antonin
  1958   *The Theatre and Its Double.* Trans. by Mary Caroline Richards. New York:
                    Grove Press.
Atanda, J. A.
  1973   The Yoruba Ogboni Cult: Did It Exist in Old Oyo? *The Journal of the
                    Historical Society of Nigeria* 6(4):365–372.
Awoyẹmi, V. O.
  1985   Pauline and Yoruba Concepts of Reconciliation: A Comparative and
                    Hermeneutical Approach. Unpublished M.A. Thesis, Catholic
                    Institute of West Africa, Port Harcourt.
  1986   Discussion, Ijẹbu-Mushin, 27 August.
Ayandele, E. A.
  1966   *The Missionary Impact on Modern Nigeria, 1842–1914: A Political and
                    Social Analysis.* London: Longman Group Ltd.
  1969   The Ideological Ferment in Ijebuland, 1892–1943. *African Notes*
                    5(3):17–40.
  1970   The Changing Position of the Awujales of Ijebuland under Colonial
                    Rule. In *West African Chiefs: Their Changing Status under Colonial
                    Rule and Independence*, eds. Michael Crowder and Obaro Ikime,
                    pp. 231–254. New York and Ile-Ife: Africana Publishing Corp. and
                    University of Ife Press.
  1979   *Nigerian Historical Studies.* London: Frank Cass and Company Limited.
  1983   Ijebuland 1800–1891: Era of Splendid Isolation. In *Studies in Yoruba
                    History and Culture.* Ibadan: Ibadan University Press Ltd.

Ayoade, J. A. A.
    1979   The Concept of Inner Essence in Yoruba Traditional Medicine. In *African Therapeutic Systems*, eds. Z. A. Ademuwagun, J. A. A. Ayoade, I. E. Harrison, and D. M. Warren, pp. 49–55. Waltham, Mass.: Crossroads Press.

Babayẹmi, S. O.
    1980   *Egungun among the Ọyọ Yoruba.* Ibadan: Board Publications Ltd.

Bakare, Chief O. Adie, Ọlọja Agẹmọ, Agọ-Iwoye
    #86.14   Taped interview, 17 July 1986.

Baldwin, David E., and Baldwin, Charlene M.
    1976   *The Yoruba of Southwestern Nigeria: an Indexed Bibliography.* Boston: G. K. Hall.

Barber, Karin
    1981a   The Challenge of Yoruba *Oriki* to Literary Criticism. Paper presented at the 24th Annual African Studies Association Conference, Bloomington, Indiana, November.

    1981b   How Man Makes God in West Africa: Yoruba Attitudes Toward the *Orisa. Africa* 51(3):724–745.

    1984   Yoruba *Oriki* and Deconstructive Criticism. *Research in African Literature* 15(4):497–518.

Bascom, William
    1944   The Sociological Role of the Yoruba Cult-Group. *Memoirs of the American Anthropological Association* 63:5–76.

    1959   Urbanism as a Traditional African Pattern. *Sociological Review* 7(1):29–43.

    1969   *Ifa Divination: Communication between Gods and Men in West Africa.* Bloomington: Indiana University Press.

    1973   The Early Historical Evidence of Yoruba Urbanism. In *Social Change and Economic Development in Nigeria*, eds. U. G. Damachi and H. D. Seibel. New York: Praeger.

Bastide, Roger
    1978   *The African Religions of Brazil: Toward a Sociology of the Interpretation of Civilizations.* Baltimore: Johns Hopkins University Press.

Bateson, Gregory
    1972   *Steps to an Ecology of Mind.* New York: Ballantine Books.

Beier, Ulli
    1964   The Agbegijo Masqueraders. *Nigeria Magazine* 82:188–199.

    1970   *Yoruba Poetry.* Cambridge: Cambridge University Press.

Belasco, Bernard I.
    1980   *The Entrepreneur as Culture Hero: Preadaptations in Nigerian Economic Development.* New York: J. F. Bergin Publishers, Inc.

Ben-Amos, Dan, ed.
    1976   *Folklore Genres.* Austin: University of Texas Press.

Berry, Sara
    1985   *Fathers Work for Their Sons: Accumulation, Mobility, and Class Formation in an Extended Yoruba Community.* Berkeley: University of California Press.

Beyioku, O. A.
    1971   *Ifa, Its Worship and Prayers.* Ebute Metta, Nigeria: Salako Press.

Biobaku, S. O.
    1956   Ogboni, the Egba Senate. In *Proceedings of the Third International West African Conference, Ibadan, December 12–21, 1949*, pp. 257–263. Lagos: Nigerian Museum.

Bloch, Maurice
    1974   Symbols, Song, Dance and Features of Articulation. *European Journal of
                Sociology* 15(1):55–81.
Bovell-Jones, T. B.
    1943   Intelligence Report on Ijebu-Ode Town & Villages, May 7 (IJE Prof.
                2/122, Confidential File C55/1), National Archives, Ibadan
                University.
Bruner, Edward M.
    1986   Experience and Its Expressions. In *The Anthropology of Experience,* eds. V.
                W. Turner and E. M. Bruner, pp. 3–30. Urbana and Chicago:
                University of Illinois Press.
Caldwell, J. C., and Caldwell, P.
    1977   The Role of Marital Sexual Abstinence in Determining Fertility: A Study
                of the Yoruba in Nigeria. *Population Studies* 31(2):193–217.
Chernoff, John Miller
    1979   *African Rhythm and African Sensibility.* Chicago: University of Chicago
                Press.
Clapperton, Hugh
    1829   *Journal of a Second Expedition into the Interior of Africa.* London: John
                Murray.
Clark, Peter B.
    1982   *West Africa and Islam: A Study of Religious Development from the 8th to the
                20th Century.* London: Edward Arnold.
Cole, Herbert M.
    1985   *I Am Not Myself: The Art of African Masquerade.* Monograph Series,
                number 26. Los Angeles: Museum of Cultural History.
Crocker, J. Christopher
    1977   The Social Functions of Rhetorical Forms. In *The Social Use of Metaphor:
                Essays on the Anthropology of Rhetoric,* eds. J. D. Sapir and J. C.
                Crocker, pp. 33–66. Philadelphia: University of Pennsylvania Press.
Crowder, Michael
    1968   *West Africa under Colonial Rule.* Evanston: Northwestern University
                Press.
Crowther, Samuel
    1852   *A Vocabulary of the Yoruba Language.* London: Seeleys.
Curtin, Philip D.
    1969   *The Atlantic Slave Trade: A Census.* Madison: The University of
                Wisconsin Press.
Czikszentmihalyi, Mihaly
    1975   *Beyond Boredom and Anxiety.* San Francisco: Jossey-Bass.
de Certeau, Michel
    1984   *The Practice of Everyday Life.* Trans. by Stephen F. Rendall. Los Angeles:
                University of California Press.
    1986   *Heterologies: Discourse on the Other.* Theory and History of Literature,
                Volume 17. Trans. by Brian Massumi. Minneapolis: University of
                Minnesota Press.
Dennett, R. E.
    1916   The Ogboni and Other Secret Societies in Nigeria. *African Affairs*
                16:16–29.
Derrida, Jacques
    1978   *Writing and Difference.* Trans. by Alan Bass. Chicago: University of
                Chicago Press.
    1984   *Of Grammatology.* Trans. by Gayatri Chakravorty Spivak. Baltimore:
                Johns Hopkins University Press.

Drewal, Henry John
  1974   Efe: Voiced Power and Pageantry. *African Arts* 7(2):26–29, 58–66.
  1982   Personal Communication, 4 July.
  1984   Art, History, and the Individual: A New Perspective for the Study of
            African Visual Traditions. *Iowa Studies in African Art* 1:87–101.
  1986   Flaming Crowns, Cooling Waters: Masquerades of the Ijebu Yoruba.
            African Arts 20(1):32–41, 99–100.
  1988   Performing the Other: Mami Wata Worship in West Africa. *The Drama
            Review: A Journal of Performance Studies* 32(2), T118:160–185.
  1989   Meaning in Osugbo Art among the Ijebu Yoruba. In *Man Does Not Go
            Naked: Textilien und Handwerk aus Afrikanischen und Anderen
            Landern*, ed. B. Engelbrecht and B. Gardi, pp. 151–174. Vol. 29.
            Basle: Basler Beitrage zur Ethnologie.

Drewal, Henry John, and Drewal, Margaret Thompson
  1983   *Gẹlẹdẹ: Art and Female Power among the Yoruba*. Bloomington: Indiana
            University Press.

Drewal, Margaret Thompson
  1986   Art and Trance among Yoruba Shango Devotees. *African Arts* 20(1):60–
            67, 98–99.
  1987   From Rocky's Rockettes to Liberace: The Politics of Representation in
            the Heart of Corporate Capitalism. *Journal of American Culture*
            10(2):67–80.
  1988   Ritual Performance in Africa Today. *The Drama Review: A Journal of
            Performance Studies* 32(2), T118:25–30.
  1989   Dancing for Ogun in Yorubaland and in Brazil. In *Africa's Ogun: Old
            World and New*, ed. S. Barnes, pp. 199–234. Bloomington: Indiana
            University Press.
  1990   (Inter)text, Performance, and the African Humanities. *Text and
            Performance Quarterly* 10(1):72–86.
  in press "Yoruba Reversionism" in New York. In *Cultural Vibrations: Yoruba
            Transformations and Continuities in the Yoruba Diaspora*, eds. Robin
            Poynor and Olabiyi Yai. Gainesville: University of Florida Press.

Drewal, Margaret Thompson, and Drewal, Henry John
  1978   More Powerful than Each Other: An Egbado Classification of Egungun.
            African Arts 11(3):28–39, 98.
  1983   An Ifa Diviner's Shrine in Ijebuland. *African Arts* 16(2):60–67, 99–100.
  1987   Composing Time and Space in Yoruba Art. *Word and Image: A Journal of
            Verbal Visual Enquiry* 3(3):225–251.

Eades, J. S.
  1980   *The Yoruba Today*. Cambridge: Cambridge University Press.

Edwards, Gary, and Mason, John
  1981   *Onje Fun Orisa—Food for the Gods*. New York: Yoruba Theological
            Archministry.
  1985   *Black Gods—Orisa Studies in the New World*. Brooklyn: Yoruba
            Theological Archministry.

Eliade, Mircea
  1959   *The Sacred & the Profane: The Nature of Religion*. Trans. by W. R. Trask.
            San Diego: A Harvest/HBJ Book, Harcourt Brace Jovanovich,
            Publishers.

Ellis, A. B.
  1974   *The Yoruba-Speaking Peoples of the Slave Coast of West Africa*. London:
  [1894]   Curzon Press.

Epega, Afolabi A.
  1987   *Ifa: The Ancient Wisdom*. New York: Imole Oluwa Institute.

Fabian, Johannes
1983   *Time and the Other: How Anthropology Makes Its Object.* New York: Columbia University Press.
Fadipẹ, N. A.
1970   *The Sociology of the Yoruba.* Ibadan: Ibadan University Press.
[1939]
Fernandez, James W.
1986   *Persuasions and Performances: The Play of Tropes in Culture.* Bloomington: Indiana University Press.
Gates, Henry Louis, Jr.
1988   *The Signifying Monkey: A Theory of Afro-American Literary Criticism.* New York: Oxford University Press.
Gbadamọsi, T. G. O.
1978   *The Growth of Islam among the Yoruba, 1841–1908.* Atlantic Highlands, N.J.: Humanities Press.
Geertz, Clifford
1983   Blurred Genres: The Refiguration of Social Thought. In *Local Knowledge: Further Essays in Interpretive Anthropology,* pp. 19–35. New York: Basic Books, Inc., Publishers.
1986   Making Experiences, Authoring Selves. In *The Anthropology of Experience,* eds. V. W. Turner and E. M. Bruner, pp. 373–380. Urbana: University of Illinois Press.
Gell, Alfred
1975   *Metamorphosis of the Cassowaries: Umeda Society, Language and Ritual.* London School of Economics Monograph on Social Anthropology, No. 51. London: The Althone Press, University of London.
Giddens, Anthony
1982   *Profiles and Critiques in Social Theory.* Berkeley: University of California Press.
1986   *The Constitution of Society: Outline of the Theory of Structuration.*
[1984]   Berkeley: University of California Press.
Goffman, Erving
1959   *The Presentation of Self in Everyday Life.* Garden City, N.Y.: Doubleday Anchor Books.
1974   *Frame Analysis.* New York: Harper & Row, Publishers.
Goody, Jack
1977   Against 'Ritual': Loosely Structured Thoughts on a Loosely Defined Topic. In *Secular Ritual,* eds. S. F. Moore and B. G. Myerhoff, pp. 28–33. Assen, The Netherlands: Van Gorcum.
Gotrick, Kacke
1984   *Apidan Theatre and Modern Drama.* Stockholm: Almqvist & Wiksell International.
Handelman, Don
1977   Play and Ritual: Complementary Frames of Metacommunication. In *It's a Funny Thing, Humour,* eds. A. J. Chapman and H. Fort, pp. 185–192. London: Pergamon.
Hobsbawm, Eric
1985   Mass-Producing Traditions: Europe, 1870–1914. In *The Invention of*
[1983]   *Tradition,* eds. E. Hobsbawm and Terrence Ranger, pp. 263–307. Cambridge: Cambridge University Press.
Hoch-Smith, Judith
1978   Radical Yoruba Female Sexuality: The Witch and the Prostitute. In *Women in Ritual and Symbolic Roles,* ed. J. Hoch-Smith and A. Spring, pp. 245–267. New York: Plenum Press.

Holy, Ladislav, and Stuchlik, Milan
    1983   *Actions, Norms and Representations: Foundations of Anthropological Inquiry.* Cambridge Studies in Anthropology, no. 45. Cambridge: Cambridge University Press.

Hopkins, A. G.
    1973   *An Economic History of West Africa.* New York: Columbia University Press.

Husserl, Edmund
    1964   *The Phenomenology of Internal Time-Consciousness.* Bloomington: Indiana University Press.

Hutcheon, Linda
    1985   *A Theory of Parody: The Teachings of Twentieth-Century Art Forms.* New York: Methuen.
    1988   *A Poetics of Postmodernism: History, Theory, Fiction.* New York: Routledge.

Iya Ṣango. Priest of Ṣango, Agoṣaga Quarter, Ilaro
    #75.6b   Taped interview, 21 November 1975.

Jelliffe, D. B.
    1953   Infant Feeding among the Yoruba of Ibadan. *The West African Medical Journal* (n.s.), 2(3):111–122.

Johnson, Samuel
    1973   *The History of the Yorubas.* Lagos: CSS Bookshops.
    [1921]

Kale, Theodore
    1986   Personal communication.

Kapferer, Bruce
    1986   Performance and the Structuring of Meaning and Experience. In *The Anthropology of Experience*, eds. V. W. Turner and E. M. Bruner, pp. 188–203. Urbana and Chicago: University of Illinois Press.

Karp, Ivan
    1986   Agency and Social Theory: A Review of Anthony Giddens. *American Ethnologist* 13:131–137.

Kirshenblatt-Gimblett, Barbara
    1976   A Parable in Context: A Social Interactional Analysis of Storytelling Performance. In *Folklore: Performance and Communication*, eds. D. Ben-Amos and H. S. Goldstein, pp. 105–130. The Hague: Mouton.
    1983   The Future of Folklore Studies in America: The Urban Frontier. *Folklore Forum* 16(2):175–234.

Klein, Ernest
    1967   *A Comprehensive Etymological Dictionary of the English Language.* Vol. II. Amsterdam: Elsevier Publishing Company.

Krapf-Askari, Eva
    1969   *Yoruba Towns and Cities: An Enquiry into the Nature of Urban Social Phenomena.* Oxford: Clarendon Press.

Kukoyi, Chief C. A., Itun-Kunni XI. Nopa, Odonopa Quarter, Ijẹbu-Mushin
    #82.95   Taped interview, 1 July 1982.
    #82.96   Taped interview, 1 July 1982.

Kuku, Fatai Adeshina
    [1977]   *Itan Igbesi Aiye Ologbe: Oloye Bello Kuku, Balogun Keji, Ilu Ijebu-Ode, 1845–1907.* Ijebu-Ode, Nigeria: By the author.

Laitin, David D.
    1986   *Hegemony and Culture: Politics and Religious Change among the Yoruba.* Chicago: University of Chicago Press.

LaPin, Dierdre
  1977   Story, Medium and Masque: The Idea and Art of Yoruba Storytelling.
              3 vols. Ph.D. diss., University of Wisconsin.
  1986   Personal communication.
Law, Robin
  1977   *The Oyo Empire c. 1600–1836.* Oxford: Clarendon Press.
  1986   Early European Sources Relating to the Kingdom of Ijebu (1500–1700):
              A Critical Survey. *History in Africa* 13:245–260.
Leacock, Eleanor B.
  1981   *Myths of Male Dominance: Collected Articles on Women Cross-Culturally.*
              New York: Monthly Review Press.
Lex, Barbara W.
  1979   The Neurobiology of Ritual Trance. In *The Spectrum of Ritual: A
              Biogenetic Structural Analysis,* eds. E. d'Aquili et al., pp. 117–151.
              New York: Columbia University Press.
Lincoln, Bruce
  1989   *Discourse and the Construction of Society: Comparative Studies in Myth,
              Ritual, and Classification.* Oxford: Oxford University Press.
Lloyd, P. C.
  1959   The Yoruba Town Today. *Sociological Review* (n.s.), 7(1):45–63.
  1961   Sallah at Ilorin. *Nigeria Magazine* 70:266–278.
  1962   *Yoruba Land Law.* London: Oxford University Press.
  1963   The Status of the Yoruba Wife. *Sudan Society* 2:35–42.
  1965   The Political Structure of African Kingdoms: An Exploratory Model. In
              Political Systems and the Distribution of Power, A.S.A. 2, eds.
              M. Gluckman and F. Eggan, pp. 63–112. London: Tavistock
              Publications.
  1967   Osifekunde of Ijebu. In *Africa Remembered: Narratives by West Africans
              from the Era of the Slave Trade,* ed. P. D. Curtin, pp. 217–288.
              Madison: University of Wisconsin Press.
  1971   *The Political Development of Yoruba Kingdoms in the Eighteenth and
              Nineteenth Centuries.* Royal Anthropological Institute Occasional
              Paper No. 31. London: Royal Anthropological Institute.
  1973   The Yoruba: An Urban People? In *Urban Anthropology,* ed. A. Southall,
              pp. 107–123. New York: Oxford University Press.
  1974   *Power and Independence.* London: Routledge & Kegan Paul.
  1977   Ijebu. In *African Kingships in Perspective: Political Change and
              Modernization in Monarchical Settings,* ed. Rene Lemarchand,
              pp. 260–283. London: Frank Cass & Co. Ltd.
Mabogunje, Akin L.
  1968   *Urbanization in Nigeria.* London: University of London Press.
MacAloon, John J.
  1984   Olympic Games and the Theory of Spectacle in Modern Societies. In
              *Rite, Drama, Festival, Spectacle: Rehearsals Toward a Theory of
              Cultural Performance,* ed. J. MacAloon, pp. 241–280. Philadelphia:
              ISHI.
MacCannell, Dean
  1976   *The Tourist.* New York: Schocken Books.
McClelland, Elizabeth
  1982   *Cult of Ifa among the Yoruba.* Folk Practice and the Arts, Vol. I. London:
              Ethnographica.
McKenzie, Peter R.
  1982   Death in Early Nigerian Christianity. *Africana Marburgensia* 15(2):3–16.

Mason, John
    1985   *Four New World Yoruba Rituals*. Brooklyn: Yoruba Theological
                Archministry.
Moore, Sally F.
    1975   Epilogue: Uncertainties in Situations, Indeterminacies in Culture. In
                Symbol and Politics in Communal Ideology, eds. S. F. Moore and
                B. G. Meyerhoff, pp. 210–239. Ithaca: Cornell University Press.
Moore, Sally F., and Myerhoff, Barbara G., eds.
    1977   *Secular Ritual*. Assen, The Netherlands: Van Gorcum & Comp. B.V.
Morakinyo, Olufemi, and Akiwowo, Akinsola
    1981   The Yoruba Ontology of Personality and Motivation: A Multidisciplinary
                Approach. *Journal of Social Biological Structures* 4:19–38.
Morton-Williams, Peter
    1960a   The Yoruba Ogboni Cult in Oyo. *Africa* 30:362–374.
    1960b   Yoruba Responses to the Fear of Death. *Africa* 30:34–40.
Mudimbe, V. Y.
    1988   *The Invention of Africa: Gnosis, Philosophy, and the Order of Knowledge*.
                Bloomington: Indiana University Press.
Myerhoff, Barbara
    1990   The Transformation of Consciousness in Ritual Performances: Some
                Thoughts and Questions. In *By Means of Performance: Intercultural
                Studies of Theatre and Ritual*, eds. R. Schechner and W. Appel,
                pp. 245–249. Cambridge: Cambridge University Press.
Nadel, S. F.
    1965   *Black Byzantium: The Kingdom of Nupe in Nigeria*. London: Oxford
    [1942]   University Press.
Nevadomsky, Joseph, with Rosen, Norma
    1988   The Initiation of a Priestess: Performance and Imagery in Olokun Ritual.
                The Drama Review: A Journal of Performance Studies 32(2),
                T118:186–207.
Newbury, C. W.
    1971   *British Policy Towards West Africa: Selected Documents 1875–1914*.
                Oxford: Clarendon Press.
Norbeck, Edward
    1976   African Rituals of Conflict. In *Gods & Rituals: Readings in Religious
                Beliefs and Practices*, ed. J. Middleton, pp. 197–226. Austin:
                University of Texas Press.
Nunley, John
    1988   Purity and Pollution in Freetown Masked Performance. *The Drama
                Review: A Journal of Performance Studies* 32(2), T118:102–122.
Odunsi, Chief O., Ekejiotu Alagemo. Ija, Imosan
    #86.20   Taped interview, 23 July 1986.
    #86.21   Taped interview, 23 July 1986.
Ogunba, Oyin
    1965   The Agemo Cult in Ijebuland. *Nigeria Magazine* 86, pp. 176–186.
    1967   Ritual Drama in Ijebu-Ode. Unpublished Ph.D. dissertation, University
                of Ibadan.
    1985   Agemo: The Orisa of the Ijebu People of South-Eastern Yorubaland. In
                Nigerian Life and Culture: A Book of Readings, eds. O. Y. Oyeneye
                and M. O. Shoremi, pp. 281–306. Ago-Iwoye, Nigeria: Ogun State
                University.
Ogunbajo, Chief S. A. G., The Olumewuro of Imewuro
    1974   Letter to Ministry of Local Government and Chieftancy Affairs, 10
                January.

Okunuga, J. A., Pastor-In-Charge
    1939   Letter to His Worship, The Regent of Ijebu-Ode. IJE Prof 1/779, pp. 57–60. University of Ibadan Library, Ibadan, June 30.

Omari, Mikelle Smith
    1984   *From the Inside to the Outside: The Art and Ritual of Bahian Candomble.* Monograph Series, no. 24. Los Angeles: Museum of Cultural History, UCLA.

Ọnafowokan, Chief A. T., Okiboro II. Ṣerefusi, Ọlọja Agẹmọ, Igbilẹ
    #86.14   Taped discussion, 18 July 1986.

Ọnafuye, Alhaji S. A. Secretary to the Awujalẹ, Ijẹbu-Ode
    #86.63   Taped interview, 25 September 1986.
    #86.69   Taped interview, 2 October 1986.

Ortner, Sherry B.
    1974   Is Female to Male as Nature Is to Culture? In *Women, Culture, and Society,* eds. by L. Z. Rosaldo and L. Lamphere, pp. 67–88. Stanford: Stanford University Press.
    1984   Theory in Anthropology since the Sixties. *Comparative Studies in Society and History: An International Quarterly* 26(1):126–166.

Osilaja, Chief William Ola. Idẹbi Olumoruwa, Ọlọja Agẹmọ, Isamoro Quarter, Agọ-Iwoye
    #86.22   Taped interview, 24 July 1986.
    #86.23   Taped interview, 24 July 1986.
    #86.57   Taped recollections, 14 September 1986.

Ọṣitọla, Ifayẹmi. Ifa devotee, Imodi
    #82.28   Taped discussion, 7 May 1982.

Ọṣitọla, Kọlawọlẹ. Babalawo, Ijẹbu-Ode
    1982   Personal communication, 3 July.
    #82.28   Taped discussion, 7 May 1982.
    #82.31   Taped discussion, 11 May 1982.
    #82.35   Taped discussion, 18 May 1982.
    #82.37   Taped discussion, 21 May 1982.
    #82.38(I)   Taped discussion, 21 May 1982.
    #82.38(II) Taped discussion, 25 May 1982.
    #82.39   Taped discussion, 25 May 1982.
    #82.42   Taped discussion, 27 May 1982.
    #82.44   Taped discussion, 31 May 1982.
    #82.45   Taped discussion, 31 May 1982.
    #82.46   Taped discussion, 31 May 1982.
    #82.47   Taped discussion, 31 May 1982.
    #82.48   Taped discussion, 1 June 1982.
    #82.49   Taped discussion, 1 June 1982.
    #82.57   Taped discussion, 8 June 1982.
    #82.58   Taped discussion, 8 & 16 June 1982.
    #82.66   Taped discussion, 16 June 1982.
    #82.67   Taped discussion, 16 June 1982.
    #82.68   Taped discussion, 16 & 20 June 1982.
    #82.70   Taped discussion, 20 June 1982.
    #82.71   Taped discussion, 20 June 1982.
    #82.78   Taped discussion, 28 June 1982.
    #82.103   Taped discussion, 20 July 1982.
    #82.104   Taped discussion, 20 July 1982.
    #82.107   Taped discussion, 23 July 1982.
    #82.113   Taped discussion, 27 July 1982.
    #82.116   Taped discussion, 28 July 1982.

#86.65   Taped discussion, 27 September 1986.
#86.66   Taped discussion, 27 September 1986.
#86.67   Taped discussion, 1 October 1986.
#86.75   Taped discussion, 17 October 1986.
#86.77(I) Taped discussion, 13 October 1986.
#86.79   Taped discussion, 13 October 1986.
#86.83   Taped discussion, 17 October 1986.
#86.94   Taped discussion, 1 December 1986.
#86.102   Taped discussion, 6 November 1986.
#86.117   Taped discussion, 9 November 1986.
#86.134   Taped discussion, 11 November 1986.
#86.138   Taped discussion, 30 November 1986.
#86.142   Taped discussion, 30 November 1986.
#86.143   Taped discussion, 30 November 1986.
#86.144   Taped discussion, 1 December 1986.
#86.145   Taped discussion, 1 December 1986.
1988   On Ritual Performance: A Practitioner's View. *The Drama Review: A Journal of Performance Studies* 32(2), T118:31–41.

Ottenberg, Simon
1988   The Bride Comes to the Groom: Ritual and Drama in Limba Weddings. *The Drama Review: A Journal of Performance Studies* 32(2), T118:42–64.

Owomoyela, Oyekan
1979   A Fractioned Word in a Muted Mouth: The Pointed Subtlety of Yoruba Proverbs. Paper read at the Annual Meeting of the African Studies Association, Los Angeles, 31 October–3 November.
1987   Africa and the Imperative of Philosophy: A Skeptical Consideration. *African Studies Review* 30(1):79–100.

Parkin, David
1982   Introduction. In *Semantic Anthropology,* ed. D. Parkin, pp. xi–li. London: Academic Press.

Peacock, James L.
1975   *Consciousness and Change: Symbolic Anthropology in Evolutionary Perspective.* New York: Halsted Press, John Wiley & Sons, Inc.

Peek, Philip M.
1981   The Power of Words in African Verbal Arts. *Journal of American Folklore* 94(371):19–43.

Peel, J. D. Y.
1984   Making History: The Past in the Ijesha Present. *Man* (n.s.) 19(1):111–132.

Pemberton III, John
1984   Odun Agemo. Typewritten manuscript.
1988   The King and the Chameleon: Odun Agemo. *Ifẹ: Annals of the Institute of Cultural Studies* 2:47–64.

Prince, Raymond
1960   Curse, Invocation and Mental Health among the Yoruba. *Canadian Psychiatric Journal* 5:65–79.

Rapoport, Amos
1982   Sacred Places, Sacred Occasions, and Sacred Environments. *Architectural Design* 9–10:75–82.

Rappaport, Roy A.
1979   The Obvious Aspects of Ritual. In *Ecology, Meaning, and Religion,* pp. 173–221. Richmond, California: North Atlantic Books.

Ray, Benjamin
    1973   'Performative Utterances' in African Rituals. *History of Religions*
                13(1):16–35.
    1976   *African Religions: Symbol, Ritual, and Community.* Englewood Cliffs:
                Prentice-Hall, Inc.
Rennaiye, Chief Philip B. Maiyegun of Imewuro, Ijẹbu-Ode
    1986   Personal communication, 17 September.
    #86.59   Taped interview, 17 September 1986.
Rosaldo, Michelle Z.
    1974   Women, Culture, and Society: A Theoretical Overview. In *Woman,*
                Culture, and Society, eds. L. Z. Rosaldo and L. Lamphere, pp. 17–42.
                Stanford: Stanford University Press.
Rouget, Gilbert
    1985   *Music and Trance: A Theory of the Relations between Music and Possession.*
                Chicago: The University of Chicago Press.
Rubin, Gayle
    1975   The Traffic in Women: Notes on the Political Economy of Sex. In *Toward*
                an Anthropology of Women, ed. R. R. Reiter, pp. 157–210. New York:
                Monthly Review Press.
Ryan, Patrick J.
    1978   *Imale: Yoruba Participation in the Muslim Tradition.* Harvard Dissertations
                in Religion, no. 11. Missoula, Montana: Scholars' Press.
Sacks, Karen
    1982   *Sisters and Wives: The Past and Future of Sexual Equality.* Urbana:
                University of Illinois Press.
Sahlins, Marshall
    1976   *Culture and Practical Reason.* Chicago: University of Chicago Press.
Said, Edward W.
    1978   *Orientalism.* New York: Random House, Inc.
Sallnow, M. J.
    1981   Communitas Reconsidered: The Sociology of Andean Pilgrimage. *Man*
                (n.s.) 16:163–182.
Sanni, Chief A., Kasan Ogunja II. Ẹwujagbori, Ọlọja Agẹmọ, Imọsan
    #86.20   Taped interview, 23 July 1986.
Sapir, J. David
    1977   The Anatomy of Metaphor. In *The Social Use of Metaphor: Essays on the*
                Anthropology of Rhetoric, ed. J. D. Sapir, pp. 3–32. Philadelphia:
                University of Pennsylvania Press.
Schechner, Richard
    1982a   Collective Reflexivity: Restoration of Behavior. In *A Crack in the Mirror:*
                Reflexive Perspectives in Anthropology, ed. J. Ruby, pp. 39–81.
                Philadelphia: University of Pennsylvania Press.
    1982b   *The End of Humanism: Writings on Performance.* New York: Performing
                Arts Journal.
    1985   *Between Theater and Anthropology.* Philadelphia: University of
                Pennsylvania Press.
    1988   Playing. *Play and Culture* 1(1).
Schwartz, Theodore
    1978   Where Is the Culture? Personality as the Distributive Locus of Culture. In
                The Making of Psychological Anthropology, ed. George D. Spindler,
                pp. 419–441. Berkeley: University of California Press.
Schwartzman, Helen B.
    1982   *Transformations: The Anthropology of Children's Play.* New York: Plenum
    [1979]   Press.

Siegel, Marcia B.
    1979   *The Shapes of Change: Images of American Dance.* Boston: Houghton
                Mifflin.
Singer, Milton B.
    1972   *When a Great Tradition Modernizes; An Anthropological Approach to
                Indian Civilization.* New York: Praeger.
Smith, Robert
    1969   *Kingdoms of the Yoruba.* London: Methuen and Co., Ltd.
    1971   Nigeria—Ijebu. In *West African Resistance: The Military Response to
                Colonial Occupation,* ed. M. Crowder, pp. 170–204. New York:
                Africana Publishing Corporation.
Ṣọtẹ, Alhaji M. O. Ọtun Balogun, Ijasi Quarter, Ijẹbu-Ode
    #86.33   Taped recollections of conversations held on 15 and 17 August, 15 and
                18 August 1986.
    #86.41   Taped recollections of conversation held on 20 August, 21 August 1986.
Strathern, Marilyn
    1981   Self-Interest and the Social Good: Some Implications of Hagen Gender
                Imagery. In *Sexual Meanings: The Cultural Construction of Gender
                and Sexuality,* eds. S. B. Ortner and H. Whitehead, pp. 166–191.
                Cambridge: Cambridge University Press.
Sudarkasa, Niara
    1973   *Where Women Work: A Study of Yoruba Women in the Marketplace and in
                the Home.* Anthropology Papers, Museum of Anthropology, #53.
                Ann Arbor: University of Michigan.
Taiwo, Raimi Akaki. Ọjẹ Egungun, Agoṣaga Quarter, Ilaro
    #75.4a   Taped discussion, 12 October 1975.
    #75.6b   Taped discussion, 21 November 1975.
    #75.11a   Taped discussion, 3 November 1975.
    #75.14b   Taped discussion, 5 November 1975.
    #75.27b   Taped discussion, 19 November 1975.
Talbot, P. A.
    1926   *The Peoples of Southern Nigeria.* Vol. I. London: Oxford University Press.
Tambiah, Stanley Jeyaraja
    1985   *Culture, Thought, and Social Action.* Cambridge: Harvard University
                Press.
Taussig, Michael
    1987   *Shamanism, Colonialism, and the Wild Man: A Study of Terror and
                Healing.* Chicago: The University of Chicago Press.
Theunissen, Michael
    1986   *The Other: Studies in the Social Ontology of Husserl, Heidegger, Sartre, and
                Buber.* Trans. by Christopher Macann. Cambridge, Mass.: The MIT
                Press.
Thompson, Robert F.
    1966   An Aesthetic of the Cool: West African Dance. *African Forum*
                2(2):85–102.
    1974   *African Art in Motion.* Los Angeles: University of California Press.
Todorov, Tzvetan
    1984   *Mikhail Bakhtin: The Dialogical Principle.* Theory and History of
                Literature, Volume 13. Trans. by Wlad Godzich. Minneapolis:
                University of Minnesota Press.
Tuan, Yi-Fu
    1977   *Space and Place: The Perspective of Experience.* Minneapolis: University of
                Minnesota Press.

Turner, Victor
  1974a   *Dramas, Fields, and Metaphors: Symbolic Action in Human Society.* Ithaca: Cornell University Press.
  1974b   Liminal to Liminoid in Play, Flow and Ritual: An Essay in Comparative Symbology. *Rice University Studies* 60:53–92.
  1977a   *The Ritual Process: Structure and Anti-Structure.* Ithaca: Cornell Paperbacks Edition.
  1977b   Variations on a Theme of Liminality. In *Secular Ritual*, eds. S. F. Moore and B. G. Myerhoff, pp. 36–52. Assen, The Netherlands: Van Gorcum & Comp. B.V.
  1982   *From Ritual to Theatre: The Human Seriousness of Play.* New York: Performing Arts Journal Publications.
  1986   *The Anthropology of Performance.* New York: Performing Arts Journal Publishers.
Verger, Pierre
  1954   Rôle Joué par l'État d'Hèbètude au cours de l' Initiation des Novices aux Cultes des Orisha et Vodun. *Bulletin de l'I.F.A.N.* Serie B, 16, 3–4:322–340.
  1969   Trance and Convention in Nago-Yoruba Spirit Mediumship. In *Spirit Mediumship and Society in Africa*, eds. J. Beattie and J. Middleton, pp. 50–66. New York: Africana Publishing Co.
  1976–77 The Use of Plants in Yoruba Traditional Medicine and Its Linguistic Approach. In *Seminar Series*, No. 1, Part 1, ed. O. O. Oyelaran, pp. 242–295. Ifẹ: Department of African Languages & Literatures, University of Ifẹ.
Wagner, Roy
  1972   *Habu: The Innovation of Meaning in Daribi Religion.* Chicago: The University of Chicago Press.
  1981   *The Invention of Culture.* Revised and expanded. Chicago: University of Chicago Press.
Wescott, Joan
  1962   The Sculpture and Myths of Eshu-Elegba, The Yoruba Trickster. *Africa* 32:336–353.
Wheatley, P.
  1970   The Significance of Traditional Yoruba Urbanism. *Comparative Studies in Society and History* 12(4):393–423.
Williams, Denis
  1964   The Iconology of the Yoruba *Edan Ogboni. Africa* 34(2):139–165.
Williams, Raymond
  1982   *The Sociology of Culture.* New York: Schocken Books.
Wirth, Louis
  1969   Urbanism as a Way of Life. In *Classic Essays on the Culture of Cities*, ed.
  [1938] R. Sennett, pp. 143–164. Englewood Cliffs, N.J.: Prentice-Hall, Inc.
Yai, Ọlabiyi
  1990   Personal communication.

Index

Aba, 27
Abeokuta, 97–98
Àbíkú (child "born to die"), 59
Abimbola, Wande, 46
Abiodun, Rowland, xiv–xv, 184
Abraham, R. C., 13
Ache, 27
Achievements, funeral rituals and deceased's, 42
Action, Yoruba theory of, xix
Actors, 32, 173–74
Adedeji, Joel, 91
Adie, 120, 125, 177, 215n
Adosu, 182
Adults, Itefa ritual and, 72–73
Agbo masks, 166–67
Age. See Seniority
Agemo festival: contention over rules, 197; cross-dressing, 177; former sociopolitical system, 135; funeral rituals, 45; hierarchies and power in Ijebuland, 138; ideological conflict, 113–15; pilgrimage, 116–19, 214n; positionality and perspective, 120–23; representations and social reality, 25; ritual precedent for mask, 94; Sote and Awùjalè 151; transformation and power, 124–25; women and ritual performances, 172, 180
Agency, improvisation and ritual, 26–28
Agere, 181
Agogo, 182
Àito (segments within ritual), 31, 197
Ajagbo, 220n
Àjé (woman with extraordinary power), 177–78
Ajobiewe, 99
Ajofunoyinbo, 94–95, 213n
Ajogún (spirits of hardship), 207n
Akoko leaves, 210n
Akonoron, 36
Alábala masks, 92, 93
Alágemo (member of Agemo society), 93–94
Aláwo (Ifá initiates), 24
Alcoholism, 72
Americans: Itefa and identity, 76; Yoruba religion and, 27, 209n
Amututu, 212n
Ancestors: change in ritual, 9–10; funeral rituals, 41; Itefa, 84. See also Egungun
Animating spirits (emi), 56, 172

Annual Rally. See Imewuro Annual Rally
Apena, 57
Apidán (performance of "miracles"), 94, 97, 98–104, 213n. See also Egúngún
Apostolic Church, 117–18, 125
Art, ritual roles and gender, 174–76, 189
Àse (performative power), xix, 27–28, 177
Asipade, 214n
Aso ologbon, 40
Authoritarianism, 199–200
Awo (esoteric knowledge), 24, 200, 210n
Aworan, 13, 15
Awoyemi, Rev. Father Valentine, 168–69
Awùjalè: Agemo festival, 114–15, 122–23, 126, 128, 151; Iléyá festival, 136, 142–43
Axe, 27
Àyànmó (associated with prenatal destiny), 208n
Ayelabola, 95–96

Baba parikoko, 22, 23
Balóguns, 137–38, 148
Barber, Karin, 103
Bariba mask, 101
Behavior, restored and repetition, 3
Beier, Ulli, 4
Ben-Amos, Dan, 12
Berry, Sara, 23
Betrothal, 187
Biobaku, S. O., 176
Blindness, 124
Brazil, 207n
Breaking the Bracelet (Itude), 181
Breast-feeding, 188
Bride: Egúngún mask, 96–97, 101, 214n; marriage and price, 187
British: adaptation of Iléyá festival to political structure, 151–52, 153; colonial strategy, 162; invasion of Ijebu, 138, 140, 217n; Islam and Christianity in Ijebu, 218n; judicial system and partrilineal descent, 220n; relationship with Balógun Kuku, 141, 142; slave trade in Ijebu, 216n; Sote's travels and appropriation of symbols, 149. See also Whites
Bullroarers, 209n

Caretaker (atejumole), 43
Catholicism, 168–69
Celebration, funeral rituals, 41–42

Margaret Thompson Drewal is Associate Professor of Performance Studies at Northwestern University. A performance theorist specializing in cultural studies, she is coauthor (with Henry John Drewal) of *Gẹlẹdẹ: Art and Female Power among the Yoruba.*